About This Book

Why is this topic important?

Making training solutions available in a timely manner is increasingly critical to add value to an organization. Training groups that are seen to be responsive and in touch with the corporation's needs are perceived to add increased value. Therefore, a consistent, replicable, and efficient instructional design model that enables rapid development is increasingly critical. Projects move faster when everyone in a training organization or project team understands, adopts, and follows a consistent model.

What can you achieve with this book?

The purpose of this book is to provide a consistent, replicable, and efficient model that will get training and performance solutions to market at the time they will provide the optimum benefit.

How is this book organized?

This book is divided into four parts. Part One is Multimedia Needs Assessment and Analysis. This part explains the activities that must be completed for twelve types of analysis and assessment and a rapid analysis model that can be used once each of the individual activities is completely understood. Tools are provided for each type of assessment and analysis to document and track the data and results of analysis. Part Two is Multimedia Instructional Design, which explains how to develop a Course Design Specification. A Course Design Specification creates the "rules" for all project members to follow to make a project run more efficiently and effectively. Again, tools are provided to complete each activity. Part Three is Multimedia Development and Implementation, which outlines the common and unique elements of producing computer-based, web-based, distance broadcast, and performance-based solutions. Useful task tracking and development tools accompany the explanation of each delivery media. Part Four is Multimedia Evaluation. This part describes how an organization can develop an evaluation strategy and, further, how to create an evaluation plan for each project. Specific instructions on how to collect and analyze data within each project plan are included to help project teams complete an evaluation that is credible, consisting of both validity and reliability. Four appendices contain completed examples of tools, and a fifth appendix shows examples of the tool templates that are included on the CD ROM.

About Pfeiffer

Pfeiffer serves the professional development and hands-on resource needs of training and human resource practitioners and gives them products to do their jobs better. We deliver proven ideas and solutions from experts in HR development and HR management, and we offer effective and customizable tools to improve workplace performance. From novice to seasoned professional, Pfeiffer is the source you can trust to make yourself and your organization more successful.

Essential Knowledge Pfeiffer produces insightful, practical, and comprehensive materials on topics that matter the most to training and HR professionals. Our Essential Knowledge resources translate the expertise of seasoned professionals into practical, how-to guidance on critical workplace issues and problems. These resources are supported by case studies, worksheets, and job aids and are frequently supplemented with CD-ROMs, websites, and other means of making the content easier to read, understand, and use.

Essential Tools Pfeiffer's Essential Tools resources save time and expense by offering proven, ready-to-use materials—including exercises, activities, games, instruments, and assessments—for use during a training or team-learning event. These resources are frequently offered in looseleaf or CD-ROM format to facilitate copying and customization of the material.

Pfeiffer also recognizes the remarkable power of new technologies in expanding the reach and effectiveness of training. While e-hype has often created whizbang solutions in search of a problem, we are dedicated to bringing convenience and enhancements to proven training solutions. All our e-tools comply with rigorous functionality standards. The most appropriate technology wrapped around essential content yields the perfect solution for today's on-the-go trainers and human resource professionals.

www.pfeiffer.com

Essential resources for training and HR professionals

Multimedia-Based Instructional Design

Multimedia-Based Instructional Design

COMPUTER-BASED TRAINING

WEB-BASED TRAINING

DISTANCE BROADCAST TRAINING

PERFORMANCE-BASED SOLUTIONS

SECOND EDITION

William W. Lee
Diana L. Owens

Pfeiffer

A Wiley Imprint
www.pfeiffer.com

Published by Pfeiffer
An Imprint of Wiley.
989 Market Street, San Francisco, CA 94103-1741
www.pfeiffer.com

For additional copies/bulk purchases of this book in the U.S. please contact 800-274-4434.

Pfeiffer books and products are available through most bookstores. To contact Pfeiffer directly call our Customer Care Department within the U.S. at 800-274-4434, outside the U.S. at 317-572-3985, fax 317-572-4002, or visit www.pfeiffer.com.

Pfeiffer also publishes its books in a variety of electronic formats. Some content that appears in print may not be available in electronic books.

ISBN: 0-7879-7069-7

Library of Congress Cataloging-in-Publication Data

Lee, William W.
    Multimedia-based instructional design: computer-based training, web-based training, distance broadcast training, performance-based solutions/William W. Lee, Diana L. Owens.—2nd ed.
        p. cm.
    Includes bibliographical references and index.
    ISBN 0-7879-7069-7 (alk. paper)
    1. Employees—Training of—Planning. 2. Computer-assisted instruction.
3. Instructional systems—Design. I. Owens, Diana L., date. II. Title.
    HF5549.5.T7L4264   2004
    658.3'12404—dc22

                                                        2004001079

Acquiring Editor: Matthew Davis
Director of Development: Kathleen Dolan Davies
Developmental Editor: Susan Rachmeler
Production Editor: Rachel Anderson
Editor: Rebecca Taff

Manufacturing Supervisor: Bill Matherly
Editorial Assistant: Laura Reizman
Interior Design: Claudia Smelser
Cover Design: Adrian Morgan
Illustrations: Lotus Art

Printed in the United States of America
Printing   10   9   8   7   6   5   4   3

CONTENTS

To Walter M. Lee

—Bill Lee

To my husband, Terry, for his feedback and support, wonderful sense of humor, and the many things I have learned from him that have contributed to this text

To my parents, Luella and Bill Dubois; my son, Rob MacKey; and his wife, Jessica, for their constant demonstrations of love, encouragement, and support

—Diana Owens

LIST OF FIGURES AND TABLES

ACKNOWLEDGMENTS

We would like to thank Bob McAvoy of Training Consulting Softek (www.trainingsoftek.com) for providing the resources for automating the Media Analysis Tool and the Objectives Analysis tool; Alex Nestor of the University of Texas at Dallas for developing the original automated the tools; and Charles Chow and Steven Liu of Training Consulting Softek for perfecting the code on the tools. Thanks to Kathy Larson of Granite Technologies, 1772 Platte St., Denver, Colorado, for permission to use Xegy, the tool that automates the step/action table in Appendix A and enables it as a Project Management Tool (www.xegy.com).

Thanks also to Centra Software, Inc., of Lexington, Massachusetts (www.centra.com), for permission to use screen shots of its synchronous web-based software. Thanks to Intellinex (www. Intellinex.com), 925 Euclid Avenue, Cleveland, Ohio, a division of Ernst & Young, for use of screens from its Rapid Development tool; to ONETOUCH Systems, Inc., 40 Airport Freeway, San Jose, California, 95110 (www.onetouch.com), for its cooperation in providing us with materials for this book; and to Global Knowledge Network, Inc., ICN Pharmaceuticals, Costa Mesa, California, and Real Learning Company of Scottsdale, Arizona.

Thanks also to Mlink Technologies, (www.mlinktechnologies.com) Inc., 550 Edmonds, Suite 204, Lewisville, Texas, 75067 for the examples of user-interface graphics shown in the book. Our appreciation goes to Claudia Dineen for the text addressing the rationale and business issue for each user-interface design and also for testing our tools and templates.

Thanks to Matthew Davis, our editor, for his belief in the value of our revisions and to Susan Rachmeler for her sound editorial advice. Also a special thank you to Carolyn Murphy of American Airlines Corporate University for her vigilance in keeping current on the latest technologies and sharing the information with us.

And to all of you whom we have worked with over the years who have mentored us, guided us, given us constructive criticism and feedback, and allowed us to experiment and be creative, you are too numerous to mention—but without all of you, we would never have gained the experience to share with others.

To our families, friends, and colleagues over the years—we couldn't have done it without you behind us and beside us.

Thank you!

February 2004

William W. Lee
Euless, Texas

Diana L. Owens
Cross Roads, Texas

INTRODUCTION:
GETTING THE MOST FROM THIS RESOURCE

WOW! So much has changed since the first edition of our book went to print in 2000 (which really means we began writing it in 1999)! Everything from changes in terminology to attempts to define consistent standards. *Learning management systems* (LMS) have proliferated since our first edition. These LMS have often incorporated *learning content management systems* (LCMS) to deliver learning activities and track them. And we have been learning too! We want to update those of you who purchased the first edition on how all of this has impacted the instructional design model.

Another unexpected surprise for us is that
the first edition of the book has been translated
into four languages: Korean, Japanese, and
two Chinese dialects. "Thanks" from the
authors to our international audience!

The major thing we have found that has not changed is how complicated the issue of e-learning is. As a matter of fact, it has become even more complicated. Figure I.1 graphically represents all of the components that need to be considered when implementing learning, including e-learning.

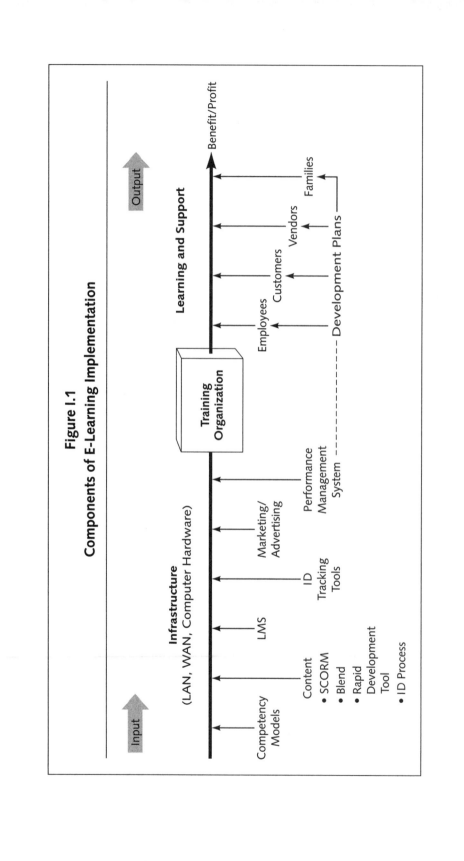

Figure I.1
Components of E-Learning Implementation

This book only deals with the learning components of this model. The inputs to implementing learning usually go through some training organization or learning function whether learning is delivered centrally, say through a corporate university, or if it is decentralized and distributed through numerous training functions within one organization. Many companies are creating new positions called *chief learning officers* (CLOs) to coordinate and implement this increasingly complex issue.

Trying to stay on the leading edge of technology is nearly impossible. But our continued involvement in the learning arena has brought many of the changes to our doorstep, and we have also gone looking to answer questions for our customers. So we thought it was time to update the book with what we have learned and to bring it more into line with our continually evolving philosophy.

When we began the first edition, the term for online learning was "multimedia." Now it's "e-learning." Multimedia now means what it always should have—"multiple media." That's how we always defined it. So we will continue using multimedia to refer to blended solutions (yet another relatively new term).

The emphasis is still very much on multimedia. Maybe even more than at any time before in the discipline of training and learning! Maybe to the extreme! We have seen many instances where "everything to the web" was the dictum. Unfortunately, most of those efforts were less than successful because insufficient thought was given to the process of translating everything in learning to one medium. Most of the edicts are for economic reasons only. While we believe that most of what can be learned can be learned through some electronic medium, given the advances in web technology, we still believe strongly that decisions should be made in a systematic manner based on what the needs are for technology-based solutions for training delivery and solving business issues.

The reason for the emphasis on multimedia is still much the same. In a global corporate environment that is increasingly becoming a virtual world whose people are connected by technology, the need for rapid communication, continuous information flow, and speed to market is critical. Maintaining the business construct of everyone in the same room at the same time is increasingly difficult and often implausible. The need for virtual training to keep people connected is imperative. Yet the physical classroom remains a major delivery method, even though, for large numbers of participants, connecting virtually can be just as effective and more economical.

Economics is a reason to use e-learning, but only if you have the infrastructure in place. Companies that upgraded their technical infrastructure for Y2K, which became a non-issue, were well positioned to move into e-learning after September 11, 2001. Those companies that decided to move to e-learning for economic reasons after 9/11 often found that the technical capabilities that were required were not there and that the investment in the required technology was too expensive.

There is still a lot of discussion about e-learning not meeting everyone's learning style. We like what our friend Susan Guest, the vice president of e-learning at Baxter Pharmaceuticals, said recently, "If you were in the financial and accounting business and you told your employer that you had a different accounting method, you would be told to use the system the company uses. However, we still say that e-learning won't work for everyone because it doesn't meet everyone's learning style, so we have to have a variety of ways to deliver training." We agree with Susan.

And with some of the great software we have seen recently, various learning styles are accommodated. It is not e-learning that has been holding learning back, but the design of e-learning. Too much e-learning has been designed using traditional methodology, much like taking an instructor-led course and delivering it through CBT or WBT. The two media require completely different constructs. Besides, instructor-led training that is basically lecture doesn't meet everyone's needs either. Auditory learners make up only about 30 percent of the total population. A well-constructed instructor-led course that uses action learning, activities, PowerPoint®, video, and games accommodates learning styles just as the same course would using e-learning. However, e-learning has the additional advantages of delivering a consistent message, is available on demand when the learner needs it, and reduces the costs and personal inconvenience associated with traveling to receive training. The "rule of thirds" is becoming pretty standard in the industry. "People retain one-third more, in one-third less time, at one-third the cost." This is well documented by the Department of Defense and can be found in Teitelbaum and Orlansky (1996).

Noonan's (1993) message is even more relevant ten years after he wrote that if the training function is ever to escape "corporate America's basement," it must transform into an organization that ties solutions to business needs and help achieve corporate goals and objectives.

WHY BUY THIS BOOK?

One of the reasons to buy this revision, even if you have the original, is that we have improved many of the tools and added even more. The Media Analysis Tool in Chapter Eleven is now automated on the CD-ROM. We have also automated our objectives analysis process in Chapter Ten. Yes, an automated tool that *almost* writes your objectives for you! The step/action table in Appendix A is also automated and is now called the Project Management Tool to track your instructional design activities and tasks. There is a special URL and password listed on the Links menu of the CD-ROM for Granite Technologies, the company that owns the tool called Xegy™ (pronounced x-è-g) that is used to automate the step/action table. This URL is available *only* to purchasers of the book. You have ninety days of free access to the Project Management Tool and can use it to track your projects and print the results. Figure I.2 shows the graphical interface of the Project Management Tool.

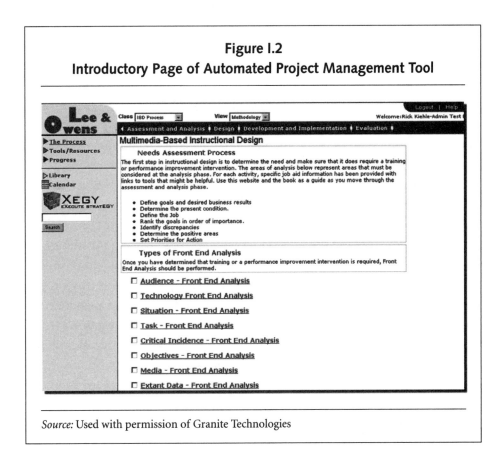

Figure I.2

Introductory Page of Automated Project Management Tool

Source: Used with permission of Granite Technologies

You can check off each activity and task as you complete it, but even more beneficial is the capability to click on any activity or step and immediately hyperlink to the online tools and worksheets that you use to complete that task. Xegy™ is a new approach to focusing business intelligence to drive performance. It provides a performance support framework for:

- Rapid prototyping of a strategy roadmap
- Communicating that roadmap uniquely to different workgroups
- Supporting ongoing management of the process
- Tracking results and capturing input for continuous improvement and innovation

Non-technical people can harness technology to build and implement their strategies.

Figure I.3 shows the conceptual framework of Xegy™. The tool can be used as a process management tool, a project management tool, or a performance support tool taking both systems and human factors into consideration. To learn more about Xegy™, see the website www.xegy.com.

We have added chapters on Issue Analysis, developing an Evaluation Strategy, and creating an Evaluation Plan. We have also created a much more robust tool for evaluating e-learning software that replaces the one in the first edition. There is now a tool for making "build or buy" decisions if the solution must be customized or can it be purchased off-the-shelf.

We have found many new examples of user interface design and restructured the section on design to reflect both the objectivist and constructivist theories of instructional design. These are only a few of the changes you will find in this edition.

Our integrated instructional design model transcends whatever media will deliver the solution and is still a major advantage of this book. There are numerous books on the market today on how to design and develop computer-based training, others for web-based training, and still others for distance broadcast training. So why buy this book rather than one of the others?

Other books are well suited for their specific delivery media, but the approach to the instructional design process differs in each one. Most use the traditional instructional design (ID) model with its phases of analysis, design, development, implementation, and evaluation, but they vary in the tasks and activities to complete during each phase.

Consequently, if you want to design for more than one medium, you have to buy a book on each and adjust or adapt your ID model depending on the medium.

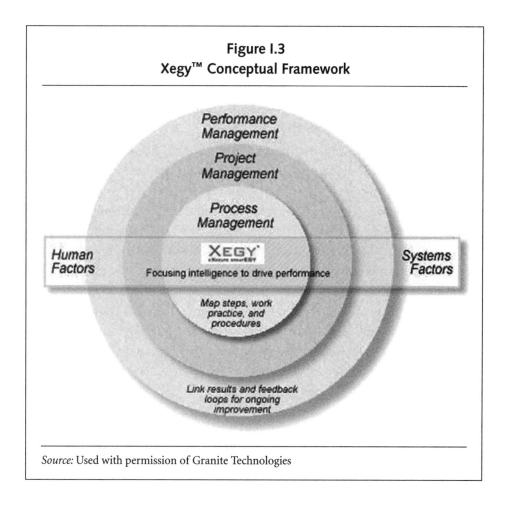

Figure I.3
Xegy™ Conceptual Framework

Performance Management

Project Management

Process Management

XEGY®
Focusing intelligence to drive performance

Human Factors

Systems Factors

Map steps, work practice, and procedures

Link results and feedback loops for ongoing improvement

Source: Used with permission of Granite Technologies

So why buy this book? Because it eliminates multiple procedures. Use the process in this book and design in any media!

Instructional designers are intelligent, creative people who eventually figure out how to meld the best components of each design model given time and experience. We all gain experience by working on multiple projects. But time is usually what we lack. We're often too rushed to reflect on what we did during a project that made it go smoothly—what we did to get over the bumps and around the roadblocks. The revised *Multimedia-Based Instructional Design* offers time-tested procedures and tools to encapsulate the experience of hundreds of course developers, thereby reducing the time required to reflect on past successes and problems. Use our book as the basis for projects, and change only those steps you find work differently and better for your group than the way we suggest. The new automated Project Management Tool allows you to make this customization.

WHO SHOULD BUY THIS BOOK?

Our revised edition of *Multimedia-Based Instructional Design* is intended for the same audience as the first, but allows us to share the updated information and knowledge we have gained since the first edition. It is for course developers (instructional designers, authors, project managers) who are beginning their first multimedia project, as well as for experienced designers of large projects that require a systematic process that everyone can follow. It is well suited for use by project teams when there is a mixture of experienced and new developers. It imparts a consistent message to those project teams that find members matrixed in and out of projects and that use a combination of internal and outsourced resources.

Although the book discusses many issues encountered by internal training departments, multimedia consulting companies should also find the tools valuable and the tips for managing customer expectations enlightening.

FOCUS OF THE BOOK

Our philosophy is to focus on the human-performance arena. This focus presents challenges to multimedia development groups whose philosophy reflects a more traditional approach. We agree with Tom Gilbert (1996) that the purpose of all instruction is to affect human performance through learning or performance support. If multimedia development groups move into the human-performance area, they open new horizons of opportunities to work within an organization and become more valuable. We recommend Judith Hale's *The Performance Consultant's Fieldbook: Tools and Techniques for Improving Organizations and People* (1998) to help your group make the necessary shift to performance consulting. Lee and Krayer's *Organizing Change: An Inclusive, Systemic Approach to Maintain Productivity and Achieve Results* (2003) is also a good companion book to this one because it uses the instructional design model and expands its use to enterprise-wide solutions that can transform a training department into an organizational development department by providing the knowledge, skills, and tools to expand the department's capabilities. We also recommend Thomas Toth's book, *Technology for Trainers: A Primer for the Age of E-Learning* (2003), and *E-Learning Tools and Technologies* (2003) by William and Katherine Horton. These books provide tactical development tips for e-learning solutions. We do not include a glossary of e-learning terms in this book because there is a very good one available on the International ASTD website (www.astd.org) that is continually updated.

We've all experienced working on projects for long hours, with budget overruns, missed deadlines, and unnecessary rework. We, too, have experienced the frustration associated with all of these situations. Our goal is to provide you with a handbook that helps you reduce cycle time for completing projects, makes your job easier, and conveys the lessons that will reduce your learning curve.

STRUCTURE OF THE BOOK

The book is organized in four parts:

1. Multimedia Needs Assessment and Analysis
2. Multimedia Instructional Design
3. Multimedia Development and Implementation
4. Multimedia Evaluation

Overall, it is structured as a step/action handbook that presents activities and the associated steps required for completing a successful project. We present tools to assist in organizing the information obtained from each activity. Appendix A is a step/action table (now automated on the CD as a Project Management Tool) that lists the steps to follow in each phase of the instructional design process. Project teams can follow the steps as listed or adapt them for their specific needs. The automated version allows you to track your progress through a project.

Each of the chapters is short. We wanted to provide you with critical information without too much extraneous information to get in the way of the way we want the book to be used—as an instructional design process manual.

The graphic that follows this paragraph appears (in varying form) at the beginning of each of the four parts of the book to identify the phase of the instructional design process to be discussed in that part. Note the circular configuration, to demonstrate the circular rather than linear nature of the process. Each phase of the ID process flows through to the next, and the last reflects back on the first. This is the concept of "congruence."

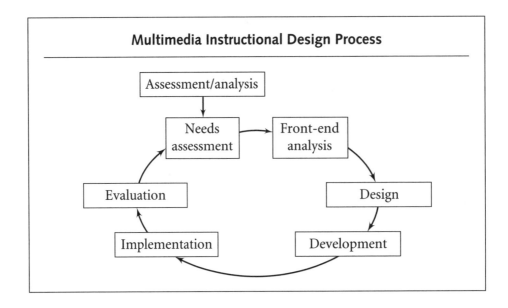

Multimedia Instructional Design Process

Assessment/analysis

Needs assessment → Front-end analysis

Design

Development

Implementation

Evaluation

In Part One we follow Dick and Carey's model (1990) of separating the analysis phase of instructional design into two parts: needs assessment and front-end analysis. Needs assessment focuses on determining the current state and the desired state and the type of business issue the need arises from. Front-end analysis then determines how to close that gap with a results-driven solution. We address ten types of front-end analysis:

1. *Audience analysis:* determining who the target population is for the solution and their demographic as well as learning needs

2. *Technology analysis:* determining the type of technology available and technological considerations and constraints for delivery of the solution

3. *Situation analysis:* determining the environmental considerations in delivering the solution

4. *Task analysis:* determining the physical and mental requirements for getting the job done

5. *Critical incident analysis:* determining which tasks require that training or information be provided to the target audience

6. *Objective analysis:* determining the performance and instructional objectives for the solution and making the distinction between the types of objectives as

well as when and where to use them; also their impact on the content as well as delivery media

7. *Issue analysis:* categorizing analysis findings into organizational, performance and training issues

8. *Media analysis:* selecting the most appropriate delivery medium (or media) for a solution

9. *Extant data analysis:* determining what materials are available and which need to be developed—basically, making a "build-or-buy" decision

10. *Cost analysis:* determining the up-front benefit the solution has in comparison to the cost of the solution

We also include a rapid analysis model (RAM) in Chapter Fourteen. We developed this model for experienced course developers who intuitively understand the step-by-step process involved in gathering data through needs assessment and the nine types of front-end analysis.

In Part Two, Multimedia Instructional Design, we have provided the activities and steps required to produce a *course design specification* (CDS) document. We include many tips on project management for course developers to fully understand the complexities involved in multimedia projects. Such information should guide them in selecting media. For example, if assessment and analysis result in a web-based solution, the project team should know what's involved so they can determine whether or not the solution is realistic for their business and can assemble the required resources before the project starts. The complexities might, though, result in choosing another solution.

Part Three is on multimedia development and implementation. Here there is divergence of methodology depending on the media. Therefore, we begin with a chapter on common elements of development and implementation and then explain the particular aspects for computer-based, web-based, distance broadcast, and performance support solutions. We also differentiate the design issues between objectivist and constructivist theories of instruction and their impact on multimedia. We also discuss SCORM (Searchable Content Objects Reference Model) standards and their impact on e-learning development.

Even if different groups perform the authoring and designing, designers should know the complexities involved in the solution they propose in order to determine whether or not the solution is feasible. Designers should also be able to carefully consider the issues related to implementing a solution. To broaden the knowledge and skills of designers, we have included a discussion on many development topics. We explain the influence of *learning management systems* (LMS) on implementation. Course developers are expected to acquire increasingly broad skill sets and are becoming the authors of what they design, so we also discuss and provide examples of *rapid development tools* (RDT) that are designed to reduce the amount of time required for developing e-learning by using templates that require less authoring.

Part Four is on multimedia evaluation. We discuss evaluation from two perspectives: the strategic and the tactical. To address strategic issues, we have included a chapter on how to develop an evaluation strategy for your organization to measure reaction, knowledge, performance, and cost. We provide the templates and a completed model of an evaluation strategy. A crossover tool from strategic to tactical is an e-learning evaluation tool that can be used if you are considering buying off-the-shelf e-learning or to be certain that you include the necessary components in custom-developed e-learning that you build internally. This evaluation tool is a companion to the new tool that assists in making "build or buy" decisions in Chapter Twelve, Extant Data Analysis.

To address tactical issues, we have included a template for an evaluation plan that you should develop for each project. The template includes all of the issues you should consider for the evaluation plan. We still have chapters on designing, developing, and delivering tests and test validity and reliability. We present the steps for constructing various types of objective tests and explain the strengths and weaknesses of each type.

Throughout, we have included sections on applicable learning and instructional design theory as a basis of "why we do what we do." People outside of the human performance arena often don't see the need for particular aspects of development. They don't understand the basic human characteristics surrounding learning that require us to include certain components. We have laid out the theory to help you explain why to them.

We also provide sections in most chapters on our personal experiences, to help you avoid the pitfalls we have experienced and replicate the successes we've had. Yet another section in each part of the book explains how e-learning, especially the Internet and web-based technologies, requires us to change the way we think about the traditional instructional design model.

In total, we present a replicable model, adaptable to any delivery medium, diverging only in the development phase of multimedia projects.

THE CD-ROM

The CD-ROM that accompanies this book contains tools we developed that are meant to be modified to meet your particular project requirements, including the following:

- *Project Management Tool:* this automated tool is a complete checklist of all activities and steps in the multimedia instructional design process as laid out in this book. The checklist is also found in Appendix A. On the CD-ROM, we provide you with the URL for a website that you can access to download the tool and use it to track your projects.

- *Tools and templates:* the tools directory contains checklists and templates for each phase of the ID process. These tools and templates can be copied and used as-is or customized to meet your needs and used for multiple projects. The directory is divided into sections for assessment and analysis tools, design tools, development and implementation tools, and evaluation tools. A hard copy of each tool is also included in the Appendix (look for the CD-ROM icon): so you can browse through and determine whether and how each one applies to your project.

- A link to Centra Software's synchronous web-based tool, which explains how the web-based delivery software works.

- A link to Intellinex, a set of rapid development templates that demonstrate the ability to create e-learning without having to possess sophisticated authoring skills

- An automated version of the Media Analysis Tool found in Part One that will calculate your responses on each of twenty-four factors regarding the content, audience, and cost of various delivery media and provide a chart that lays out a hierarchy of potential components of a blended learning solution

- An automated version of the objective analysis process we outline in Part One that will assist you in writing measurable performance, terminal, and lesson objectives

Hardware/Software Requirements and Launch Instructions

The tools found on the CD-ROM require you to have access to a PC running Microsoft Word.

System requirements for the automated objectives tool include:

1. Pentium 100 MegaHertz CPU or above with minimum of 64M of memory and 5M free hard drive space.

2. Microsoft Windows® Operating System (WIN9x/2000/ME/XP).

3. Internet Explorer® 5 or above.

4. Java Runtime 1.3 or above.

Instructions to Run Automated Objectives Tool

If you have a high-speed Internet connection:

1. Launch objWizard.htm from CD directly by double clicking on the file. Follow the instructions on screen to download and install Java Runtime 1.3.

2. Automated Objectives Analysis Tool content will show up after Java Runtime 1.3 is successfully installed.

If you don't have a high-speed Internet connection, or if Java Runtime download fails:

1. Run j2re-1_3_1_06-windows-i586.exe program from CD directly. Follow the instruction on screen to install Java Runtime 1.3.

2. Launch Automated Objectives Analysis Tool by double clicking on objWizard.htm from CD.

System Requirements for Automated Media Analysis Tool

1. Pentium 100 MegaHertz CPU or above with minimum of 64M of memory and 5M free hard drive space

2. Microsoft Windows Operating System (WIN9x/2000/ME/XP)

3. Internet Explorer 5 or above

Instructions to Run Media Analysis Tool

Simply double click on MediaAnalysisTool on the CD ROM Menu.

part one

Multimedia Needs Assessment and Analysis

Introduction to Multimedia Needs Assessment and Front-End Analysis

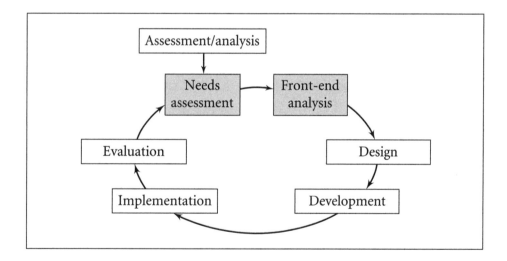

O ur approach to analysis breaks the phase into two parts. The first is needs assessment, a systematic way of determining the gap that exists between where the organization is and where it wishes to be. The second is front-end analysis, a collection of techniques that can be used in various combinations to help you bridge the gap by determining what solution(s) will be required.

In completing the activities in this phase you will

- Find the customer's business issue
- Decide how to satisfy the business issue
- Decide the delivery mechanism for the solution
- Write objectives
- Complete cost analysis

During needs assessment, it is critical to focus on gathering the information you need to be able to make informed decisions. The information from needs assessment provides input into front-end analysis in that, once the need for an intervention is established in needs assessment, front-end analysis explores deeper levels of information needed for the design of the solution. To perform needs assessment and front-end analysis you will need to:

1. Make a judgment about how much assessment and analysis is required to make an informed decision based on your time frame, project size, and project constraints
2. Determine the appropriate sources for collecting information
3. Establish a technique for collecting and assembling information

E-LEARNING'S IMPACT ON ASSESSMENT AND ANALYSIS

Assessment and analysis before multimedia technologies consisted of the instructional designer gathering information from subject-matter experts (SMEs) and organizing it in such a manner that it could be delivered in a meaningful way and that learners would retain the information. In the absence of an expert, a great deal of time was spent researching information in libraries and plowing through existing materials. The Internet has aided designers in finding information more quickly and reducing the amount of time required for analysis (Lee, Owens, & Benson, 2002).

In the training world before the technology explosion, only a few delivery methods needed to be considered during analysis. Today, with so many new media to choose from, thorough media and technology analyses are required. A *technology analysis* yields information about the infrastructure capabilities of a company and the current technologies being used. *Media analysis* yields information on the most appropriate delivery systems for a particular application.

Analysis also includes *vendor analysis*. Today there are many companies in the industry that claim to have total solutions that will solve all problems. Implementing any e-learning technology has obstacles that will cause huge problems if a company does not do its research on any product it is considering. Vendor research should include investigating the venture capital of a company, its financial standing, and how long it has been in the industry. Discover their goals and objectives. Are they looking to establish themselves in the industry or become a large enough player to be bought out? Often the reasons for buyouts are to eliminate competing products. You may purchase a product that will some day have no technical or customer support, and you may not be able to do it yourself. Also check out the vendor's customer base. Ask for the names and *visit* customers who have repeatedly engaged the vendor, as well as customers who have used them only once. Find out how often the vendor plans to upgrade its product. How many upgrades are included in the original purchase price? And how long will it take for your product to become obsolete if you decide not to upgrade?

chapter TWO

Needs Assessment

Needs assessment is the systematic process of determining goals, identifying discrepancies between actual and desired conditions, and establishing priorities for action (Lee & Roadman, 1991).

Briggs (1977) identified five types of need, illustrated in Table 2.1.

Table 2.1
Five Types of Need

Need	Description
1. Normative need	A need that is compared to a standard.
	Example one: industry standards establish that it should take 750 hours of development time for each hour of computer-based training delivery. Company X currently takes 1,500 hours to do this, so it needs to find ways to reduce the time to meet this standard in order to bid competitively.
	Example two: bank A is not as competitive as bank B in offering a variety of services to customers because it is not automated enough to efficiently process the paperwork required to deliver those services. Bank A needs automation to bring it to the same level as bank B.
2. Felt need	What people think they need.
	Example: the executives of a sales-and-marketing firm believe that their sales representatives need training in interpersonal

Table 2.1
Five Types of Need, Cont'd.

Need	Description
	relations because they don't share valuable information that can help others increase their sales. They feel a need for this training to solve their problem.
3. Expressed or demanded need	Supply and demand. Example: insurance company Y is looking for ways to improve the speed of processing claims because a private consulting company delivered the results of a survey it conducted, showing that motorists use this as the number-one criterion in selecting an insurance company.
4. Comparative need	Some people have a particular attribute; others don't. Example: retailer A finds that its customer service representatives resolve customer inquiries at an average of ten resolutions per measurement unit. The range among representatives, however, is from five to fifteen resolutions. The retailer needs to bring all customer service representatives to a maximum level of efficient processing while maintaining customer satisfaction.
5. Anticipated or future need	Projected demands. Example: a steering committee of bank A has decided that for it to be competitive it must automate the data-processing function to provide more services to customers. They state this goal in their five-year strategic plan.

PROCESS

There are six activities in the process of conducting a needs assessment:

1. *Determine the present condition.* Identify the root causes of the expressed need.
2. *Define the job.* What knowledge and skills are required to successfully complete the work?

3. *Rank the goals in order of importance.* Show how goals are interrelated.

4. *Identify discrepancies.* How do the expected performance and the actual performance encountered in meeting a goal differ? List all discrepancies, as well as missing tasks.

5. *Determine positive areas.* Identify areas related to the business issue in which the company is doing well, and document their existence.

6. *Set priorities for action.* Set them against the backdrop of the job goals, desired results, and other relevant factors.

Needs assessment is accomplished by developing assessment questionnaires, establishing procedures for collecting data (such as mailings, telephone and personal interviews), and analyzing data to produce meaningful information.

Consider using the data-collection techniques presented in Table 2.2. Appendix D provides instructions for these data-collection techniques:

- Self-completion questionnaires
- Direct interviews
- Focus groups
- Observation

Table 2.2
Data-Collection Techniques

Interviews		
Technique	Advantages	Disadvantages
Phone	Fast and inexpensive	Less sensitive; no visual information
	Easy to supervise	Must be short—fifteen minutes or less (participants do not like to be kept on the phone longer)
		Requires trained interviewers
In person	High response rate, most accurate	Can be time consuming
		Sometimes yields extraneous information
	Highest volume of information	Requires trained interviewers

Table 2.2
Data-Collection Techniques, Cont'd.

Questionnaires

Technique	Advantages	Disadvantages
E-mail	High rate of return	Requires explicit instructions
	Yields large amount of data	Allows collaboration among respondents (if individual responses are desired)
	Does not require trained interviewers	
Paper questionnaire	Yields large amount of data	Requires explicit instructions
	Does not require trained interviewers	Returns tend to be low

Observation

Technique	Advantages	Disadvantages
Video camera	Find out what people actually do rather than what they say they do	Time consuming
		Those who analyze the results must be trained
	Less bias of what is observed because more than one person can view the video	Workers may perform differently while being observed
		Does not allow you to question job performers in real time or experience some of the environmental factors that affect performance
		You can only see what the lens of the camera sees, not everything on the periphery
Observer	Find out what people actually do rather than what they say they do	Time consuming
		Requires skilled observer
		Workers may perform differently while they are being observed

Table 2.2
Data-Collection Techniques, Cont'd.

Simulation

Technique	Advantages	Disadvantages
Inexpensive mock-up or talk-through	Permits collecting job performance information before equipment is developed	Results may not transfer directly to job performance because mock-up is not realistic
		Requires skilled determination of what should be simulated
		Will not account for motivational factors
Use actual equipment or software, but not in the work environment	Only opportunity to observe behavior under controlled conditions of stress, system failure, etc.	Can be very expensive
		Requires skilled determination of what should be simulated
		Does not account for motivational factors

Confidentiality is important. To assure employees that none of their individual responses will be reported, use a confidentiality agreement similar to the one in the Assessment and Front-End Analysis Tools section of Appendix E. The organization's representative signs the agreement and a copy is shared with each participant in the needs assessment.

NEEDS ASSESSMENT PROCEDURE

Follow these activities:

Activity One: Determine the Present Condition

Step one: Identify the knowledge and skill needed to perform the task(s).

Step two: Identify the job-related knowledge and skill areas used to select people for the task(s).

Step three: Check for discrepancies between steps one and two. This step depends on whether there is a match between the results of steps one and two. If there isn't a match, then identify the skills that are missing and review for possible training or performance support applications, and consider revision of employee-selection criteria.

Step four: Look for environmental causes of the problem if there is a match between steps one and two. Visit the work environment and compare average performance with exemplary or ideal performance. Identify gaps in performance, and continue with step five.

Step five: Document task performance that is affected by such environmental factors as:

- Noise
- Equipment
- Tools
- Temperature
- Work space

Step six: Review all results and identify areas of need.

Step seven: Gather data from employees about:

- Management support
- Existing training
- Teamwork and empowerment
- Workflow and processes
- Safety

Step eight: Review all results and identify areas of need.

Activity Two: Define the Job

Define the ideal situation of the job, and compare the ideal to the tasks currently performed.

Activity Three: Rank the Goals in Order of Importance

List goals in order of importance, and show how they interrelate.

Activity Four: Identify Discrepancies

Determine the differences between ideal and actual performance. List all discrepancies as well as missing tasks.

Activity Five: Determine Positive Areas

Use the appreciative-inquiry technique (Hammond, 1996) and document what is working. Appreciative inquiry identifies an organization's strengths, which is important for two reasons. First, the solution might be as simple as applying the same principles and procedures from those strengths to the current issue. Second, it focuses and allows organizations to reflect on and appreciate the positive aspects of what they do rather than focusing only on the negative.

Activity Six: Set Priorities for Action

Step one: List all possible solutions suggested by the needs assessment. Identify the impact on performance goals of not providing a solution.

Step two: Define the impact of each solution in terms of time, money, and customer satisfaction.

Step three: Make recommendations, keeping in mind job goals, desired results, and other relevant factors.

FROM OUR EXPERIENCE

Using the activities and steps outlined in this chapter, you will be surprised by how often the solution is not training. Spend the time you need to gather enough information to make enlightened suggestions for solving the stated business need.

Taking the time to systematically uncover the root of a perceived problem keeps you from wasting your time and your organization's resources on multimedia projects that do not solve a business need. Use the Needs Assessment Report form in the Assessment and Front-End Analysis Tools section of Appendix E as a starting point to document and report your needs-assessment results.

Those duties and tasks that the company performs well should be analyzed to determine how the successful skills are learned or taught at present. A possible recommendation might be that the successful learning techniques be replicated and included in training, or that where current performance is successful there is no need for training on those skills.

We often begin a needs assessment by analyzing the job descriptions that are usually already available for positions within a company. These descriptions generally detail the types of duties that members of the audience for the training are expected to perform. Job descriptions usually contain a catch-all phrase that reads something like ". . . and other duties as assigned." Be certain to identify whether these other duties fall within or outside the scope of the stated business problem. Generic descriptions can be modified to accurately reflect the job using data collected during interviews or observations.

The status of the job description is a critical issue. If it is current, it probably accurately reflects the duties of the persons holding the position. If it is not current, you should determine its accuracy. The issue of accuracy might well be raised in any case, given the rapid pace of change and growth in business and industry today. More jobs now require people to assume multiple duties and perform tasks once performed by several employees.

At a minimum, the job descriptions you analyze should contain:

- Position title (the job name). This should be part of an overall organizational structure or hierarchy.
- Position description (generic). This can be a broad description or listing of the job actions and activities required for successful job performance.
- Knowledge, skills, and attitudes (KSA) required for the job.
- Proficiency measures. This is a list and explanation of the performance measures used for the job tasks.

If job descriptions do not exist for a position, they should be developed during the needs assessment.

From the job description, make a flowchart of the job, starting with the goal or final product and working backward. Use this flowchart to identify any prerequisite job skills as well as all critical steps in the job process and their related skills.

You can verify the job-description flowchart you have developed by asking the job performers and their supervisors to confirm the current duties and the correct entry-level skills for the job.

An electronic database is often helpful in assessment and front-end analysis efforts. A database format enables you to store, manipulate, and organize data to report your findings clearly and concisely.

We have found the techniques in Table 2.2 useful for data collection. Analyze them to determine what would work best in your unique situation.

After collecting all relevant data, verify that the information is adequate for recommending a solution and (if appropriate) designing the intervention. Document your conclusions with as much detail as time, resources, and project constraints allow.

If you are an experienced instructional designer and if you determine that your project warrants a streamlined process for needs assessment and front-end analysis, use the rapid analysis method outlined in Chapter Fourteen and the information in Chapter Nine on Issue Analysis.

SUMMARY

At this point, you have determined whether or not there is a gap between the desired performance and the current state of a job. If a gap exists, move to front-end analysis and determine the type of intervention required to close the gap. If there is no gap, or if the gap is outside the range of interventions permissible for the multimedia development or training group (which might be the case for a performance or systemic issue, as outlined in Chapter Nine on Issue Analysis), then so inform the stakeholders.

Note that instructional developers and multimedia development or training groups should expand their repertoire of skills to assist with issues other than training. At the very least, they need to be aware of other sources of help. If some aspect of the solution is within the purview of the training group, remain involved in the project and stay informed of the changes that occur. In this way, your group can move quickly to implement your portion of any solution once the changes are completed.

Front-End Analysis

Once needs assessment determines that training or performance support intervention is required, the next step is to obtain more detailed information about exactly what is to be developed. Table 3.1 is a summary of the types of front-end analysis and what you will know at the conclusion of front-end analysis.

Table 3.1 **Types of Front-End Analysis**	
Type	**Purpose**
Audience analysis	Identify the background, learning characteristics, and prerequisite skills of the audience.
Technology analysis	Identify existing technology capabilities.
Task analysis	Describe the job-related tasks performed as a result of the training or performance support.
Critical-incident analysis	Determine what skills or knowledge should be targeted in the multimedia intervention or training program.
Situational analysis	Identify environmental or organizational constraints that may have an impact on goals and multimedia design.
Objective analysis	Write the objectives for the job tasks to be addressed.
Media analysis	Select the appropriate media delivery strategy.
Extant-data analysis	Identify existing training materials, manuals, references, and syllabi.
Cost-benefit analysis	Identify cost and benefit, and return on investment.

At the end of front-end analysis, use the Analysis Report Tool in the Assessment and Front-End Analysis Tools section of Appendix E to organize your findings.

FROM OUR EXPERIENCE

Once the need has been established, use the tools of front-end analysis to collect and analyze all relevant data regarding a business need. To avoid expensive rework, we recommend you complete all front-end analysis, including content gathering, before beginning design.

We often find front-end analysis to be the "hidden phase" of the ID process. Many organizations decide to eliminate assessment and analysis altogether and begin immediately with design "to save time." But have you ever heard of tweaking the design? What usually happens is that the team gets to a certain point in the project and realizes there's not enough information or there's been an error. So the team members decide to go back and revisit their initial ideas and then move forward. The team may have to gain permission to make the changes, which is usually obtained because of the investment of time and resources. So the project moves on—but suddenly, another stop! More tweaking. Then at some point the project is determined to be so far off target that it is abandoned because the usefulness is no longer worth the effort or money, or it is finally completed—over budget and late.

The revisiting is really analysis. Time taken to complete a thorough analysis at the beginning is invariably more than made up in time savings later. It's sort of "Pay me now, or pay me later." Somewhere, the team is going to do the analysis. Our experience has been that if you spend adequate time completing a proper needs assessment and front-end analysis, the time required for the design and development phases can be greatly reduced. Those projects that go immediately to design simply spend more time there, and the result is a rushed development phase.

During development, it is usually the quality assurance (QA) reviews that are eliminated or rushed, resulting in an inferior product fraught with errors. We have found a more appropriate ratio is one-third analysis; one-third design and development; and one-third implementation, evaluation, and maintenance (Figure 3.1).

We have been asked how to respond to management or customers' position when they don't want to spend so much time on assessment and analysis. Our answer is that, so long as you incorporate the time and activities into the project, you

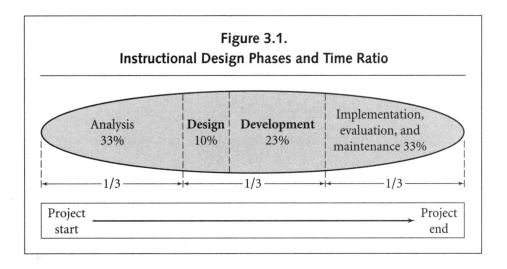

**Figure 3.1.
Instructional Design Phases and Time Ratio**

Analysis 33%
Design 10%
Development 23%
Implementation, evaluation, and maintenance 33%

|← ——— 1/3 ——— →|← ——— 1/3 ——— →|← ——— 1/3 ——— →|

Project start → Project end

can call it whatever the decision makers are comfortable with. If you keep decision makers informed of the valuable information you are gaining from the assessment and analysis activities, they will be satisfied in seeing progress on the project.

The next ten chapters deal with the nine types of front-end analysis. We examine each type closely and explain the information derived from it. We also explain how all of the data collected during front-end analysis fits into the design of the project.

In Chapter Fourteen we present a method for reducing the time required to complete an analysis without sacrificing quality. Our rapid analysis method can be used only after you thoroughly understand the methodology and information derived from the nine types of analysis.

chapter FOUR

Audience Analysis

Remember sitting through training sessions that were way over your head, or that proceeded so slowly you had trouble staying focused? It's not a favorite experience, but one we all have had. Audience analysis identifies the background and some of the learning characteristics of the target population.

This information helps you design a solution appropriate to the intended audience. Examples of information about the target audience that has an impact on the final solution are

- Experience with the training medium, as with CBT (computer-based training) or self-instructional materials. You may have to add additional material to the solution to acclimate the audience to the medium.

- Learning preferences (such as team versus individual learning). If the job requires people to work together, the solution should use the team approach.

- Language ability or preference (for example, considerations of English as a second language). Extra reference material, online dictionaries, or translations may be required.

- Previous training or job experience. If there are widely varying skill levels among those who perform the job, the solution has to accommodate the variations by guiding the audience to the appropriate level of materials.

- Special requirements (signing, Braille, and so on). If you have special conditions among the target audience that need to be met, the solution must be adapted to meet those requirements.

PROCESS

There are four activities in the procedure for conducting an audience analysis:

1. Analyze audience demographics and special requirements.
2. Determine attitudes toward content.
3. Analyze the language skills of the audience.
4. Document the results.

AUDIENCE ANALYSIS PROCEDURE

Follow these activities:

Activity One: Analyze Audience Demographics and Special Requirements

Step one: Begin with the job task information you collected during needs assessment and use it to verify the audience.

Step two: Confirm how many individuals will participate in the program and their general education and background.

Step three: Collect data on the native language, tone, use of humor, and graphics that are most appropriate for the audience. Pay particular attention to this aspect of the analysis if the audience is global, is predominantly male or female, or has a narrow age range. We recommend you become knowledgeable about cultural differences and make certain you address special requirements for cultural sensitivity for audiences from various cultures.

Step four: Note any special physical, ergonomic, or environmental audience requirements.

Activity Two: Determine Attitudes Toward Content

Step one: Determine whether or not the learners are likely to have misconceptions or misinformation about content that need to be addressed.

Step two: Determine whether there are negative or positive attitudes toward the content.

Step three: Go on to determine whether there is content-specific terminology or vocabulary that must be used or learned. Pay particular attention to this aspect if a large percentage of the audience use English as a second language.

Activity Three: Analyze the Language Skills of the Audience

Developing interventions at appropriate levels of readability is important to ensure that learning occurs. Analyzing language skills requires a two-step approach: (1) determining your audience's primary spoken and written language and (2) confirming the reading levels of the audience members in their primary language.

An effective method we employ to ensure that language is used consistently is the Fog Index (Gunning, 1968), one of many readability scales available. Instructions for using the Fog Index are found in the Assessment and Front-End Analysis Tools section of Appendix E. Also, most sophisticated word-processing systems contain components that analyze readability.

Activity Four: Document the Results

Record the results of your analysis for use by the design team (graphic artists, instructional designers) during the design phase and for the development team (interface designers, authors, videographers) in the development phase.

FROM OUR EXPERIENCE

Audience analysis is an area where assumptions are often made without validation. If your assumptions about the audience are not correct, problems will show up during testing and evaluation, at which time it is often too late or too expensive to fix the product. Attention during analysis to determining the audience language, tone, and delivery format can make the difference between great multimedia for the wrong audience and great multimedia that hits the mark and solves a business need.

When developing training for a global audience, we recommend you consider (1) recruiting for the project team someone who is from the appropriate culture(s) and speaks the language(s) well to be certain the product meets the cultural and language requirements of the audiences or (2) producing one version of the product and sending it to a vendor or development team from the target culture to enculturate and translate it.

SUMMARY

You now know the characteristics of the target audience with respect to their language, cultural, and educational background, as well as their attitude toward the content of the job and learning in general. All of these factors influence, and must be taken into account in, the media you use to deliver the solution.

Next, you analyze the technology considerations from the perspective of what is available or required for the solution, what the customer is willing to entertain as technology, and what the audience is familiar with and comfortable using.

chapter FIVE

Technology Analysis

There is a widening gap between training technologists and instructional designers. We assume the latter have the ability to produce "regular" training media, such as instructor and participant guides, job aids, overhead transparencies, or flip charts. But if you are typical of professionals in the instructional design field, your background is not "technical." Still, to meet the challenge of supporting business needs in today's business environment, you will discover it is critical to have a basic understanding of your unique technology environment.

Analyzing the level of technology in the organization:

- Brings the flexibility needed to solve business problems in the context of your unique technology environment
- Allows for a measured and phased approach to multimedia technologies, depending on who and how many in the organization have access to technology
- Provides the information you need for media selection

PROCESS

There are seven activities in conducting a technology analysis:

1. Analyze available communication technology.
2. Analyze the technology available for reference or performance support.

3. Analyze the technology available for testing and assessment.

4. Analyze the technology for distribution.

5. Analyze the technology for delivery.

6. Analyze the expertise.

7. Document the results.

TECHNOLOGY ANALYSIS PROCEDURE

Follow these activities:

Activity One: Analyze Available Communication Technology

To assess available technology for basic communication, determine which of these technologies are currently being used:

- *Phone conferencing.* Are employees able to phone in from their desks or a convenient location?

- *E-mail.* Are employees able to use their e-mail and attach documents to mail messages? Most employees have an e-mail address, and e-mail is accepted as just another communication tool, like the telephone. This media can very effectively constitute a communication channel between the instructor and student(s). E-mail was one of the earliest Internet applications to be widely used and is still one of the most powerful applications.

- *Chat room technology.* Chat room technology allows users to carry on text-based, online conversation with one another from within their web browser, similar to a phone conference.

- *Newsgroup technology.* Newsgroups (discussion groups) are similar to chat rooms, but discussions are posted on a server for anyone to read and learn from. Most web browsers include features that let users interact with a newsgroup from the browser.

- *List-server technology.* List servers use e-mail to enable a group to carry on discussions around a common area of interest. List servers are another form of discussion group and are also one of the original Internet applications.

Activity Two: Analyze the Technology Available for Reference or Performance Support

Step one: Determine whether or not online reference materials in hypertext markup language (HTML) and linked documents are available: company websites with links to other references or websites; graphics, videos, and photos in databases; on-line phone lists; and online course catalogs, schedules, abstracts, course notes, and instructor's notes.

Step two: Determine whether or not employees have access to performance support files or help systems. If so, what software is available for development? "Robohelp," "Doc-to-Help," or similar software applications are often used to develop this type of help file or online performance support system.

Activity Three: Analyze the Technology Available for Testing and Assessment

What technology is available for testing and assessment?

Step one: Determine whether or not electronic self-assessment, testing, or certification is available. If applicable, determine database and record-keeping requirements. If the tests are developed internally, determine the languages used. HTML, Java, and Shockwave are applications used in test development, along with off-the-shelf testing and assessment generators.

Step two: Define the issues of security. They make web-based testing and assessment challenging. Security issues are often the purview of an information systems (IS) department responsible for the computing needs of the entire business. A multimedia development organization's need to be able to test participants remotely and with security may find that its requirement is not a high priority for an IS department struggling with system integration or similar problems. Two security issues related to testing and assessment via the Internet or an intranet are quite commonly encountered. The first is user authentication. Authenticating (confirming) users' identities and access privileges is one way to control access to the site. Users are asked to authenticate themselves by providing information unique to them along with a private password. Determine the requirements for authentication.

The second issue is information confidentiality. The type of security that receives the most attention is information privacy. Web encryption is the technology used to ensure that information remains private as it passes over the Internet. Encryption does this by scrambling information so only the sender and receiver can make sense of it. More and more, web browsers and web servers are being developed with encryption capabilities built in. Determine the requirements for information confidentiality.

Activity Four: Analyze the Technology for Distribution

What technology is available for distribution of training or performance support?

Step one: Determine whether CD-ROMs, disks, or other materials are used for courses, reference material, or help files and, if so, how they are distributed.

Step two: Determine whether file transfer protocol (FTP) is used to download courses or files. FTP is a program with standardized features and functions used to transfer files from one computer to another on an intranet or the Internet. FTP technology is widely available and used routinely for distributing courseware. The potential for security-related issues is particularly acute for courses that contain sensitive or company-proprietary information. FTP technology can be used internally, though, to transfer content among members of a production team.

Activity Five: Analyze the Technology for Delivery

What technology is available for delivery of training or performance support?

Step one: Determine whether dedicated audio and video servers are used for delivering courses. If appropriate, note the requirements for file type and size.

Step two: Determine whether employees have access to multimedia PCs. Be sure to note the delivery platform with the lowest common denominator, so that configuration can be used for a minimum development-and-testing standard. Remember that the performance of a course is only as good as the slowest computer on which it is delivered.

Don't assume that the corporate computer is the only one that most employees have available. Many home PCs are more multimedia-capable than their corporate counterparts. Determine alternate access to PCs.

Step three: Find out whether a video teleconferencing or educational TV system is used for distribution of information. If applicable, pay particular attention to scheduling requirements.

Activity Six: Analyze the Expertise

Analyze the technology design and development and maintenance expertise. Determine if the equipment, hardware, software, and maintenance required for each technology is available. Include vendors or resources in other departments within your organization. Here is a sample checklist to use for determining availability of resources:

- ☐ Video production personnel, hardware, equipment, and software
- ☐ Audio production personnel, hardware, equipment, and software
- ☐ Graphics production personnel, hardware, equipment, and software
- ☐ Help or reference-system development personnel, hardware, equipment, and software
- ☐ CBT authoring and development personnel, hardware, equipment, and software
- ☐ Web and HTML development personnel, hardware, equipment, and software
- ☐ Testing, database, and statistical-programs personnel, hardware, equipment, and software

Activity Seven: Document the Results

Document all your results, and all contacts, with appropriate detail. Use the Technology Assessment Tool in the Assessment and Front-End Analysis Tools section of Appendix E to document findings, and note any additional technologies in use for

- Communication
- Reference material
- Testing and assessment
- Distribution
- Delivery
- Special design and development expertise

FROM OUR EXPERIENCE

It's impossible to meet business goals using multimedia without knowing technology details, such as the baseline configuration of user PCs or your company's ability to perform secure testing. Producing multimedia that doesn't transmit correctly, can't be maintained, or is inappropriate for the delivery platform wastes time, money, energy, and company resources. Understanding and documenting available technologies as well as current development expertise yields design specifications that ensure the effectiveness of your solution. A technology assessment can also uncover technology and resource gaps that are not readily apparent. This can have a big impact on cost analysis.

The assessment can be performed periodically and reused in multiple projects to lower overall analysis costs.

SUMMARY

You have now captured the technology capabilities of your group or target organization. These capabilities are important in determining which components you can include in a solution—indeed, in determining the very form of the final solution. For example, if the target audience has low-end computers with no sound or video capabilities, a high-level computer-based training solution is of no use.

Next, you look at the physical surroundings where actual work takes place and the availability of facilities in the event training is required.

chapter SIX

Situational Analysis

When you analyzed the job and tasks being performed during needs assessment (Chapter Two), you noted the physical conditions under which the job is performed. If you uncovered physical or environmental factors that have an impact on job and task performance, then conducting additional situational analysis will help you gather information to:

- Take these factors into consideration in developing realistic goals and objectives
- Design an effective performance support strategy or multimedia delivery strategy
- Produce insight into the design phase to ensure successful job performance
- Help uncover barriers to transferring and performing job skills

PROCESS

Before you can begin to design your solution, you need to examine the work environment for factors that either detract from or else enhance how successfully an employee performs specific job-related tasks. Visiting the work environment is the best way to conduct a situational analysis.

There are three activities in performing a situational analysis:

1. Analyze the job environment.
2. Analyze delivery environment.
3. Document the results.

SITUATIONAL ANALYSIS PROCEDURE

Follow these activities:

Activity One: Analyze the Job Environment

Familiarize yourself with the environment where the job is typically performed. Analyze task performance that is affected by these environmental factors:

- Physical and environmental factors such as noise, ventilation, or temperature
- Management support of training and employee development
- Teamwork
- Empowerment
- Delegation and control
- Feedback
- Work processes and policies
- Safety issues
- Coaching and mentoring

Activity Two: Analyze Delivery Environment

What factors in the training delivery environment can influence transfer of learning to the work environment? For example, a telecommunications training lab might boast fine equipment that nevertheless does not replicate the real world of work in the company. Or a lack of proper training facilities might be obvious in a noisy retail environment.

In your review, you should consider a number of factors:

- Access to training facilities
- Availability of instructors, coaches, and mentors
- Physical and environmental factors such as noise, ventilation, and temperature

Activity Three: Document the Results

Document the results of your analysis for use in the design, development, and implementation phases. Be particularly sensitive to employee confidentiality and how results of the analysis are reported.

FROM OUR EXPERIENCE

The best multimedia in the world cannot overcome a network that constantly crashes, management that gives little support to the tasks being targeted, or lack of equipment and tools for performing the tasks on which you are targeting. Develop observation and survey instruments such as those explained in Appendix D to uncover the information you need about the environment.

If you suspect that environmental or situational factors are inhibiting performance, conducting this analysis can keep you from wasting time and resources targeting training when in fact the effort should be directed at improving the workplace environment or organizational, management, or work-process issues.

SUMMARY

You now have information on the environment where the work is done and where any potential learning might take place. This information is pivotal in designing a solution. For example, you wouldn't want to design an instructor-led class in a facility where there are no classrooms. Neither would you want to present a hands-on workshop on the work floor of a noisy factory.

Now that you know about the audience, the technology, and the environment, you're ready to find out what the work consists of through task analysis.

Task Analysis

T ask analysis involves breaking the job down into duties and tasks, as well as determining the knowledge, skills, and attitudes (KSA) that job performers must have.

The job is what is outlined in a job description. Duties are major categories outlined in the description; tasks are the steps required to complete a duty. As for KSA, knowledge is the intellectual information a job performer must have. Skills are the behaviors required. Attitude is the demeanor or spirit with which the job performer completes the job.

ADULT LEARNING THEORY

From behavioral and developmental theory come our knowledge of adult learners. Although adults have gone through the developmental stages and their thinking has been affected by those experiences that gave them the pieces of information they integrated into their present intellectual scheme, nevertheless adults differ in numerous ways because of experience. When they are learning something completely new, they go through the same developmental stages as young children—although they pass through them much faster because of certain intellectual processes that are already in place from previous experiences. This means, for example, that adults need fewer examples of a concept than children do to completely grasp it.

The components of adult learning (Knowles, 1990) are outlined in Table 7.1.

Table 7.1
Adult Learning Theory

Component	Description
Relevance	Adult learners must see a direct relationship between the topic or information to be learned and the real world where the knowledge is used.
Involvement	Adult learners must be actively involved in the learning process, rather than sit passively and listen or watch the instructor.
Control over learning	Adult learners must have independence to learn where, what, and how they learn best.
Nontraditional learning situation	Adult learners need privacy for learning and individualized, self-paced instruction so that they can learn at their own rate.

Adult learning theory is applied to multimedia instructional development in two ways. First, material is less effective if written at a level above the stage where learners are functioning. Second, objectives must match appropriate levels if adults are to enjoy the best learning (see Lee, 1990).

PROCESS

A well-structured task analysis should give you the information needed to construct a list of all the tasks required for successful completion of a specific job. The activities to complete during task analysis are to

1. Define the position title.
2. Identify all job-related duties.
3. Identify all tasks.
4. Order the tasks.
5. Document the results.

Figure 7.1 may help you visualize the relationships among job, duty, task, and KSA.

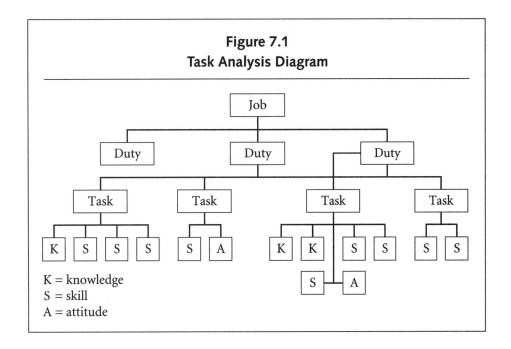

Figure 7.1
Task Analysis Diagram

K = knowledge
S = skill
A = attitude

TASK ANALYSIS PROCEDURE

Follow these activities:

Activity One: Define the Position Title

State the position title from the job description established during needs assessment. An example of a position title is "instructional designer."

Activity Two: Identify All Job-Related Duties

Break the job down into major areas of responsibility, and then write a duty statement for each area using a verb ending in –ing, followed by an object of the action. (*Example:* specific duties of an instructional designer may be "writing course objectives" and "writing course storyboards.") Ensure that each duty is independent of other duties. If you can find no tasks to list under a duty statement, the duty is probably a subordinate task of another duty.

Activity Three: Identify All Tasks

Step one: Use questionnaires, interviews, and observations to confirm or identify primary tasks. Use subject-matter experts (SMEs), exemplary performers, or incumbent workers as your information sources. Be certain to

- Include references such as the names of tools or forms

- Avoid abbreviations and jargon

- Be brief

Step two: Ensure that each task statement stands alone. To write task statements, use an action verb and add clarification statements as necessary. For example, a task associated with the duty of an instructional designer who is writing objectives might be to "use all five parts of an objective (the situation; the learned capability; the object; the action verb; and the tools, constraints, and conditions)."

Step three: Determine the KSA the job performer must have. For example, the knowledge associated with writing a five-part objective is knowing the five parts of the objective and being able to include those items in writing objectives.

To review, using our example:

Job	Instructional designer
Duty	Writing course objectives
Task	Write a five-part objective
Knowledge	The five parts of the objective

Activity Four: Order the Tasks

Create a task hierarchy by listing all superordinate tasks with their subordinate tasks. Tasks should be ordered in the sequence in which they will be performed, if there is a preferred or required sequence. Order the tasks by using one of the methods listed in Table 7.2.

Activity Five: Document the Results

Document what you find in your analysis, using the Job or Task Breakdown Tool and the Task Inventory Tool, both found in the Assessment and Front-End Analysis Tools section of Appendix E.

SUMMARY

You now have the job broken down into its component parts. Now you can move on to critical incident analysis, to determine which of the components you want to include in the solution.

Table 7.2
Task Order

If tasks . . .	Then . . .
Are mostly related to procedures (such as steps performed to process an order),	Order the tasks in the same sequence by which the procedures are completed (job-task order).
Are concepts related to an overall skill or task (such as using active listening techniques to improve team communication),	Order the tasks from the simplest to the most complex (simple-to-complex order).
Require application of rules or principles (such as following guidelines of a policy for returned merchandise),	Order the tasks by grouping related content (psychological order).

chapter EIGHT

Critical Incident Analysis

You've assessed and analyzed your audience and the job from a number of perspectives. Now that you have completed the task analysis, you must decide which tasks to teach and which ones not to teach.

It is important to focus on tasks that improve performance and are essential to solving the business need. Otherwise, money and resources that could be used to address other problems are wasted on extraneous design and development. Also, your audience wastes energy wading through information that is simply not useful. As a consequence, the effectiveness of the solution is degraded.

In critical incident analysis, analyze the task list to determine the duties and tasks that are presently performed well, and also those duties and tasks that are important but lacking.

Critical incidents are areas of performance that are completed either effectively or ineffectively, and behavioral descriptions of instances of extreme cases (characterized by success or failure) in performance. To perform a critical incident analysis, use focus groups, observations, direct interviews, and questionnaires (or any combination of these that you feel is necessary) to determine the critical aspects of the solution. Instructions for developing these observation instruments, interview forms, and questionnaires are in Appendix D, along with instructions for conducting focus groups.

PROCESS

The basic process is to review the tasks that were generated during the task analysis and perform four activities:

1. Determine the critical tasks.

2. Determine important but nonessential tasks.

3. Determine the tasks you will deselect.

4. Document the results.

PROCEDURE

Follow these activities:

Activity One: Determine the Critical Tasks

Which tasks are critical to the job? Uncover those tasks the employee must be able to complete to successfully perform the job, under typical conditions and to the standard required. High-priority tasks that show up as weak areas of performance definitely should be included in the solution.

Because there are no universally accepted criteria for criticality, you have to construct one or more for your specific situation. You might consider these ideas in establishing your norms:

- How often the task is performed (the more often, generally the more critical)

- The severity of the consequences for failure to perform the task (the greater the consequence, the more critical the task)

- Restrictions within the organization on what jobs, tasks, and duties certain people can perform (for example, presence of union agreements usually indicates a higher level of criticality for those tasks)

Activity Two: Determine Important but Nonessential Tasks

Identify which tasks are nice to know but are to be included only if time and budget permit. Determine the criteria for marginal tasks, such as those that

- Are performed occasionally

- Constitute background

- Provide supporting knowledge not directly related to job tasks

Activity Three: Determine the Tasks You Will Deselect

Determine the tasks to deselect and not include in the solution.

Here are some typical reasons for task rejection:

- It is rarely performed.
- It is not critical to job performance.
- It is easily learned.
- It is a prerequisite skill that the learner has as a condition of employment.
- It involves skills beyond the range of capability or permissibility of the members of the target audience.
- It involves skills that are presently performed at a marginal, but high enough, level of proficiency.

Activity Four: Document the Results

The outcome of the critical incident analysis should be documented as a list of tasks used for developing objectives.

FROM OUR EXPERIENCE

Critical incident analysis is used most effectively to define performance in technical areas. The focus-group strategy is useful in situations where expert performers can describe their own performance. There are times, however, when what is considered expert performance is difficult to describe or capture. For example, what is it exactly that distinguishes the tasks of an effective salesperson or a top manager from an average or poor one?

Analyzing target-audience skill levels before going into design helps you produce a solution that is both appropriate and effective. Lists of prerequisite skills are important because, although expert performance sets the upper limits of knowledge and skill, prerequisite skills set the lower limits. Keep in mind that entry-level skills that the job holders are presumed to have usually do not require training and are in the nice-but-not-necessary category.

SUMMARY

Critical incident analysis keeps things focused as you develop objectives. With the information from this analysis, you concentrate on what is most important for improving performance and what you will include in your solution.

Issue Analysis

A ll of the data collected through the analyses thus far need some structure in order to examine all of the aspects of the issue being examined. This is called issue analysis.

You must examine three levels to fully understand any issue: organizational, performance, and training. There is an Issue Analysis Tool in Appendix E to complete this analysis.

PROCESS

The process for completing an issue analysis consists of the following activities:

1. Collect data from audience, technology, situational, task, and critical incident analyses.
2. Place the data in the appropriate category of the Issue Analysis Form.
3. Document your results.

ISSUE ANALYSIS PROCEDURE

Activity One: Collect Data from Audience, Technology, Situational, Task, and Critical Incident Analyses

Collect all reports from the various analyses and have them available for the project team.

Activity Two: Place the Data into the Appropriate Category of the If Analysis Form

Step one: Discuss the appropriate categorization of each issue into one of the three categories:

1. *Organizational:* enterprise-wide issues that impact the entire company
2. *Performance:* those issues that enable people to do their jobs better
3. *Training:* the knowledge, skills, and attitudes required to solve an issue

Step two: Determine any interdependencies between issues at the different levels.

Step three: Complete the Issue Analysis Form found in the Assessment and Front-end Analysis Tools found in Appendix E.

When you determine the solution that will bridge the gap, be certain that you work on issues at each of the three levels that impact the solution simultaneously or start from the top down, as the Issue Analysis Model in Figure 9.1 indicates. For example, you might find that there is a high turnover rate in an organization. You find that there is very little training provided to entry-level employees, their jobs are high stress, and they are paid minimum wage. The organizational issue is in-centives—that is, employees aren't paid enough. The performance issue is that their job is high stress because they do not have the processes and procedures in place to access information easily. In this example, solving the organizational and per-formance issue will probably solve the problem. The only training that might be required would be training on a technology system that might be developed to as-sist employees in accessing the information.

Appendix B presents a completed case study including an issue analysis for a customer service issue. The example consists of three parts: the scenario, the analy-sis results, and the solution. The issue analysis produces information that might be found through analysis. The information structure gives examples of each level in the model to be taken into consideration in developing the solution.

Activity Three: Document the Results

FROM OUR EXPERIENCE

Upper management typically controls organizational issues; middle management typically controls performance issues; and the training department typically con-trols training issues. If you are a multimedia developer, the issues at the upper two

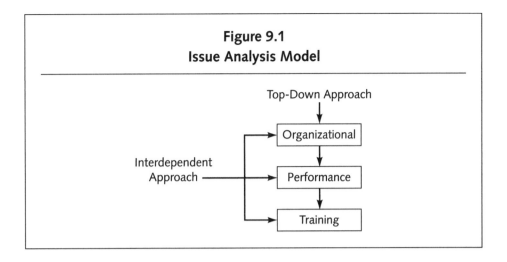

Figure 9.1
Issue Analysis Model

Top-Down Approach

Organizational

Interdependent
Approach

Performance

Training

levels may be outside of your control, but you need to be aware of them because they are going to impact the effectiveness of the solution you develop.

We recommend that the training group still complete an issue analysis and inform management of the issues that exist and of the degree of impact they will have on the solution. Too often management's expectation is that training will solve the entire issue. Training will seldom rise to that expectation.

Analyzing only the training issues during analysis might lead to developing a solution that addresses only a symptom of the problem, making the outcome of the intervention less effective. It would be ideal if every issue could be solved by one solution. However, in the real world things are seldom so simple. And seldom is beginning at the bottom level and working up as effective as it could be. Often if you solve the organizational and performance issues, there will be no need for training.

SUMMARY

You now have all of the data from all the analyses completed so far categorized into the appropriate level. You already have a good idea of the impact a multimedia training solution will have. You are now moving on to writing the objectives for the solution. Objectives need to be written for each of the three levels so that you will be able to convince management about the need for changes at these levels. If you cannot influence changes at the organizational and performance levels, you have at least set management's expectations for the degree of difference the solution you develop will have.

Objective Analysis

Writing clear, measurable objectives is critical to developing effective solutions. Objectives determine what you include in the content, whether the solution produces knowledge or performance, how the effectiveness of your solution is measured, and the media you choose to deliver the solution. All of your analyses done thus far now culminate in formulating your objectives.

Remember to write objectives for the training, performance, and organizational levels.

We have developed a system for writing objectives with two primary purposes: first, to get you to think about objectives before you write them, and second, to write objectives that are meaningful. There is now an automated Objectives Analysis Tool on the CD-ROM that accompanies the book. Instructions for this tool are found in the Introduction and also in the "readme" file on the CD-ROM. Figure 10.1 is a flowchart of our system.

RELATED THEORY

Of all that is written on objectives, Mager provides the basics in his 1962 book, *Preparing Instructional Objectives.* Gagné, Briggs, and Wager (1988), in *Principles of Instructional Design,* have, in our opinion, improved on these basics better than anyone.

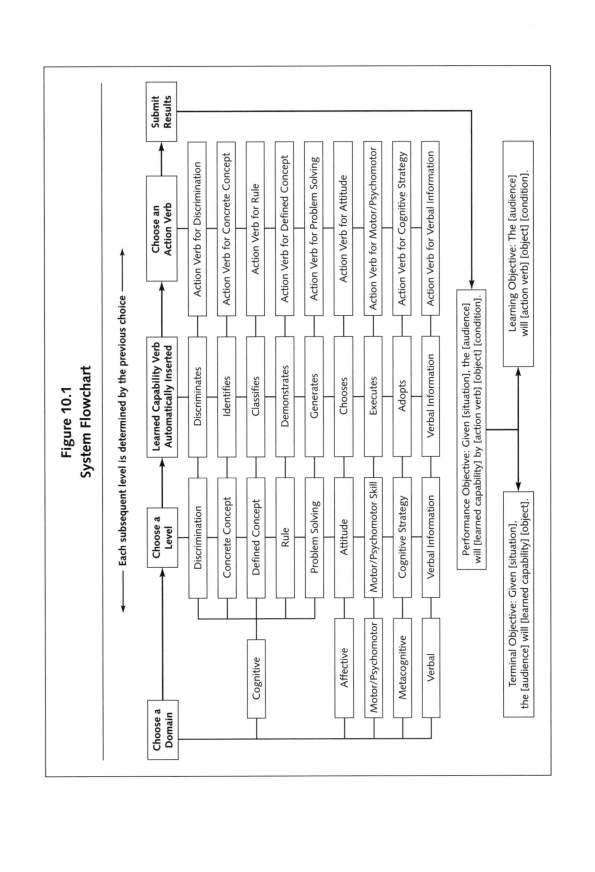

**Figure 10.1
System Flowchart**

There are five domains in which learning occurs: cognitive, affective, motor, psychomotor, and metacognitive. These domains, which are explained in Table 10.1, form the basis for an objectives analysis.

Table 10.1
Domains of Learning

Domain	Dealing with . . .
1. Cognitive	The thought processes
2. Affective	Feelings and attitudes
3. Motor	Learning physical movements
4. Psychomotor	Cognitive thought processes involved in physical movements that have been brought to the automatic level (can be done without thinking)
5. Metacognitive	Cognitive thought processes involved in "learning how to learn" that have been brought to the automatic level (strategies for approaching learning tasks that one uses without thinking about them)

The Cognitive Domain

Gagné, Briggs, and Wager (1988) present an outline of the various levels of intellectual skills required for learning within the cognitive domain. Table 10.2 explains the seven levels.

The Affective Domain

Krathwohl (1964) edited *A Taxonomy of Educational Objectives,* which outlines levels within the affective domain. Although he lists five levels, we combined the first two, receiving and responding, in Table 10.3 because receiving cannot be measured unless (1) the student responds and (2) we write only measurable objectives. Table 10.3 explains the four levels.

Table 10.2
Levels in the Cognitive Domain

Level	Intellectual Skill
1. Discriminations	Being able to see, hear, or feel the differences between incoming stimulus situations
2. Concrete concept	Being able to identify one or more instances of a class of items
3. Defined concept	Being able to classify objects or events according to certain attributes and functions
4. Rule	Being able to form classifications that distinguish relationships between and among concepts (concrete or defined)
5. Problem solving	Being able to apply rules to new situations
6. Cognitive strategies	Applying problem-solving strategies when approaching a learning situation
7. Verbal information	Information that can be verbally repeated with comprehension of what is verbalized

Table 10.3
Levels in the Affective Domain

Level	Description
1. Receiving and responding	Verbally stating the learner is sensitive to or has adopted a value or attitude
2. Valuing	Demonstrating by behaviors and actions that one is sensitive to or has adopted a value or attitude
3. Organization	Making comparisons, theorizing, organizing, balancing, defining, and formulating criteria to evaluate behaviors, codes of conduct, and standards for values determination
4. Characterization	Changing behavior as a result of reorganization, and establishing consistent, increasingly mature behavior patterns

The Motor and Psychomotor Domains

Harrow (1972) published a taxonomy of levels of functioning within the motor and psychomotor domains. Three are listed here as examples; we deal with only these levels because they seem to us the most relevant to writing objectives. (Refer to Harrow's book for a complete discussion of all the levels.) There is an important distinction for instructional designers, in that motor objectives are those that emphasize actually teaching the motor (movement) skill. Psychomotor has as its basis the intellectual knowledge and skills that underlie the motor activity. Psychomotor skills are motor skills that have been brought to the automatic level through learning that integrates them with cognitive processes. Table 10.4 explains these motor and psychomotor domain levels. Psychomotor has one level—perceptual—with five sub-levels.

The Metacognitive Domain

Metacognition (Alley & Deschler, 1979) is the integration of the cognitive, affective, motor, and psychomotor domains. It involves the internal strategies one employs when approaching a task or solving a problem—that is, learning how to learn. Metacognition is probably the least written about and least understood (but, in our opinion, the most important) learning domain because it integrates all of the others. The best learners develop these strategies on their own. However, mastering them should not be left to chance.

Superior multimedia instruction should go beyond simply presenting the knowledge and skills necessary for a task. Superior multimedia should teach processes and problem-solving strategies that individuals can generalize to other situations. Here is Alley and Deschler's basic eight-step metacognitive strategy to teach someone how to learn:

1. Observe the student performing the task.
2. Explain the student's approach (verbalizing each step).
3. Explain the desired approach.
4. Demonstrate the new approach (verbalizing each step).
5. Encourage questions before, during, and after the demonstration.
6. Have the student verbally rehearse the steps until he or she can state them without error (provide corrective feedback to the student during rehearsal).

Table 10.4
Levels in the Motor and Psychomotor Domain

Level	Sub-level	Description
1. Reflex movements		Voluntary or involuntary physical movements or actions
2. Basic movements		Coordinated movements such as reaching, grasping, crawling, manipulating physical objects, walking
3. Perceptual		Distinguishing between the self and surroundings:
	(1)	Kinesthetic discrimination: the relation of one's body to surrounding objects and controlling one's body in relation to the surrounding space
	(2)	Auditory discrimination: the ability of the learner to differentiate among various sounds—their pitch, intensity, directionality—and to reproduce the sound if necessary
	(3)	Visual discrimination: distinguish between form and details of objects; visually track an object; remember the attributes of an object; select the dominant figure from the background; recognize the consistency of shapes and forms
	(4)	Tactile discrimination: the ability to differentiate between the textures or forms of objects through the sense of touch
	(5)	Coordinated abilities: the coordination of two or more of these perceptual capabilities

7. Have the student practice with simulated materials (again offering corrective feedback immediately).

8. Have the student practice with actual materials.

Writing Objectives Within the Domains of Learning

There are four types of objectives for any solution, as listed and explained in Table 10.5. Write objectives in the order outlined in the table.

Table 10.5
Ordering Objectives

Objective	Description
Goals and course objective	Concisely states the goal for the entire course in one or two sentences, clearly indicating what the students should know (KSA) or be able to do (behaviors, performance) after completing the entire course. Statements describe the intended outcome of the learning from a learner's perspective.
Performance objectives	These objectives never actually go into the course; they are written for instructional designers to communicate with each other. These are the five-part objectives that eventually make up the terminal and lesson objectives, as explained in the process approach described in this topic.
Terminal objectives	This objective states the KSA that a student is to demonstrate when he or she returns to the job.
Lesson objectives	The specific KSA that the student demonstrates during a lesson.

PROCESS

Here is the process to follow when writing objectives:

1. Decide on domains.
2. Decide on level.
3. Write goal statement.
4. Write performance objectives.
5. Engage in a group discussion.
6. Separate terminal objectives from performance objectives.
7. Separate lesson objectives from performance objectives.

OBJECTIVE ANALYSIS PROCEDURE

Complete the following activities and steps.

Activity One: Decide on Domains

Decide on the domain of each task, using the task listing to determine KSA. Match the domains to each task.

Activity Two: Decide on Level

Determine the level within the domain of each task.

Activity Three: Write Goal Statement

Write the overall course goal statement.

Activity Four: Write Performance Objectives

Write the performance objective for each task. Use the five elements in Table 10.6 to construct a performance objective for each task.

Table 10.6 Five Parts of an Objective	
Element	**Description**
1. Situation	The stimulus situation, the given, or the circumstances under which the behavior will be observed
2. Learned capability	The type of learning outcome the demonstrated behavior represents, strictly defined by certain verbs for each level of intellectual skill
3. Object	The content of the learner's performance
4. Action verb	How the performance will be completed (*note:* a complete list of action verbs corresponding to each level of Gagné's hierarchy is provided in Appendix A)
5. Tools, constraints, and conditions	The special tools needed, the constraints to, or the actual conditions under which the performance will be observed

Table 10.7 lists the verbs that are used exclusively as capability verbs. Use the appropriate learned-capability verb for the level you intend. Gagné (1985) restricts these verbs to focus the objective writer on what the solution addresses, from discriminations to attitudes.

Table 10.7
Gagné, Briggs, and Wager's
Learned Capabilities and Accompanying
Verbs for Developing Performance Objectives (1988)

Learned Capability	Capability Verb
Discrimination	Discriminates
Concrete concept	Identifies
Defined concept	Classifies
Rule	Demonstrates
Problem solving	Generates
Cognitive strategy	Adopts
Verbal information	States
Motor skill	Executes
Attitude	Chooses

Use an appropriate action verb from the list at the beginning of Appendix B.

The following are examples of performance objectives that use adult learning situations in the technical-skills and soft-skills training environments and model objectives in each domain and at each level.

Objectives for Technical Skills. Training in technical skills usually involves developing training for software, a piece of equipment, or machinery. The manufacturing examples we use here involve maintaining a piece of electronic equipment. The domain and the level are identified for each objective.

- *Cognitive domain, discrimination level.* Given a diagram of the electronic instrument (situation), the student will discriminate each functional part (learned capability) by circling (action verb) each major part (object) with complete accuracy (special condition).

- *Cognitive domain, rule level.* Given a defined problem in a major part of the electronic instrument (situation), the student will demonstrate (learned capability) knowledge of troubleshooting procedures (object) by describing (action verb) the troubleshooting procedure with complete accuracy (special condition).

- *Affective domain, valuing level.* Given an identified problem with the electronic instrument (situation), the student will choose (learned capability) to perform (action verb) the emergency-shutdown safety procedures (object) before beginning to repair the problem (constraint).

- *Psychomotor (perceptual) domain, visual discrimination level.* Given an identified problem in the electrical distribution system of the electronic instrument (situation), the student will execute (learned capability) the diagnostic procedures by correctly attaching (action verb) the voltmeter to the ground and appropriate resistor or lead point (object) with the correct ends on the correct terminals (constraint or tools).

- *Metacognitive domain.* Given an unidentified problem in an electronic instrument's electrical system, but without identifying a specific instrument (situation), the student will develop (learned capability) a strategy for approaching the situation (object) by verbally listing (action verb) the steps necessary to approach the problem without prior instruction (constraint).

Objectives for Soft Skills. Soft-skill training covers those intangibles such as delivering quality service, management techniques, leadership skills, or interpersonal skills. The examples here demonstrate how the objective-writing process is adapted to supervisory skills.

- *Cognitive domain, defined concept level.* Given a selected work unit (situation), the learner will identify (learned capability) internal and external customers (object) by verbally listing (action verb) all (condition) customer characteristics.

- *Cognitive domain, problem-solving level.* To ensure that work group members have the information, training, responsibility, and resources to accomplish their assignments (situation), the learner will generate (learned capability) strategies for deducing (action verb) routine elements (object) of workgroup performance with customer requirements using quality standards (conditions).

- *Affective domain, organization level.* Given a workplace situation where quality standards could be ignored (situation), the student will choose (learned capability) to endorse (action verb) the benefits of following quality standards (object) to another individual, using words that adhere to company philosophy (conditions).

Activity Five: Engage in a Group Discussion

Engage the project team, or a neutral party, in discussion of each performance objective to clarify and verify correct assumptions.

Step one: Review the objectives in a group setting to validate the relevance to job tasks.

Step two: Rewrite performance objectives as necessary after discussion.

Activity Six: Separate Terminal Objectives from Performance Objectives

The terminal objective and lesson objective exist within the performance objective. The terminal objective comprises the situation and learned-capability portions of the performance objective.

Separate the terminal objectives from the performance objectives. Let's use the sample objective we have written for the manufacturing course:

Cognitive domain, discrimination level. Given a diagram of the electronic instrument (situation), the student will discriminate each functional part (learned capability) by circling (action verb) each major part (object) with complete accuracy (special condition).

In this case, the terminal objective would read, "Given a diagram of the electronic instrument, the student will discriminate each functional part."

A terminal objective lists the observable performance that the learner will possess at the end of the course, when he or she returns to the job.

The terminal objective is written into the student materials to inform learners about what they will achieve. For this purpose, the objective should be rewritten to appear less formal; the terminal objective in the student materials might read, "After concluding this lesson, you will be able to discriminate each functional part of an electronic instrument."

The terminal objective focuses the instructional designer on the upper level of learning the concept—in this case discrimination (recognizing the parts).

Activity Seven: Separate Lesson Objectives from Performance Objectives

Separate lesson objectives from the performance objective by removing the learned capability from the latter.

Lesson objectives identify what activity occurs within a lesson that leads the learner to achieve the terminal objective. Continuing to use the performance objective from Activity Six, we suggest the lesson objective could read, "Given a diagram of the electronic instrument, the student will circle all major parts with complete accuracy."

The lesson objective focuses the instructional designer on the activities within the lesson that lead to accomplishing the terminal objective.

Note: The structure of the Objectives Analysis Tool is different from the structure in Tables 10.2, 10.3, and 10.4. This seeming discrepancy is purposeful to merge the five domains and the levels, since they come from different sources.

The tool combines *motor* and *psychomotor.* When you are developing objectives, focus on action verbs that describe the actual physical act or the coordination of mind and body when you select a verb. Some verbs are better suited for one or the other.

Cognitive strategies is moved to the *metacognitive* domain because a strategy is an approach. Gagné considered all of his learned capabilities to be cognitive. We think they need to be further discriminated to best develop objectives.

Verbal information has become its own *verbal* category.

FROM OUR EXPERIENCE

Our system for writing objectives is designed as a way to think about objectives. All project team members have to understand the system for it to work. Where our system has been used, it eliminates confusion in two ways: (1) designers and subject-matter experts have a clear understanding of the intended level of the training and (2) terminal and lesson objectives are developed concurrently.

This process emphasizes the team approach because objectives written by one person are (in our experience) not as effective as those written by a team.

After objectives are written, you may find that some do not align with the task order you created. Move and group objectives and their accompanying content as appropriate.

Objectives relate directly to any testing and measurement of the effectiveness of your solution. Testing and measurement concepts are discussed in Part Four.

SUMMARY

Once the objectives are written, you know precisely what the end user of your solution should know when he or she returns to the workplace to perform the job. You also know what must be included in your solution in the form of information and activities.

Now that you know the content of the solution and what to include in delivering it, you are ready to choose the medium or media for delivery.

Media Analysis

A systematic and careful media selection decision is essential to successful and cost-effective resolution of business problems. We have developed a media analysis tool that addresses many considerations regarding learner and cost factors relevant to delivery media.

There are many types of media to be considered in making the appropriate selection. Although multimedia is frequently used to refer to CBT, remember that the word media is plural. You should always consider using a blended solution consisting of whatever media are required.

The media discussed in this chapter are presented in Table 11.1.

Table 11.1 Types of Delivery Media	
Media	**Description**
Instructor-led	Materials intended to be presented by a teacher or facilitator. They may be used in a traditional classroom setting or on the job. Presentations can include lecture, discussion, demonstration, workshop, as well as other types for other media.
Computer-based	Any form of delivery involving use of a computer. Options include computer-assisted instruction (CAI), which also supports printed materials or instructor, or

Table 11.1
Types of Delivery Media, Cont'd.

Media	Description
	totally computer-based instruction, where all content is presented by computer.
Distance broadcast	General term for the category of instruction delivered over television, telephone, or via satellite to remote locations. Specific media are video or audio tele-conferencing and interactive distance broadcasting.
Web-based	Use of the Internet or intranets to distribute training over wide-area networks (WAN) or local-area networks (LAN).
Audiotapes	Use of prerecorded audiotapes to deliver instruction with or without the supporting materials.
Videotapes	Use of prerecorded video to deliver instruction with or without supporting materials.
Performance support systems (PSS) Electronic performance support systems (EPSS)	Job aids, either electronic or paper-based, used to help and support people on the job. These do not require any formal training or instruction other than on the job-aid tool.

PROCESS

To perform a media analysis, complete the following process.

1. Rate the factors.
2. Summarize findings.
3. Place the media in a hierarchy.

4. Match media advantages and limitations.

5. Calculate costs.

6. Determine final media selection.

7. Match media to the appropriate objectives.

8. Document the results.

MEDIA ANALYSIS PROCEDURE

Complete the following activities and steps.

Activity One: Rate Each of the Factors

Have the project team, including the subject-matter expert, and possibly the customer, rate the factors on the Media Analysis Rating Form in the Assessment and Analysis section of Appendix E. Each factor relates to the user, the cost, or the content. (See the completed case study in Appendix B.)

Rate each factor on a scale of 1 to 5 regarding importance to the issue. Use the Considerations column for clarifications and for thought starters. A rating of 5 means the factor is very important. A rating of 1 indicates the factor is not important at all. A rating of 3 is a neutral rating. Use a rating of 3 if you can honestly say that the factor makes no difference one way or another. As you will see this becomes important, because ratings of 3 are not calculated in the final analysis.

> The rating scale has built-in redundancy and asks you to consider numerous factors from the standpoint of both the learner and cost. It is designed to focus your decision, not make it for you. The considerations provided ask you to question what you really mean when you rank a factor on the scale.

Activity Two: Summarize Findings

Use the Media Analysis Summary Sheet in Appendix E to calculate the results of the ratings.

Step one: If you rated a factor as 4 or 5, put a mark in the High column for each medium that is associated with that factor.

Step two: If you rated a factor as 1 or 2, put a mark in the Low column for each medium that is associated with that factor.

Step three: Subtract the Low occurrences from the High occurrences for each medium and record the number in the Difference column.

Step four: To achieve a weighted percentage, divide the difference by the number in the All Occurrences column (all occurrences are the number of times a particular medium is listed in the Media Analysis tool). Convert the decimal to a percentage and place the number in the Weigh column.

Activity Three: Place the Resulting Media in a Hierarchy

Make a list of the ranked media from the highest percentage to the lowest. The highest ranked media are the most likely possibilities for your solution.

Activity Four: Match Media Advantages and Limitations

Match the strengths and weaknesses of the media to business requirements.

Analyze the advantages and limitations of each type of medium. Factors vary depending on your location, the size of the organization, internal and external resources, and your level of development experience.

Table 11.2 is a starting point for analyzing each available media type and its advantages and limitations. Feel free to expand the table with additional media, details, clarification, or considerations that are important in your unique business environment.

You will conduct a full-scale cost analysis in Chapter Thirteen. For the purposes here, simply review the various costs to eliminate any of the delivery media from the analysis results before arriving at the delivery of the solution.

Table 11.2
Advantages and Limitations of Media

Media	Advantages	Limitations
Instructor-led	Allows social interaction.	Scheduling may not meet the needs of all who require the information or instruction.
	Useful with variable-size audiences.	
	Personalized feedback.	Not enough time to give everyone feedback they may need.
	Integrates a variety of media.	
	Materials can be tailored to the group or adjusted by the instructor while in progress.	Moves at one pace, or at the pace of the majority of the class, and does not account for individual rates and styles of learning.
	Short development time.	
	Traditional method of teaching that is comfortable for students and instructors.	Lack of transfer to the workplace.
		Relies heavily on instructor knowledge.
	Because learners are removed from work environment, they can focus on the course free of distraction.	Inconsistent delivery and certain areas stressed or deemphasized, causing gaps in learning and varied levels of learner involvement.
		Inconsistent evaluation.
		Travel time and expense, whether for participants to attend at a centralized location or for instructor travel.
		Only limited numbers can participate at one time.

Table 11.2
Advantages and Limitations of Media, Cont'd.

Media	Advantages	Limitations
Computer-based	Consistent delivery.	May be too text based.
	Accommodates individual time schedules.	Expensive due to the number of design-team members required, authoring platform hardware and software, and cost of added media.
	Extensive multisensory capabilities.	
	Learner-controlled pace.	
	High degree of interactivity and involvement by the learner.	Long design and development time, with range from 250–750 design and development hours per hour of delivered instruction, depending on the complexity of the content. For a first project, even more time has to be scheduled.
	Adapts to learner performance.	
	Consistent testing and record keeping.	
	Unlimited opportunity for review.	
	Overlearning through multiple presentations and examples of the same concept.	Specialized computer skills of programmers and authors are required.
		Feedback specific to content and context may be limited.
		Any poorly designed user interface makes navigation difficult (that is, extensive menu layers) or interferes with learning (that is, uses too many bells and whistles).

Table 11.2
Advantages and Limitations of Media, Cont'd.

Media	Advantages	Limitations
Distance broadcast	Transcends geographical boundaries. High level of interaction and immediate feedback to questions in spite of distance. One instructor for a large group of participants. Reduced travel for participants and instructors (reduced cost and more convenience). Trains large numbers in a short period of time. Incorporates a variety of media. Two-way video permits instructor to see participants and participants to see each other.	Large time-zone differences require some participants to view at inappropriate times. May rely on a "talking head" with little or no interaction, which becomes boring; participants lose interest. Special training of instructor to handle technology, or large staff to handle broadcast equipment, is often required. Much preparation by instructor is needed to coordinate technology. Satellite time is very expensive. One-way video does not allow students and instructor to see each other.
Video teleconferencing	Less expensive than satellite broadcasting with use of existing telephone lines. Transcends geographical boundaries. High level of interaction and immediate feedback to questions in spite of distance.	Delays due to compression and decompression rates of video may result in video and audio out of synchronization. Large time-zone differences require some to participate at inappropriate times.

Table 11.2
Advantages and Limitations of Media, Cont'd.

Media	Advantages	Limitations
Video teleconferencing (cont'd.)	One instructor for a large group of participants. Reduced travel for participants and instructors. Trains large numbers in a short period of time. Incorporates variety of media. Two-way video permits instructor to see participants and participants to see each other.	May rely on a "talking head" with little or no interaction, which becomes boring; participants lose interest. Special training of instructor to handle technology, or large staff to handle broadcast equipment. Much preparation by instructor to coordinate technology. One-way video does not allow students and instructor to see each other.
Web-based	Includes chat rooms, where participants and instructor can have dialogue or interactive, real-time, collaborative discussions. Includes electronic mailboxes, where participants can pose questions to instructor or participants. Includes reference and data-storage capabilities.	Much preparation by instructor to coordinate and plan course elements. Requires specialized design skills of programmers and authors. Security, testing, and feedback may be limited. A poorly designed user interface may be difficult to navigate (i.e., extensive menu layers) or interfere with learning (i.e., too many bells and whistles).

Table 11.2
Advantages and Limitations of Media, Cont'd.

Media	Advantages	Limitations
Web-based (cont'd.)	Includes sharing of files and data. Course material can incorporate audio, video, and graphics. Material is easily updated.	Slow video compression and decompression rates cause video and audio to be out of synchronization.
Audiotapes	Flexible in delivery; participants can get information anywhere there is a tape player. Inexpensive to develop and deliver.	Only one sensory modality used for learning.
Videotapes	Flexible in delivery; participants can get information anywhere there is video playback equipment. Inexpensive to duplicate and deliver after initial development costs. Good for role-modeling behavior and motivation.	Only two sensory modalities used for learning. Expensive to produce because of highly specialized skills of videographers, editors, producers, and script writers. Industry range is from $500–2,000 per finished minute of video.
Performance support systems (PSS) Electronic performance support systems (EPSS)	Provides information on an as-needed basis. Does not require formalized training that removes people from their jobs.	Not good for delivering concepts, principles, or demonstrations. Specialized programming and authoring skills on the part of members of

Table 11.2
Advantages and Limitations of Media, Cont'd.

Media	Advantages	Limitations
Performance support systems (PSS) Electronic performance support systems (EPSS) (cont'd.)	Best for providing information on procedures and processes or reference material. Ready source for information that may be used infrequently or is complex.	design team are required for EPSS. May have a user interface or be constructed such that it is too complex to navigate. May not be organized in a way that allows users to quickly access the information they need.

Table 11.3 lists costs associated with various training media.

Step two: Consider delivery factors (see Table 11.4).

Step three: Consider maintenance factors (see Table 11.5).

Activity Five: Compare Results and Decide on the Media

Compare the results of the media selection with the cost factors and decide on the appropriate media.

You may be able to deduce more from the results of the media analysis than from a hierarchy of media for a solution. For example, if *all* of the media for training, such as synchronous and asynchronous web, CBT, and instructor-led, rank low on the hierarchy, you can conclude that training is not a solution at all for this issue. The performance and organizational components may be where the problem lies. When the objectives at these levels are achieved, the problem will be solved.

Table 11.3
Cost Factors Associated with Media

Category	Factors	Consideration
Development-team resources	Project leader Instructional designer Subject-matter expert Deployment representative Media specialists (audio technician, video technician, graphic designer, system designer, etc.) Programmer (author, interactive designer, system engineer, etc.) Publisher (editor, etc.)	Hourly costs for team members involved in development activities
Administrative resources	Manager Clerical	Hourly costs for administration of development activities
Production	Reproduction of videos, diskettes, or CD-ROMs Postproduction Narration Studio rental Video equipment rental Videotaping Facilities costs	Production costs for developing media
Materials	Diskettes CD-ROMs Videotapes Audiotapes Software Hardware	Materials cost

Table 11.4
Delivery Factors Associated with Media

Category	Factors	Consideration
Logistics	Expected lifetime of course (years)	The longer the course will be useful, the more cost-effective it is to develop.
	Course length	More content is more expensive to develop.
	Number of users	The greater the number of students, the lower the cost per student.
	Times when course is held each year	Calculate deployment costs.
	Geographic location of audience	Calculate travel and other deployment costs.
	Materials	Consider reproduction, postage, and transmission costs.
Cost per training unit	Average annual salaries of Students Instructor Clerical staff Manager	Determine the cost for each person involved.
	Average per diem expenses of Students Instructors	
	Average travel expenses of Students Instructors	
	Facilities cost	
	Number of instructors per class	
	Cost per hour of development of each unit	

Table 11.5
Maintenance Factors Associated with Various Media

Category	Factors	Consideration
Ongoing reproduction	Cost of producing additional materials such as videotapes, audiotapes, diskettes, CD-ROMs, print materials	Who reproduces materials as needed?
Material	Additional cost of materials purchased: CD-ROMs Paper Diskettes Audiotapes Videotapes	Who purchases additional materials for ongoing reproduction? Who pays for additional materials?
Storage	Cost of storing materials	Where are originals and extra materials warehoused until distribution? Who maintains storage?
Distribution	Cost of distributing materials	Who is in charge of distribution materials? Do users know where to order materials?
Revision	Cost of revising materials	Who is responsible for required revisions to materials? Who is responsible for version control? Cost of disposal of outdated inventory?

Activity Six: Match Media to the Appropriate Objectives

Use the Media/Objectives Mapping Tool on the CD-ROM to match objectives with the most appropriate media. Remember that you may choose to deliver one objective using more than one medium.

Activity Seven: Document the Results

Document the results making a list of the final media choices.

An analogy to how the media analysis tool works would be to imagine a box with all of the various media on individual blocks in it. If a factor associated with a medium is rated as 4 or 5, one of each of the media associated with the factor is placed in another box. If a factor is rated 1 or 2, an example of each of those media are taken out of the second box and placed back in the original box. A factor rated 3 leaves the both boxes undisturbed. When you are finished if you took all of the blocks out of box 2 and grouped them by similar type, the media on the most blocks would be ranked the highest down to the media on the fewest blocks that would be ranked lowest.

Validity and Reliability of the Media Analysis Tool

The media analysis process has achieved a high degree of validity and reliability. (See Part Four of this book for more information on validity and reliability.) It has a high degree of content validity because we used a team of twelve highly experienced instructional designers who used consensus to arrive at the factors and the associated media. The factors were associated with the media by using concept mapping and information structure concepts. Predictive validity was established by using the tool with six hundred participants in workshops over the last five years. Using the same four case studies based on actual solutions, these participants came to the same, or nearly the same, solution 95 percent of the time as the actual solutions.

FROM OUR EXPERIENCE

We advocate a rational approach to selecting media. By rational, we mean that a decision is arrived at through a process that considers all relevant aspects.

Here is an excerpt from a conversation in a project room in a training department:

A: Let's develop it [a training course] in CBT.

B: Yes, and let's include a game so people will enjoy it.

A: We can use all of the authoring system's capabilities, such as high-resolution graphics, animation, and video.

B: And CBT is so much more fun to design than those other courses. I'm so bored developing workbooks, I could scream! CBT experience looks better on a résumé, anyway.

Notice that there are a few elements missing from this conversation. As a matter of fact, in this situation the conversation continued, but the important elements never came up. The discussion never turned to learning design, solving a business problem or performance need, or effectiveness in terms of time and cost. The major criterion seemed to be that the team should have "fun" developing the training.

True, there is something to be said for enjoying your work, but it is much more vital for effective and efficient use of technology to enhance performance and solve an organization's business need. Either it isn't important to A and B and their team of designers that the end users of the training need to learn something in a cost-effective and timely manner, or it is assumed that learning takes place magically. Both beliefs are erroneous.

We are here to tell you that the medium is *not* the message, contrary to Marshall McLuhan's statement of some years back. This one aphorism—often misunderstood—started a rampage of multimedia development from which students and developers alike are still suffering.

We believe the message is the *content* that needs to be delivered through a certain medium or media. The content might be a process, procedure, principle, concept, fact, or system. Each type of content requires a particular instructional strategy. The medium is dictated by objectives. All of the capabilities and features of a particular medium are useless unless the product teaches something that the learner needs so as to enhance performance.

Here is an example. Company X has just adopted a new policy that must be communicated to all employees immediately so that the company can comply with a new government regulation. Question to you: What medium or media should the company use to deliver this information to employees?

In simply reading the description and the question, do you find yourself immediately deciding on the media? Does a choice at least occur to you in the back of your mind? Or do you begin to ask yourself such questions as the following:

- How many people are in the target audience?

- How geographically dispersed is the audience?

- Do employees only need to be informed of the policy, or do they need to be taught the skills to use it?

- What physical capabilities does the company have for holding large meetings?

If you began by raising these questions, then you're thinking in the right direction. In contrast, an impulse to begin immediately reaching a decision means a good chance of developing an inappropriate solution.

By jumping immediately to a solution, you make certain assumptions about the content, the context of the training, and the constraints you will face in designing and delivering the training. If you make the correct assumptions, great! The solution will be a success, and everyone will be happy. But what are the consequences if your assumptions prove to be incorrect? The solution will be ineffective in solving the targeted issue.

For the sake of demonstration, here is some additional information about Company X's situation:

- There are three thousand employees who need the information.

- All employees must know about the regulation within a week.

- Employees only have to be aware of the regulation; they don't need the skills to carry it out.

- All of the employees are in one geographic location.

- There is an auditorium in the company's facilities that holds one thousand people.

If you were to immediately determine the media before being given this information (although we're sure you aren't in that impetuous group!), what impact would this information have on your decision? Suppose you had quickly decided to use interactive distance broadcasting, before you had this information. You might unnecessarily have spent thousands of dollars on satellite time and development costs.

With the information in this list, though, you can make a better decision: to have a meeting in the company's thousand-person auditorium. Now you can either hold the meeting three times or hook up television monitors in training rooms (if available) and encourage employees to call or fax in their questions.

The best solution for any issue is nearly always a blended solution. We recommend the model outlined in Figure 11.1.

Figure 11.1
Four Levels of a Blended Solution Learning Environment

Level 4   **Face to Face Environments**
- Classroom
- Workshops
- Conferences

Level 3   **Virtual Learning Environments**
- Synchronous web-based
- Online learning communities of practice
- User groups
- Chat rooms
- Email
- Video teleconference
- Audio teleconference
- Web conferencing

Level 2   **Self Instructional Environments**
- Programmed learning materials
- Asynchronous web-based training
- Asynchronous computer-based training

Level 1   **Performance Support Environments**
- Online help systems
- Reference manuals
- Help desks
- Internet

You should attempt to begin at Level 1 and move up through the levels. Performance support environments are those media that allow users to learn for themselves through direct information sources. Level 2 are self-instructional environments where users can learn on their own, at their own pace. Level 3 are virtual learning environments where people can learn and exchange information collaboratively. Whatever learning remains should be completed in Level 4, in a face-to-face format.

We live in a society that expects to be entertained. The same entertainment principles follow when adults attend training classes. The courses or instructors who are the most entertaining usually receive the best reviews from their students. We are suggesting that "edutainment" not be your primary instructional strategy. Edutainers lose sight of the fact that their overarching objective is for learners to obtain knowledge and skills to improve their performance. Multimedia with content that is presented logically, with appropriate practice and feedback, is far more effective than edutainment. Likewise, instructors who present training with confidence, expertise, and true enjoyment for what they are doing, and who can relate to students on a personal level, are more effective than those who spend much of their time practicing for a stand-up comedy routine.

We don't want to imply that you shouldn't use humor. If you can work in a relevant story or theme that is humorous, do it. However, making the graphics the focal point in a CBT or using your audio resources for irrelevant jokes detracts from the business goal of cost-effective and efficient performance support intervention.

SUMMARY

You have now determined the delivery media for your solution. There is one more analysis to perform before you begin to design your solution. Products may already exist that you could use in their entirety or in part. Analyzing extant data reveals information on what is already available. You should only design and develop new materials if you cannot use material that has already been produced by others.

chapter TWELVE

Extant Data Analysis

Remember: your primary purpose is not to design multimedia, but rather to solve a business need. Therefore you must determine whether the solution, or parts of the solution, already exists (is extant), which avoids unneeded development costs. A search for what is available used to be a rather daunting task, but with advances in telecommunications and computer technology the search, or extant data analysis, has become relatively simple. Completing such an analysis can save you time and money, and it often yields an added level of confidence that you are not reinventing the wheel.

PROCESS

To conduct an extant data analysis, complete these activities:

1. Identify likely sources of information.
2. Collect information and existing course materials.
3. Compare information.
4. Make a buy-or-build decision.
5. Evaluate off-the-shelf solutions.
6. Document your decision.

EXTANT DATA ANALYSIS PROCEDURE

Follow these activities:

Activity One: Identify Likely Sources of Information

Decide what you are looking for: Is it an entire solution, or one or more pieces of the solution? Make this determination according to (1) the size and complexity of your solution (a large and complex solution means searching for one or more pieces of the total solution) and (2) the amount of proprietary company material to be included (the more proprietary the content, the less likely you are to locate existing, intact, useful content elsewhere).

Activity Two: Collect Information and Existing Course Materials

Web search engines are an excellent place to begin. Information searches can be conducted using a bulletin board service (BBS) and special-interest groups (SIGs) on the Internet, provided you have an online account or access to one. Search costs vary from free to a fixed fee per search—that is, a charge per unit of search time and amount of information generated.

The numerous guides and indexes to periodicals found in libraries are excellent sources of information. Most libraries offer online computer searches for information on nearly any topic.

Use the Extant Data Analysis Form in the Assessment and Front-End Analysis Tools section of Appendix E to document the results of your search.

Activity Three: Compare Information

Evaluate the collected information, being mindful of objectives, audience, and business needs.

Step one: Rate the appropriateness and usability of the materials you locate. Determine whether the materials in fact contain the required information. Again, use the Extant Data Analysis Tool to compare audience, objectives, and media to the requirements of the solution. Also determine whether the hardware, software, or scheduling required by the off-the-shelf material matches your organization's available technology.

Step two: Determine whether the availability of the information matches the time constraints of the project. The shorter the time frame for development, the more appropriate an off-the-shelf solution might be if it is readily available.

Step three: Determine whether the cost is appropriate to the project's budget. Ensure that a technology requirement does not include acquiring or implementing hardware that extends the delivery timeline or costs beyond what is practical.

Activity Four: Make a Buy-or-Build Decision

You now decide whether, in essence, to buy (if the results of your analysis determine that the off-the-shelf material is usable as is or can be modified to meet the business need) or build (develop materials if the results of your analysis show that an off-the-shelf product is not appropriate for the solution). Use the Buy-or-Build Decision Matrix in Appendix E to help you make this decision.

Step one: Place an X in the Yes or No column to answer each question.

Step two: Total the number of X's in each column. If the number of X's in the YES column is greater than those in the NO column, you might consider buying the solution. If the opposite is true, you might consider building the solution. If the numbers are fairly even, you might determine that you should purchase the off-the-shelf solution and develop only what is not available in the purchased solution.

Activity Five: Evaluate the Off-the-Shelf Solutions

Whatever you decide to purchase must be evaluated for its quality and suitability. Use the Extant Data Materials Review Tool in Appendix E to complete this activity. This tool may be used in either of two ways:

1. End users may use the tool to evaluate a solution from their perspective.

2. Developers may use the tool to evaluate a solution from their perspective.

> If developers use the tool, they must be very objective and evaluate the solution based on the qualities of the instructional design (see Part Two of this book for elements of instructional design), rather than from their personal taste or learning style.

Step one: Complete the information at the top of the form.

Step two: Rate each category on the Courseware Evaluation Tool by placing an X in the appropriate column according to the key that is provided.

Step three: Record your overall comments at the end of the tool.

Step four: Select the overall rating for the solution based on the four categories. Your overall rating should be Great or Good in order to consider purchasing it.

Activity Six: Document Your Decision

Document the results by listing the sources, rationale, and decisions reached during the analysis.

FROM OUR EXPERIENCE

There is no need to develop a solution that already exists in an off-the-shelf product or a course that can be purchased and adapted to meet your particular business need.

There are many sources of information available to complete an extant data analysis, from web search engines to advertisements and vendors at professional conferences. The key to successful web searches is organizing the search. Sometimes the time available for an extant data analysis is limited. Take time to focus your search by listing key words or phrases and asking specific questions. It is vital to reduce the amount of material you have to review by collecting only the most relevant information as efficiently as possible.

In developing questions for a computer search, narrow your questions for the search. Web searches can only give back information based on the key words searched. To take a whimsical example, consider how much time you will spend and how many hits you will get from searching for "mice" as opposed to searching for "mouse AND computer BUT NOT rodent."

Schedule and plan your analysis so that you do not spend too much time researching and gathering information at the expense of analysis of the search results. Remember, once you find the sources, someone still has to sort through the results, analyze the content, and make appropriate recommendations.

SUMMARY

While analyzing, don't forget to include the costs of off-the-shelf materials in your cost analysis. You now know what is available, what to include in your solution, what can be purchased, and what the project team has to develop. You are now ready to calculate the cost of your solution.

chapter THIRTEEN

Cost Analysis

This chapter gives you a high-level overview of two commonly used formulas for determining the benefit of a solution:

1. *Cost-benefit analysis* (CBA) is used to determine whether or not you will undertake a project.

2. *Return on investment* (ROI) is often measured after a project has been implemented, in order to determine its actual benefit.

Business is concerned with cost. If a solution does not add benefit to the organization, it should not be developed. As a professional instructional designer, you should be ready to justify the value added by your proposed solution. Document your cost-analysis results, and share them with your stakeholders in order to

- Request and obtain the support necessary to successfully complete the project
- Demonstrate that the proposed solution is cost-effective and adds value
- Maintain credibility and a business focus within your development organization
- Be seen as a solution provider and revenue generator rather than an overhead expense

PROCESS

To determine value added by a proposed solution, complete these cost-analysis activities:

1. Conduct a cost-benefit analysis (CBA).

2. Determine the return on investment (ROI).

3. Document the results.

COST ANALYSIS PROCEDURE

Follow these activities:

Activity One: Conduct a Cost-Benefit Analysis (CBA)
Before the Project Begins

Determine the anticipated benefit of the project in relation to the cost of producing the activity.

Step one: Calculate the anticipated total cost the project. Total cost consists of assessment, design, development, implementation, and evaluation.

Step two: Calculate the anticipated benefit of the project.

Step three: Divide the total anticipated benefit by the total cost. The formula is

$$\frac{\text{(Total Anticipated Benefit)}}{\text{(Total Cost)}}$$

Step four: Express the CBA as a ratio.

> For example, if you determine the anticipated value of your proposed solution to the organization to be $1 million and the actual cost to complete the solution is budgeted at $100,000, the CBA equals a ratio of $10 of anticipated value for each dollar spent.

You must determine with your stakeholders whether or not this is a high enough ratio. Some organizations set minimums on what they are willing to spend in relation to the return they anticipate receiving.

Activity Two: Determine the Return on Investment (ROI)
at Some Point After the Solution Is Implemented

Prepare for ROI analysis by collecting data on the cost of the issue the intervention is intended to solve. The formula to calculate ROI is

$$\frac{[\text{(Total Net Value)} \times 100]}{\text{(Total Cost)}}$$

Step one: Determine the *total net value*. The total net value is the total actual benefit minus the costs.

Step two: Divide the total net value by the total cost.

Step three: Multiply the answer by 100 to compute a percentage.

For example, if the customer actually realized a profit of $10 million and the cost was $1 million, the total net value was $9 million. If you divide these numbers, the ratio is 9:1. Multiply that by 100 to obtain a percentage and you realize a 900 percent ROI.

Activity Three: Document the Results

Document the results in the format appropriate to your audience. If the audience is a management team, use a presentation package style familiar to the team members to communicate the cost-analysis results.

FROM OUR EXPERIENCE

If numbers are not your thing, get some help from your accounting group or set up some basic spreadsheets. Once set up, cost analysis can give you what you need to demonstrate your value, obtain the funding you need, and effectively focus your multimedia efforts. Detailed literature on the factors and calculations used with both formulas is available on the web, on business publication bookshelves, and from such professional organizations as ASTD, formerly the American Society for Training and Development.

Some people believe that not everything can be quantified. We believe *everything can be measured.* Certain soft skills, such as leadership, may be more difficult, but they can nonetheless be quantified. With a soft skill, the true value may be more than one level removed from what can be directly observed. Consider the following example:

Assume that having better leaders results in greater employee satisfaction (unobservable) and that satisfied employees are less likely to leave a company (observable). Therefore, statistics about employee attrition and employee satisfaction should show some correlation—that is, as satisfaction increases, attrition should decrease. Employee satisfaction can be measured by administering an employee satisfaction survey, a component of which assesses employees' satisfaction with their leaders.

The average cost of replacing an employee times the attrition rate can be calculated. Keeping statistics on the employee attrition level before and after an intervention that trains leaders on leadership skills yields information on increased or decreased attrition, along with associated cost savings. Thus, a goal to reduce employee attrition by a certain amount while increasing employees' satisfaction with their leaders by a certain amount is measurable.

SUMMARY

Using the CBA formula, you have now calculated whether (and, potentially, how much) the benefit of the solution you propose meets the customer's criteria. If it does, you are ready to begin designing and developing the solution. If your proposed solution does not meet the criteria, you must look for another solution—possibly a second one that you considered during media analysis. Before moving on to the design phase, we'll look at a method for shortening the time it takes for the analysis phase after you are thoroughly familiar with the activities and steps in each of the types of analysis.

chapter FOURTEEN

Rapid Analysis Method

With the pace and number of changes occurring in business and industry today, it is incumbent on a training function to quickly respond to the needs resulting from those changes. Therefore, we present a rapid analysis method, or RAM, which is designed to significantly reduce the amount of time required to conduct analysis while still obtaining valuable information.

There are benefits and advantages to the RAM:

- It facilitates collecting data from all levels of the organization (management and employees) and from all methods (interviews and observations) simultaneously.
- It identifies gaps between the actual and desired situations.
- It identifies differences in perception among various levels of the organization.
- It reduces cycle time for analysis by about two-thirds when used effectively.

Several essential factors must be present for this method to be successful. If any one is missing, the data retrieved may not hit the target. The first factor is that the training function must employ highly experienced analysts who intuitively understand what aspects of the assessment and analysis process are functioning in each question. The RAM is not for the novice or inexperienced analyst. Complex analysis processes are integrated in the RAM. Even though the method requires only five questions, each one represents a high-level view of all information gained from needs assessment and front-end analysis. The difference is that the analyst must be able to ask the required follow-up questions.

The second factor is that certain conditions must be true of the organization being analyzed:

- It must have a clearly articulated strategy that embodies core processes.
- Owners of core processes (for example, the core owner of the marketing process is the marketing vice president) are charged with managing the operation of infrastructure and personnel.
- The training-and-development function must be involved and aware of strategies regarding operation of the core business.

If these essential factors are not present, the analyst can only be partially successful in suggesting interventions, because they may bring only a short-term solution to long-term problems.

For the RAM to work effectively, analysts must be aware of the organization's direction. At a minimum, analysts must thoroughly understand the business, the core processes, and the organization's objectives. This understanding is necessary for the background needed to rapidly analyze any situation requiring an intervention. If the analysis team is not integrated into the business, it takes too long to come up-to-speed on the requirements for solving the business need. Inadequate or, worse yet, no analysis, often the result of time pressures, increases the chance of developing an incorrect solution or a "Band-Aid™" applied to a much larger "sore."

Critical success factor number three is that the RAM assumes your customer has a clear idea of the direction in which to proceed. If not, the RAM can help articulate it, but the need to clarify direction lengthens the time required to develop and implement a solution. Some good organizational development work must often be performed before successful analysis of any type of intervention. For example, if a solution must tie into an organization's vision and mission, the vision and mission statements must be written, available, and articulated. Or if processes and procedures are not producing the desired results for an organization, they must be changed.

Most RAM information must be gleaned from letting people talk. Analysts must have good listening skills and be able to probe for an appropriate level of detail. Questions must be succinct to capture all the needed information and to avoid repeatedly calling on those interviewed. The word rapid means just that: You get in, get the information you need, get out, and don't bug people again. Repeated calls to collect additional information indicates interviewers do not have the experience to successfully employ the RAM.

Table 14.1 outlines the RAM. It lists:

- The activities and approximate amount of time spent on each one relative to the overall analysis
- The operations, or what should actually happen during each activity
- The anticipated outcomes of each operation

Table 14.1
Rapid Analysis Method

Activity	Percentage of Total Time	Operations	Outcomes
Ask	9%	Ask upper management, middle management, and employees these questions: "What is the source of the need?" "What do people have to do to respond to this need?" "What must people know to respond to this need?" "What is the value of a solution to the organization?" "How will you measure the success of the solution?"	Validate responses from all groups and reconcile the gaps.

Table 14.1, Cont'd.
Rapid Analysis Method

Activity	Percentage of Total Time	Operations	Outcomes
Listen	50%	Categorize responses according to these categories: 1. Felt need 2. Normative need 3. Anticipated need 4. Comparative need 5. Expressed or demanded need	Complete information about the issue to use during observation phase to validate and reconcile difference between what is said and what is actually done.
Observe	40%	Observe exemplary performers and others selected randomly. Determine if the environment supports what each group says people need to know and do. Task analysis (is the task being performed effectively and efficiently by some segment of the employee population?) Situation analysis (conditions under which the work is being performed)	Validate responses from various groups; identify gaps between the various needs and the actual situation in the environment.

Table 14.1
Rapid Analysis Method, Cont'd.

Activity	Percentage of Total Time	Operations	Outcomes
Observe (cont'd.)		Instructional analysis (learner characteristics: education, background, culture)	
		Critical incident analysis (what employees actually need to know)	
Report	1%	Compile results.	Groups' acceptance or rejection of recommendations (*note:* at this point the design of the intervention can begin at the appropriate level of training, performance, and organization; includes partial acceptance of recommendations with all groups understanding how much impact intervention(s) can have at the accepted level).
		Explain findings and make recommendations.	
		Explain and recommend on three levels:	
		1. Training	
		2. Performance	
		3. Systemic	

PROCESS

There are five activities that occur during the RAM:

1. Prepare for the analysis.
2. Ask primary questions and probing questions as appropriate.
3. Listen and record responses.
4. Observe actual performance.
5. Report results.

RAPID ANALYSIS METHOD PROCEDURE

Follow these activities:

Activity One: Prepare for the Analysis

Step one: Discuss the focus of the assessment with your customer and team to make sure they are aware that training, performance, and organizational levels will be assessed. You will need a completed Issue Analysis as outlined in Chapter Nine.

Step two: Prepare for the analysis by having a kickoff meeting attended by everyone involved in the project (except those who will be interviewed and observed).

Use the Roles and Responsibilities Matrix template included in the Assessment and Front-End Analysis Tools section of Appendix E to determine what tasks need to be done and by whom.

Once participants have accepted all roles and associated responsibilities, develop a project plan and project schedule to let each person know when his or her tasks begin and end.

Use the legend on the Roles and Responsibilities Matrix template to identify which participants are responsible for the task (R), consulted about the task (C), or simply informed (I) of the outcome of the task. More than one person can be consulted or informed, but only one is responsible for completing the task. Having everyone responsible for at least one task achieves buy-in from project members and gives everyone a stake in the success of the project. The person who is responsible also has the authority for determining how the task gets done. Hammer and Champy (1994) state that assigning responsibility to someone without also giving the person authority is inconsistent. Getting things done requires that people be empowered to act and also be answerable for their actions. Figure 14.1 is an example of a completed Roles and Responsibilities Matrix.

Step three: Divide the work so that each analyst (if more than one) interviews and observes all three vertical groups (upper management, middle management, and employees) of a segment of the target audience. Using this vertical structure for analysis permits analysts to most readily identify inconsistencies between what is said and what is actually happening.

Activity Two: Ask Primary Questions

Step one: Ask the five primary questions listed in Table 14.1, in the first cell of the Operations column. Some probing questions may also need to be asked as follow-on

Figure 14.1
Sample Roles and Responsibilities Matrix

Project: Telecommunications
Phase: Analysis

Name: **Role:**	J. Doe Analyst	S. Doe Analyst	K. Sue Analyst	J. Black Analyst	R. Roy Analyst	K.Levy Analyst	P. Roy Editor	K. Lee Manager
Tasks:								
Audience Analysis	I	I	I	I	R	I	I	I
Develop Observation Instruments	R	I	I	C	C	C	I	I
Validate Observation Instruments	I	C	R	I	C	C	I	I
Conduct Observations	I	I	I	R	C	C	I	I
Summarize Data	I	I	I	I	C	C	R	I
Write Audience Analysis Report	I	R	I	I	C	C	I	I

R = Responsible   C = Consulted   I = Informed

to obtain complete information. In the overall process, this activity should only take about 9 percent of the total amount of analysis time. Ask the same questions of people at all levels of the organization: upper management, middle management, and employees. You are looking for congruence across what each group says.

Step two: Identify inconsistencies (gaps) among the answers of those interviewed at each level.

Activity Three: Listen and Record Responses

Step one: Begin this activity by listening to the responses. Listening involves fully half of the time for analysis. Too often, most of the time in analysis is spent questioning. We have found that if you just listen, people tell you what you need to know. Asking too many specific questions often biases what people say because of how the question is worded. In other words, you find out what you *expect* to find out, not what you *need* to find out.

Step two: Categorize responses into each of the five need categories in the Listen section of Table 14.1 to be certain that you have all the information needed.

Activity Four: Observe Actual Performance

Step one: Watch people complete tasks. You have probably heard the phrase "walk the talk." What people say often does not match what they do. People may tell you what they wish for ideally, or they may be out of touch with what is actually happening.

Step two: Reconcile gaps between verbal responses and actual performance. It is the analyst's job to reconcile any differences. Determining the mismatch between what people say and do is the reason for carrying out Activity Four.

Activity Five: Report Results

Review your notes and prepare to report your findings and recommendations. There may be a lot of data to analyze, depending on the size of the project and the number of analysts, interviews, and observations. Even so, this step of the RAM should only take about 1 percent of the total time for analysis if your notes are complete and you have collected all the information you need in all areas. Use the Analysis Report tool in the Assessment and Front-End Analysis Tools section of Appendix E to summarize your findings.

FROM OUR EXPERIENCE

If you conduct only a training analysis, it is an extremely narrow view of what your function is capable of contributing to your organization. We advise our customers that all three levels of issue analysis outlined in Chapter Nine need to be addressed.

After we complete our assessment, we make it very clear to the customer how much of the total issue can be solved by addressing each level of the organizational assessment. Typically, the percentage of improvement increases as the performance and organizational levels are addressed.

There are times when training alone is the solution that solves the problem. This is the exception rather than the rule. Because organizations are so complex, changing one part nearly always affects another. For example, suppose you implement an electronic performance support system (EPSS) that greatly reduces the time required to produce automotive parts in a foundry. You must check to determine that the company has storage space for the parts. Otherwise, the amount of money you save in one area of the company may be lost in the expense of storing car parts until the assembly line can use them to build cars.

SUMMARY

In using the rapid analysis model, you are conducting the equivalent of all of the other analyses covered in Part One.

By asking just five questions, carefully listening, recording answers, and mentally categorizing them as you ask the questions (to be certain you obtain all the information you need), you have shortcut the needs assessment and analysis process.

Using the RAM gets you to the design phase much more quickly than does completing each step of the nine analyses presented earlier in this part of the book. Whichever methods and strategies of assessment and analysis you use, you are now ready to begin designing the solution.

part two

Multimedia Instructional Design

Introduction to Multimedia Instructional Design

When you have documented all of the information from assessment and analysis and made the required decisions, you are ready to enter the design phase.

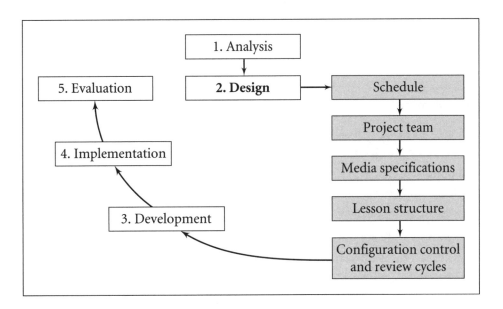

The design phase is the planning phase of your multimedia project. Planning is probably the most important factor in the success of your project. Projects often founder because of failure to adequately plan.

The outcome of this phase is a *course design specification* (CDS) document that details how the intervention will look when it is complete. In completing the CDS you will

- Schedule project activities
- Identify project team members
- Develop a project plan
- Write detailed instructional outlines (if your solution includes a course)
- Create an interface design (if appropriate)
- Review the design for the technical content accuracy with subject-matter experts (SMEs)
- Review the design for instructional or performance support soundness
- Establish the standards for the development phase
- Establish the validity methodology of any tests

We recommend you complete the design phase with as much detail as project constraints (such as time or budget) will allow, thus avoiding expensive rework during development. Course design specifications are especially critical in projects where the planned multimedia development will be phased. A phased approach, in which the content is designed, developed, and implemented in sections, is appropriate when:

- Development begins on a core set of content, skills, or knowledge with plans to add on additional content at a later date. For example, the development of a performance support tool with time-tracking procedures useful to all employees may contain plans and specifications for follow-on additional development of department level time-tracking guidelines.
- A solution is being developed in conjunction with the development of the content. This is often termed "concurrent development" and is often the case in projects that involve software or new product development. When using a multimedia solution for concurrent development, it is best to provide a framework via design specifications so that the content can be "plugged in" as it becomes finalized and available.
- The multimedia development is ongoing in response to rapid changes in the business environment. For example, a web-based tool that provides up-to-date

price or scheduling information that must be regularly updated. The design specification provides the "recipe" for updates.

- When rapid prototyping is used to "try it," "sell it," or to move forward quickly, a course design specification provides a mechanism for capturing the decisions and documenting the design for follow-on development.

All specifications governing the production of materials should come from the work group that will be implementing them. Specifications should never be imposed on a work group by another group without their input. In addition, specifications should be developed in cooperation with internal or external stakeholders.

After specifications are completed, the design and development team and the stakeholder should approve the CDS document. Approval clarifies expectations among all parties and serves as a baseline as the project moves forward. Finally, the specifications should be delivered to the group that will perform quality control and product review.

The course design specification consists of the elements shown in Table 15.1.

Table 15.1
CDS Elements

CDS Element	Content
Schedule	Describes the project and lists milestones, deliverables, and deliverable dates
Project team	Lists roles and responsibilities of project team members and contacts
Media specifications	Documents types, general presentation styles, text, grammar, graphics, fonts, themes, editing symbols, and so on
Lesson structure	Describes how the content is grouped, ordered, linked, or navigated: • The type(s) of information to be taught and methodology for delivering instruction

Table 15.1
CDS Elements, Cont'd.

CDS Element	Content
Lesson structure (cont'd.)	• The lesson flow with respect to events of instruction; course flowcharts; unit, lesson, and detailed content outlines ready for storyboarding or scripting • Feedback, user control, user interactivity, and testing methods and types
Configuration control and review cycles	Describes version control and how media elements are designated and managed; also documents the types of review and process for conducting reviews

Depending on the type of multimedia project, you may need to add to the design specifications suggested in the table. For example, a distance learning project might require a more detailed scheduling component; the addition of video in a multimedia project might require detailed specifications for scripts, set design, lighting, and shot locations. A course design specification template is available on Training Consultants' Softek website at www.trainingsoftek.com.

NEW CONSIDERATIONS

There are many more things that need to be considered during design than there were just a few years ago. Now you must consider issues like the *Searchable Content Objects Reference Model* (SCORM) and *learning management systems* (LMS).

SCORM

SCORM standards are receiving a great deal of attention. Customers are asking if vendors are "SCORM compliant," and nearly all vendors testify that they are. However, the truth is, the standards are not set yet and compliance means many different things.

The history of SCORM began in 1997 when the Department of Defense (DoD) and the White House Office of Science and Technology established the Advanced

Distributed Learning (ADL) initiative. The DoD uses many courseware vendors in all branches of the military. Its goal is to be able to purchase courseware from one vendor that can be used with any LAN anywhere in the world, in any branch of the military. The military had been expending large portions of its budget to develop the same courses for different branches. Figure 15.1 demonstrates the desired result.

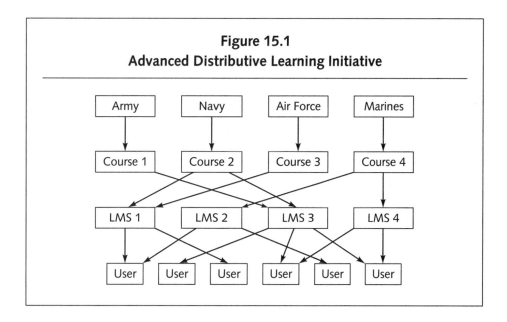

Figure 15.1
Advanced Distributive Learning Initiative

The DoD called all of the vendors together who wished to conduct business with the federal government and explained its ADL initiative and charged them with developing a common set of standards for courseware development. The goal was to have content that was available without modification. The common standards became known as the Sharable Content Object Reference Model or SCORM. SCORM also contained standards to break content into small learning objects that could be reused in numerous courses but only developed one time. These objects were called *reusable content objects* (RCO). That meant that all courses had to be developed using small "bits" (objects) that could be accessed from courses that had been developed by different vendors and incorporated into one course using a searchable database. The standards called for doing this with a system of meta-data that were each tagged in a way that a search would identify all relevant objects and combine them automatically.

Shackleford (2002) explains the ADL's goals for SCORM capabilities:

1. *Accessibility:* content should be available anywhere in the world not on a LAN or CD-ROM.

2. *Interoperability:* the content should work on all platforms, browsers, and LMSs.

3. *Reusability:* content should be used wherever needed not just in a course or lesson.

4. *Adaptability:* agility of content to configure itself depending on learning progress and preferences.

5. *Affordability:* reduce production costs for e-learning and make quality learning widely available at significantly lower costs.

How meta-tagging might work is demonstrated by the following example. When a user wants to learn about a certain subject, he or she can take a pretest. For each question that is missed, the database will automatically search for content objects associated with that question. All of the associated content objects will be compiled into a course that is automatically launched for the user. Figure 15.2 demonstrates this example.

Now that is easier to say than to do. It requires tagging all of the content in a certain way that will associate it with the questions. That is why the DoD required all of its vendors to work together to establish the standards. What would be considered a content object? These are still defined differently by different vendors. You can determine whether courseware is truly SCORM compliant by download-

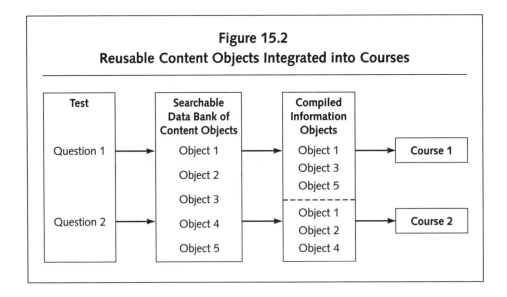

Figure 15.2
Reusable Content Objects Integrated into Courses

ing the SCORM Compliance Test Suite from the Advanced Distributive Learning website (www.adlnet.org). Run a vendor or internally developed course through this suite and receive a diagnostic on its conformity. The current version of SCORM (1.3) identifies navigation rules within the content without having to set up the rules independently in an LMS. However, the current version does not fulfill true adaptive sequencing and navigation, although it does provide a degree of flexibility comparable to most current e-learning. It seems it is going to be a while before the SCORM standards are truly solidified.

What designers should be concerned with is that courses can now be constructed in many ways for many uses and thus create more value. For example, a user may take a complete course but then can go back and review information that is either complex or infrequently used. Or the course can be used as an EPSS, where users can log on, access only the information needed, and then use the information.

Learning Management Systems

Learning management systems (LMS) are increasingly appearing on the e-learning scene. LMSs are sometimes misunderstood in terms of what they can and cannot do. What an LMS does do is automate all of the tactical processes involved in delivering training. Think of an LMS as a registrar's office at a university. Figure 15.3 outlines the capabilities of an LMS.

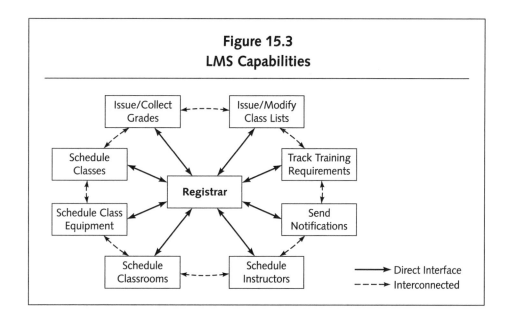

Figure 15.3
LMS Capabilities

Content that is compliant with an LMS can be accessed through it. The interface that allows the user to access the content is known as a portal. (See Figure 15.4.)

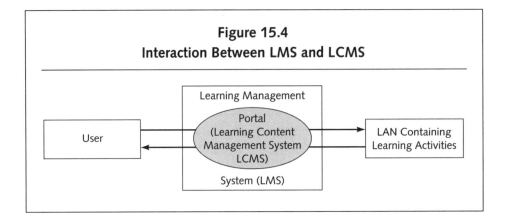

Figure 15.4
Interaction Between LMS and LCMS

E-Learning's Impact on Design

The web and other interactive technologies have necessitated rethinking how solutions are designed (Lee, Owens, & Benson, 2002). Much discussion has been generated regarding whether *objectivism* or *constructivism* is the best approach to designing e-learning. The philosophy you adopt will have a profound effect on the way you use the instructional design model and the user interfaces of the solutions you produce.

If you follow the objectivist's philosophy in applying the model, you will create products where there is one best path for learning derived from the mind of an expert on the subject. If you follow the constructivist's, you believe that everyone derives his or her own reality from a learning experience and therefore should be permitted to explore and learn from experience. Both of these camps seem to feel they have discovered something new. Yet, objectivism is the didactic approach to learning and constructivism is the discovery learning method that John Dewey (1916) wrote about when he said that all new learning must be approached from the standpoint of trial and error. In other words, learning by doing, and yes, making mistakes. Think of your own most significant learning. It was probably the result of you doing something and making a mistake. And, for the record, neither approach is the "best." It depends on the situation, the content, and the learner.

The web is certainly a pliable vehicle for the constructivist approach to designing solutions. With so many websites and so much information available on just about every topic imaginable, the web can be used very effectively to allow users to explore topics and draw conclusions from their own research. This design is, on the one hand, more simple because the designer does not have to create as much material, but it is more complicated because the designer must conduct more research during the analysis phase to determine the availability of information and guide users to the various sources of information. The designer must provide the motivation by setting up scenarios where questions are raised, curiosity aroused, and impetus given to the need to search out information.

Another impact of the web is the level of knowledge about instructional design that is required to develop solutions. One camp believes that only professional instructional designers who understand the instructional design model can develop effective solutions. It is not the knowledge, they would say, but the way it is fit together to be delivered. However, with web-based technologies, someone knowledgeable in the subject who understands principles of good research and where to find information may be just as suited to creating web-based solutions as a formally trained instructional designer.

In the traditional model, companies often felt that only SMEs could understand their business and therefore chose to use those experts to design and deliver training—usually with mixed results, and often with disastrous ones. We believe "The best thing about being a subject-matter expert is that you know everything about the subject and the worst thing about being a subject-matter expert is that you know everything about the subject." An expert will make quantum leaps over information that the novice needs to know. Because the SME is so familiar with the subject, much of the information is now intuitive to him or her, but it will not be evident to the user of the solution.

Companies that have taken the time to provide training on the principles of learning to SMEs seem to have better success with the "SME-as-designer" approach. Indeed, some industries are so highly specific that it would take a great deal of time to bring someone who knows nothing about the subject up-to-speed on the content and would require the use of an SME anyway to provide information to the designer, decreasing the productivity of two people. An SME who knows where to point users to find information may be as effective as an instructional designer. And, using the constructivist philosophy, learners take more responsibility for their learning and fill in the gaps themselves that were left out by the SME.

Designing goal-based scenarios or performance-related problem-solving systems should be considered when deciding whether the solution is context-sensitive or context-independent. When designing context-sensitive systems, the designer must anticipate the users' questions. For example, a transportation company that implements a context-sensitive help system to support a piece of hardware or software must anticipate when decisions or information might be needed for a particular activity and program along with the appropriate links.

When designing a context-independent system, such as a problem-solving system, the designer must focus on structure, tables, menus, and searches so that the information can be accessed effectively from various sources. For example, a telecommunications company that implemented a product development support system had to create links to related information, cross-references, browse paths, and calls to other support systems.

Performance support systems should supplant training on processes and procedures. We believe no one should tell anyone else something they can look up for themselves. This is in alignment with the four-level model we introduced in Figure 11.1. Moving from memorizing numerous procedural steps to providing online help so users can obtain information for themselves is a major capability of the web. Yet memorization in a instructor-led class is still prevalent.

FROM OUR EXPERIENCE

There are several reasons your entire team should work together to develop a course design specification:

- To capture innovative and creative design ideas before it is too late in development to make it practical to incorporate them. If project members begin creating individually, each might have good ideas that are not leveraged in the design of the entire project. Including the team in course specifications prevents good ideas from being overcome by events or being used inconsistently.

- To obtain consensus and shared understanding of the design specifications. Everyone on the team needs to understand the design specifications prior to beginning the development phase. Otherwise, you will set the project team up for needless rework and inconsistency in the final product. Design meetings that give everyone a chance to ask questions and give their input increase the chances of the specifications being adhered to because all team members buy in.

- To create an appreciation for the necessity for a consistent approach. A consistent approach is important in order to create a comfortable learning or support environment and to ensure the transfer of learning. A consistent approach speeds development by documenting the degree of consistency necessary to meet project goals.

You may find that once you begin implementing the specifications during development, some things you thought would work well do not produce the desired results. Remember, however, as development progresses, the longer you wait to change design standards, the harder, more costly, and more time-consuming implementing the change will be.

A basic course design specification template can be saved and modified to meet the requirements of subsequent projects. Modifying an existing course design specification for follow-on projects can result in significant project time savings.

Regarding SCORM, the important thing from a design standpoint is to develop courses that can be used in many ways and that can be combined into many different courses using pieces that already exist.

We also believe that the concept of the LMS has been oversold. Maybe all you need is a good database that can access information and that you can feed information into. If you have large numbers of employees and have many tracking requirements, an LMS might be the solution. Otherwise, look to other solutions.

Regarding the interaction of the LMS and content, be certain that you require your content provider to work with your LMS provider to be certain the two are compatible before you accept the content.

SUMMARY

The design phase uses the conclusions from the project assessment and analysis phase to build a roadmap for development. The design process is an opportunity to design your intervention, document a plan, build consensus, and clarify expectations before beginning development. The rest of the chapters in Part Two provide suggested steps and activities that will provide you with a roadmap for your project.

chapter SIXTEEN

Project Schedule

You'll recall from the preceding chapter that the design specification phase begins with a description of the project and a list of milestones, schedule, deliverables, and deliverable dates; definition of the scope and vision of the project; and details of the plan for how the vision is achieved. It often serves as a communication tool among stakeholders, internal and external customers, sponsors, vendors, and project team members.

Whatever the delivery medium or media, use the same basic principles for developing a project schedule. Each component of project planning must be integrated and coordinated, but in a different manner. For example, although CBT and web-based courseware are structured around learning components, distance broadcasting and teleconferencing are structured around timed events. Each must be carefully scheduled for effective development and implementation, regardless of the resulting product.

Project scheduling at the activity level is often the result of design decisions and compromises made on the basis of the cost, availability, and capability of key personnel and tools. For example, the number and design of graphic elements, use of clip art, or the decision to use an off-the-shelf graphic interface may be determined by the availability and talents of key graphic development personnel. Interactivity and testing design decisions may be based on the development ratio required for one design versus another. The decision making during design affects deliverables and the supporting activity scheduling. Often the project activities are created and revised iteratively throughout the design phase. As design decisions are made, project activities are confirmed, developed in more detail, or revised to reflect design decisions.

Creating a project schedule is an important aspect of multimedia instructional design. The design must be not only effective, but also achievable within the context of the business need, time frame, and personnel and resources needed to perform the work. When completed, schedules decrease the chance of "scope creep," which ultimately prevents you from meeting project deadlines. Schedules also communicate shared understanding of how the design affects goals, project tasks, and team members' roles and responsibilities.

PROCESS

There are three activities in the process of creating a project schedule:

1. Document general project information.
2. List project deliverables.
3. Schedule project activities.

PROJECT SCHEDULE PROCEDURE

To create a project schedule, perform the following activities and steps.

Activity One: Document General Project Information

Develop and include a brief statement about

- The purpose of the project and what business need is addressed
- The current performance gaps and obstacles
- The desired outcome and high-level performance requirements
- Any project constraints or issues
- The assumptions you are making that have an impact on time lines or project success

Activity Two: List Project Deliverables

List the deliverables or milestones and associated dates, specific to your project. Deliverables and milestones might include developing, reviewing, and approving

- Audio scripts
- Storyboards
- Prototype screen interface
- Programming templates or models
- Video scripts
- Video broadcast schedule and script

Activity Three: Schedule Project Activities

Especially for large projects, it is important that activities be well organized and that all team members (1) know their roles and responsibilities, (2) be aware of the project timeline, and (3) deliver their project components at the appropriate time. If the Roles and Responsibilities Matrix has been developed during the analysis phase, revise and enhance it to produce the level of task detail needed to begin development. The matrix is outlined in the rapid analysis method (Chapter Fourteen) and is included in the Assessment and Front-End Analysis Tools section of Appendix E.

Be sure to establish review cycles with adequate time for revision as part of the schedule. Reviews are an important aspect of multimedia project success because they ensure the quality of the instruction design and the validity of content.

Include time in the schedule for reviewers to gain a clear understanding of what is to be reviewed, time allowed for conducting the review, time to record observations and suggestions, time to determine which suggestions are implemented, and time to perform the rework. The importance of adequate review and revision cycles cannot be stressed too strongly. If project deadlines narrow or are overrun, never encroach on the time necessary to ensure the quality of the design and final product. Remember, a good ratio for allocating time on multimedia projects is one-third analysis; one-third design and development; and one-third implementation, evaluation, and maintenance.

Plan for these reviews in your schedule:

- A technical or functional review
- An ID review
- A standards review
- An editorial review
- A management review

Templates with instructions for each of these reviews are included in the Design Tools section of Appendix E.

There are many useful software scheduling applications available, such as Microsoft Project® or Microsoft Scheduler Plus®. Automating scheduling is especially important when it becomes necessary to adjust the schedule; you can change one project date and all others that are affected by that change are adjusted immediately.

FROM OUR EXPERIENCE

Project management and project scheduling are complex disciplines that require a unique set of skills. Instructional designers or other multimedia team members often find themselves serving as project manager or team leader without the experience, aptitude, or tools necessary for success in this role. It is important to recognize that the project-manager or team-leader role is not a simple add-on for a team member having other duties in a multimedia development project. Because of the increased requirements for tracking, scheduling, communicating, and monitoring project activities, most multimedia projects require a skilled, full-time project manager.

It is best to construct the project timelines with those who will be performing the work. A team approach to constructing schedules takes advantage of the group's expertise and experience and affords the buy-in needed to get project development off to a good start. Chapter Seventeen presents a list of typical multimedia team members and roles and responsibilities. We refer you to Lee and Krayer's (2003) book on organizing change for help with project management.

We recommend that the team develop a basic schedule and project task list and modify it for subsequent multimedia projects. Modifying existing schedules for later projects generally results in significant time saving and allows benchmarking and accurate project scheduling.

There is a lot to be gained from analyzing the schedule during and after completion of the project. Tracking and comparing actual time and costs with scheduled time and costs gives you the data you need to (1) accurately estimate the scope of future development efforts and (2) point out areas where you can increase productivity, maintain quality, or improve cost-effectiveness.

Lack of time-tracking data can be a real barrier to getting the scheduling information needed to do accurate planning. Scheduling isn't accurate if project time is not tracked, or if it's tracked inconsistently or haphazardly, or if it doesn't track scheduled tasks.

Considerations for time tracking include:

- Determining how the time data are captured
- Determining what level of data should be collected and analyzed
- Deciding who has access to the time-tracking information
- Determining how time tracking is implemented

We recommend doing a quick survey of how long team members think a project task normally takes or should take. Then establish benchmarks and move forward by scheduling, tracking, and analyzing the team's performance against scheduled estimates. At the conclusion of the project, debrief the team and analyze how the benchmarks can be revised if needed. Review on a project-by-project basis provides the data needed to accurately schedule multimedia design and development tasks.

SUMMARY

The project schedule—especially the section outlining project-development tasks—reflects the decisions made during analysis and design. Schedules are an important tool in assessing whether multimedia ID decisions are achievable and appropriate to unique personnel, time frame, and business constraints. Regardless of your role on the multimedia design team, it is important to understand and have input into the activities that are planned and scheduled. The next chapter presents typical roles and responsibilities that are assigned to activities on a multimedia instructional design and development team.

chapter SEVENTEEN

Project Team

The second undertaking in design specification (recall Table 15.1) is to define typical roles and responsibilities for project team members and associate them with project tasks. If you are using scheduling software that facilitates assigning resources, then it's efficient to add the resources to the schedule.

In a perfect world, multimedia teams would design solutions without the constraint of using only what is available in tools and resources. In reality, multimedia ID teams must design solutions that consider not only the problem but also the resources at hand to solve the problem.

PROCESS

There are three activities in the process of defining roles and responsibilities for project team members:

1. List team roles.
2. List project tasks.
3. Assign roles and responsibilities.

PROJECT TEAM PROCEDURE

Follow these activities:

Activity One: List Team Roles

As a team, list the roles required. Review the typical roles and responsibilities of a design team in the (alphabetical) list that follows, and then select those appropriate for your particular project.

Audio Producer or Technician

- Produces all audio
- Generates final audio scripts
- Casts talent
- Schedules audio recording sessions
- Mixes, edits, and digitizes audio
- Finds sources of music and sound effects
- Identifies existing media
- Controls and archives audio libraries
- Arranges licensing of existing audio materials
- Reviews the product from an audio perspective
- Has working knowledge of the authoring tool

Author (Publisher, Materials Developer)

- Produces written or electronically mediated instructional materials
- Integrates media elements and creates the product using an authoring tool
- Works with the graphic designer to incorporate graphics into the product
- Constructs interactions and makes revisions
- Has advanced skills with, and knowledge of, the authoring tool
- Works with the creative director to integrate audio and video elements into the product

Creative Director

- Works closely with the interactive designer and graphic designer on design and development of the human/computer interface
- Works with the interactive designer and audio and video producers on creating storyboards and scripts
- Collaborates with the graphic designer regarding media elements
- Ensures all media elements are produced and integrated into the product
- Carries responsibility for the overall quality of the media elements of the product

- Reviews the product from a quality perspective
- Has working knowledge of the authoring tool

Editor

- Edits written or authored material
- Creates or reviews writing specifications

Evaluation Specialist

- Develops or reviews the evaluation plan and tools
- Develops or reviews the testing plan

Graphic Artist

- Works with the graphic designer to create content graphics
- Creates screen or interface designs
- Creates illustrations and animations for the product
- Has some knowledge of the multimedia authoring tool

Graphic Designer

- Designs and produces graphics for instructional materials
- Designs the overall visual look of the product
- Works with the instructional designer and creative director to conceptualize the main interface and content graphics
- Designs the main interface as well as the typography and buttons for all screens
- Creates content art, illustrations, and animation
- Identifies opportunities to use existing artwork
- Maintains libraries of graphics
- Works with the instructional designer to determine all graphic standards
- Has working knowledge of the authoring tool

Implementation Representative

- Weighs implementation alternatives with organizational priorities, issues, and concerns to offer input on the best solution

- Identifies implementation activities according to the medium or media selected
- Defines the time schedule for implementation activities
- Works with support groups and organizations to ensure timely, smooth transition of the intervention from the development phase to the implementation phase
- Creates or carries out implementation, marketing, and communication plans and schedules
- Implements maintenance and evaluation plans

Interactive Designer, Instructional Designer
- Prepares objectives as part of the project team
- Defines content
- Selects and sequences activities for a specific intervention
- Writes (or works with subject-matter experts) to develop instructional material
- Develops multimedia instructional design
- Works with SMEs to develop content for the product
- Develops the interactive design of the product (for example, interactions within the product, how the interactions work, and how the user interacts with the product)
- Works with the systems designer to design flow diagrams to support the instructional and interactive design
- Creates storyboards with the graphic designer, creative director, and video and audio producers
- Works with the creative director to write audio and video scripts
- Bears responsibility for the overall quality of the instruction and interactivity of the product
- Has working knowledge of the authoring tool

Performance Analyst
- Identifies ideal and actual performance conditions
- Determines the cause of any discrepancy and recommends solution(s) and evaluation strategy

Project Manager, Project Leader

- Manages the project (including people, resources, schedule, and processes)
- Estimates the project costs
- Creates CDS with the support of the team
- Creates and maintains the project schedule with the support of the team
- Keeps the project on track by holding regular meetings of the team
- Ensures the team has sufficient resources and tools
- Keeps the customer and sponsors informed of all decisions
- Communicates regularly with management on the status of the project
- Maintains an atmosphere conducive to creativity, productivity, and quality
- Arranges for reviews of the product
- Sets the goals for the team and defines the roles and responsibilities of team members
- Maintains records and motivates team members
- Plans and coordinates resources for developing, acquiring, or deploying a developmental product or service
- Supports a group's work and links that work with the total organization
- Supports evaluation, measurement for success, and benchmarking
- Establishes ground rules for the team and reports on the project to senior management
- Resolves conflicts among team members and various departments, functions, managers, and so on
- Ensures recognition of project team members

Quality Reviewer or Evaluator

- Identifies what impact an intervention has on individual or organization effectiveness
- Reviews the product from an educational and quality perspective

Sponsor

- Owns resources and sets the direction of development activities for the project
- Interfaces with the project team on all decisions, status of project, and signoffs

Subject-Matter Expert (SME)

- Reviews the content in various stages for accuracy and gives feedback to interactive designer
- Functions as a content expert throughout the development process

Systems Designer

- Designs how the product works from a technical standpoint
- Decides what development tools are used
- Decides how the program logic and flow is structured and how it is produced
- Manages authors
- Creates the base logic for the product and unit models for the authors
- Works with the instructional or interactive designer to design flow diagrams for the product
- Conducts technical reviews of the product
- Has extensive technical knowledge of the authoring tool

Systems Engineer, Application Developer

- Provides information-technology services, primarily application development and support

Video Editor or Technician

- Digitizes and edits all video
- Integrates video elements into the final product
- Has extensive knowledge of the online editing tool
- Has working knowledge of the authoring tool

Video Producer

- Produces and directs all video for the product
- Generates final video scripts
- Casts talent
- Schedules shoots
- Assembles a video crew
- Obtains costumes and makeup
- Reviews final product from a video perspective

- Has working knowledge of the online editing tool
- Has working knowledge of the authoring tool

Activity Two: List Project Tasks

List all of the tasks that will be required during each phase of the project. You should develop a separate matrix for each phase of the project.

Activity Three: Assign Roles and Responsibilities

Assign roles to project team members. Depending on the size of your project, the timeline, and the skills and resources needed, you may find that team members fill multiple roles or that you require more than one person to fill a role. The project timelines reflect the number of responsibilities assumed by individual team members. If a few key players assume most responsibilities, this generally lengthens the timeline on a small project. Develop a Roles and Responsibilities Matrix for each phase of the project, tailored to the needs of the project.

FROM OUR EXPERIENCE

Clearly defining roles and responsibilities can reduce conflict and confusion and focus team members on their unique role in successfully completing a project. Individual roles and responsibilities for design vary, depending on the size of the project, the number and type of media elements, and the number of available personnel (along with their talent).

Organizations that assume that "a couple of people with the right skill sets" can design and produce multimedia are misinformed about the number and complexity of skill sets needed for even a minimal multimedia design and development project. It is rare, in fact almost impossible, to staff a design team with a couple of people who can competently act as subject-matter expert, instructional designer, media expert, authoring software expert, system engineer, and so on. The more likely scenario is a team-based approach with a much larger group of people who are not dedicated 100 percent to the project, lending expertise only when it is needed.

SUMMARY

Determining who performs project-development tasks affects the decisions made during design. Design decisions must be achievable and appropriate to the project's unique personnel, time frame, and business constraints.

chapter EIGHTEEN

Media Specifications

The first three elements of the course design specification describe the project, the schedule, and the roles and responsibilities of project team members.

The next undertaking, media specification, describes standards and design for multimedia elements such as:

- Theme and interface design and functionality
- Writing style and grammar guidelines
- Feedback and interaction standards
- Video and audio treatments
- Text design and standards
- Graphic design and standards
- Animation and special effects

The design decisions on these multimedia elements are a set of compromises that weigh theories and best practices in learning and performance support; knowledge of the audience and content; project team member preferences, skills, and talents; and project realities such as the budget, timeline, and stakeholder preferences.

An appropriate goal is to design a performance support environment or learning environment that:

- Engages the learner's modalities
- Provides a comfortable and stress-free environment in which to learn or perform

- Presents the content at the right level and sequence, and with as much fidelity to the real environment as is possible
- Meets the constraints and requirements of the project goals

RELATED THEORY

The optimum design engages as many of the senses as possible. Barring any type of impairment or disability on the one hand and any extrasensory abilities on the other, we may assume that the learner has five senses. He or she uses all five senses to learn or perform.

Over the years, everyone develops a preference for using certain senses, because of types of instruction received, the parts of instruction attended to, and an inborn disposition to learn using some senses more than others. Whatever the reason, people learn in different ways. Learning through more than one sense is known as a multisensory approach.

The best learning occurs through using more than one of the senses. Even though one sense might be preferred, learning is reinforced through secondary sensory learning methods. Because the best learning occurs through more than one sense, the best instruction stimulates as many senses as possible.

In the typical learning situation, you have learners who represent preference for the full spectrum of modalities. The most efficient learners are those who can maximize integration of all of these modalities. It is the instructional designer's responsibility to help students maximize their learning by presenting content that stimulates as many learning senses as possible. Students can use their preferred sense to learn the majority of the material and their secondary senses for reinforcement.

FOUR APPROACHES TO LEARNING

Here are the five senses, grouped into four approaches to learning:

1. *Visual:* presenting instruction using anything learners can look at. Visuals include video, graphics, animation, and written text (on a computer screen, whiteboard, flip chart, overhead transparencies, books, posters, and so on).

2. *Auditory:* presenting instruction using anything students can listen to (tapes, audio teleconferencing, CBT, lecture, sound effects, music, and so on).

3. *Olfactory:* presenting instruction using anything students can smell or taste—as when a student discerns that equipment is overheating, or something is burning, or something has been prepared with too much spice, and so on. (Olfactory is usually not a primary sense for learning, especially in regard to multimedia, but because some people are more sensitive to smells and odors, learning is enhanced and stimulated by their olfactory sense.)

4. *Tactile or kinesthetic:* presenting instruction using anything students can touch or manipulate (models, actual parts or equipment, having students perform demonstrations, role plays, and so on).

PROCESS

Defining the media elements determines the look and feel of the final product. There are seven activities in the process of defining media specifications:

1. Define the look and feel of the theme.
2. Define the interface and functionality.
3. Define the interaction and feedback standards.
4. Define the video and audio treatments.
5. Indicate text design standards.
6. Prepare the graphic design standards.
7. Decide on animation and special effects.

MEDIA SPECIFICATIONS PROCEDURE

Follow these activities:

Activity One: Define the Look and Feel of the Theme

Step one: Brainstorm a list of themes. Delete any theme that could offend culturally sensitive audience members or be viewed as religious or sexist in nature.

Narrow the list to the top three or four themes. Use the information you have gained in analysis to define a theme (or metaphor) and general presentation style. The goal in defining a theme is to

- Add interest and relate to the audience and content
- Supply a thread that links the course elements
- Support learning with a unified look and feel
- Constitute a starting point for creating multimedia analogies, graphics, set and costume design, text styles, activities, and so on

Themes should be associated with the actual job the solution is designed for. Job-related themes enhance transfer of learning to the job. We do not recommend or support "fantasy themes"; teaching principles of leadership by way of space creatures coming from Mars to interact with humans does not make the connections that people need to learn—indeed, a far-out theme may be so intriguing as to interfere with learning. It is much more challenging to make the course engaging, yet keep it related to the jobs that people do.

Step two: Mock up text styles, ideas for an interface design, set design, costumes, and analogies or graphic styles that support each theme on paper.

Step three: Decide on the theme.

Activity Two: Define the Interface and Functionality

The interface design for multimedia should be representative of the theme, audience characteristics, and organizational environment. In addition, the interface design should

- Be as simple as possible, with adequate white space, uniform spacing, and adequate margins (top and bottom, left and right)
- Use consistent screen areas for repeated screen elements such as titles, feedback, links, menus, or prompts
- Include a consistent navigation design so users become comfortable within the learning or support environment
- Keep in mind that most people from western cultures view screens using a Z pattern, as shown in Figure 18.1. This is an important consideration in placing screen elements. Generally, the most important information, such as graphics or photos, are placed at the upper left and text or supporting information on the right, followed by prompts and navigation at the bottom. The most-often-used navigation button is placed at the lower right. This placement facilitates mouse-click navigation for right-handed mouse users.

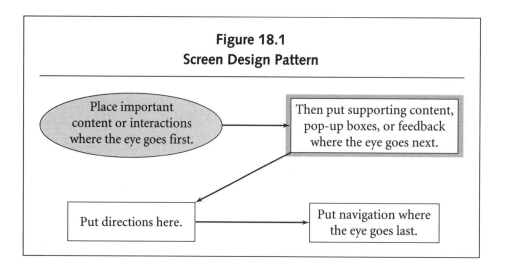

Figure 18.1
Screen Design Pattern

Place important content or interactions where the eye goes first.

Then put supporting content, pop-up boxes, or feedback where the eye goes next.

Put directions here.

Put navigation where the eye goes last.

Many of the interface design and navigation options in this chapter are available in authoring software. Consider these options when designing an interface:

- A frame identifier such as "3 of 25," so users can judge how close they are to completing a section or segment. (Remember, multimedia is not like text, where a user can judge how much remains by leafing forward in the text.)

- Exit, Next, Menu, and Back buttons, to facilitate navigation.

- Bookmarking so that students can return to a course and navigate to the last topic or frame they completed.

- A Glossary button, if the terminology used is likely to be unfamiliar to the audience.

- A Help button with navigation tips, supplemental information, links to other websites, or graphics that remind students of their location in the flow of the course.

- An Audio Repeat button, so students can listen to the audio again on any particular frame. Repeat capabilities are a particularly good strategy if the audience uses English as a second language, if screens include complex audio instructions, or if screens contain long audio sequences.

- A Flash Card button, allowing users to mark frames for printing or review. This is appropriate if the application is deployed in a location such as a learning lab, where screens are not readily available for review or refreshment.

- A More Info button, for access to additional, detailed explanations. This strategy is successful with audiences having varying levels of expertise.
- A Print button, which allows printing job aids, course-completion certificates, or reference materials.
- Lesson and Topic buttons, to aid students in navigation through complex curricula.
- Audio Record, Stop, and Play (playback) buttons, useful when students are practicing audio responses and then listening to their responses and self-evaluating them against a prerecorded example.

One of the best sources of design insight is to review existing web and CBT programs. Note how content, theme, and interface satisfy the audience and meet the business need that they address. Here are a few sample interface designs, with information about the audience and the business need in each case.

- The purpose of the CBT program illustrated in Figure 18.2 is to market the company's products. CD-ROMs were sent to prospective sales partners.

  Completely open navigation is critical to the effectiveness of this program; therefore the interface is designed for easy access to all areas of content. Displaying the menu structure down the left side of the screen enables users to retrieve the specific information they need from any point in the program. Although this program was designed and produced prior to the growth in popularity of the World Wide Web, the general navigation layout it illustrates has become standard for most website design.

- The purpose of the CBT program illustrated in Figure 18.3 is to train operators in performing startup procedures for a steam turbine.

  The user interface for this course (displayed across the bottom of the CBT screen) is designed to resemble the steam seal system control panel that operators use on the job. This brings a level of comfort to operators who are unaccustomed to using CBT for continuing-education purposes.

- The purpose of the CBT program illustrated in Figure 18.4 is to offer training and marketing information regarding AST Computer's Ovation Program.

  Because of the competitive nature of its industry, AST chose a "Business Olympics" metaphor to compare its products and services to those of the competition. This includes a sportscaster-on-television theme, which in turn inspires the remote-control navigation interface. Users click through different "events" in the "competition" as if switching channels.

- The purpose of the CBT program illustrated in Figure 18.5 is to train new hires at an ophthalmology supplier and extend continued-education support for sales representatives. Areas of education include products, basic concepts and tools related to the field of ophthalmology, and the anatomy of the eye.

The course structure is presented as a tour of an optometrist's office. Users visit various rooms and explore the topics by selecting objects. Navigation is simplified for ease of use, and so as not to conflict with or distract from the

Figure 18.2
Sample Interface One—Stratus

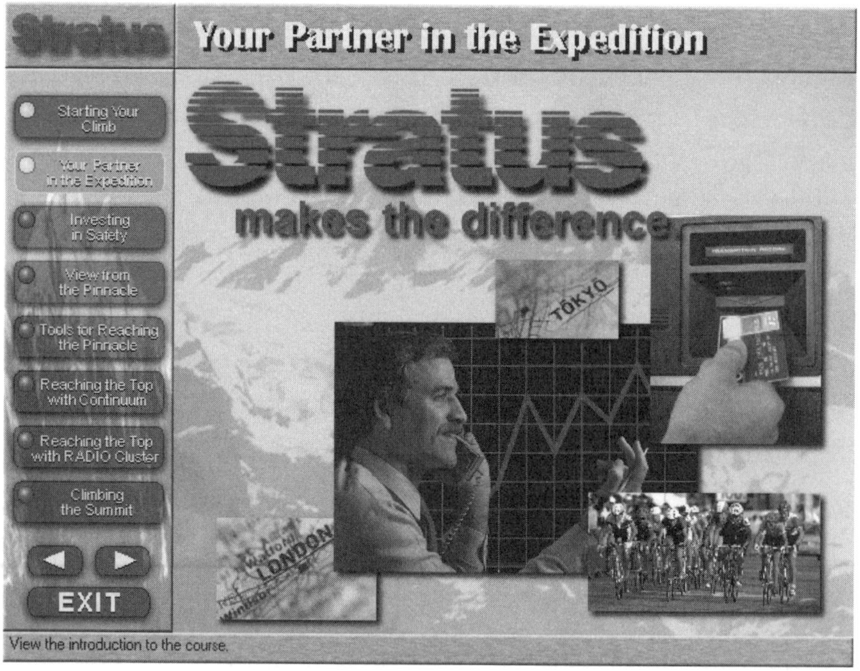

Source: Courtesy of Mlink Technologies

sometimes-complex content presented on screen. This interface also includes a briefcase (icon in the lower left corner of the screen) that contains reference materials and product and medical glossaries the student can access at any time.

The previous interface designs represent the Objectivist approach design. (See Figures 23.2 and 23.3 for a representation of the Constructivist perspective.)

Activity Three: Define the Interaction and Feedback Standards

Begin by defining the standards for interaction and feedback.

One of the strengths of multimedia is the capacity for interaction. A lot of exciting work is being done in the area of intelligent interfaces; virtual reality; and

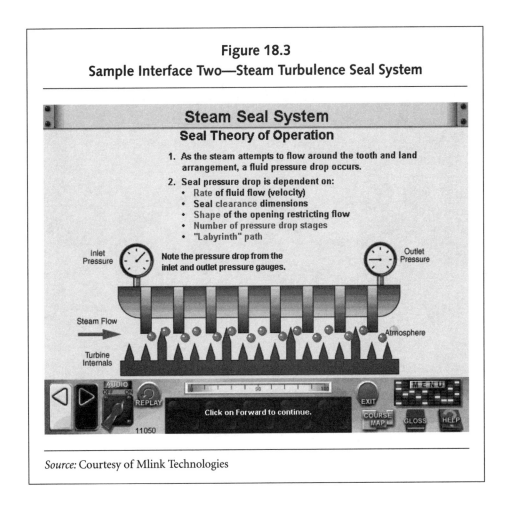

Figure 18.3
Sample Interface Two—Steam Turbulence Seal System

Source: Courtesy of Mlink Technologies

various means of interaction such as natural-language interface, voice and speech technology, gesture recognition, and even biological interface. For the time being, multimedia interaction is typically entered through a microphone, keyboard, or mouse. Whatever the input method, interaction must capture a user's attention and help him or her form associations. In multimedia courses, interactions should be frequent and produce student involvement. We recommend student-controlled pacing and branching.

Objectivism uses structured questioning techniques. There are clear instructions, and the question contains only one correct response. Indicate the format for

Figure 18.4
Sample Interface Three—AST Computer

Source: Courtesy of Mlink Technologies

the sentence containing the question and possible answers in your standards so that they have a distinct and consistent screen format. Most questions are a variation of text entry, clicking on an object, multiple choice, or matching; they permit one or two tries before the user is given the correct answer and allowed to move on. All questions should be titled, worded clearly, and easy to understand.

Constructivists' approach to questions is to put questioning in control of the user himself or herself. One piece of information raises another question in his or her mind, which causes him or her to explore further. Or the content will form a situation that the user then explores.

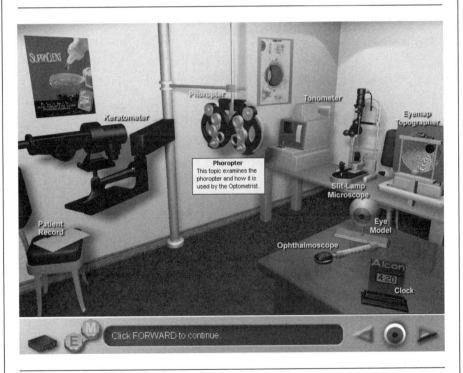

Figure 18.5
Sample Interface Four—Ophthalmology

Source: Courtesy of Mlink Technologies

Objectivism uses structured feedback. Feedback should neither be distracting nor reward incorrect responses. It should be immediate, informative, and positive and motivational. There should be no excessive delay from the time the user performs an action to when the feedback occurs. Constructivists provide feedback through permitting the user to see the consequences of failing. Feedback from failure is often in the form of a story, the reasoning being that we think in the form of stories anyway based on personal experiences we have had.

Objectivists would likely create traditional question-based tests to evaluate learning, and thus would benefit from the record-keeping capabilities of most multimedia systems, which allow interaction or test-item results to be saved for later reporting. Indicate the items that are to be recorded and in what format the information is exported. Reporting ensures desired, consistent outcomes. The ability to prove consistent learning is especially critical for organizations that must comply with changing regulations. Items that can be recorded include student identification, number of items missed, frequency at which items are missed, and seat time.

Constructivists would probably not use a traditional question-based test. As with feedback, the questioning would arise from the situation and learning would be through "doing" using situationally based computer simulations.

Activity Four: Define the Video and Audio Treatments

Define the audio, photography, and video standards. Here are standards to be established, depending on the media and the technology specifications you are using:

- *Audio:* narration style and tone—for example, male narrator, British English. Indicate sound file types and file-naming conventions. Determine how sound effects and music are used. Music is an especially good tool for signaling the beginning or end of an instructional sequence. As with a motion picture, it can also set the tone and support a graphic style and theme.

- *Photography:* file type, file-naming conventions, and size requirements.

- *Video:* file type, file-naming conventions, and size requirements. Any video should clearly support the goals of the project. Video should be shot with enough detail to demonstrate the objectives of the training. It should be used as an aid in and support for text, graphic, and audio presentation of the content. The length of the motion segments should not detract from the content; short segments that play a supporting role are best.

Activity Five: Indicate Text Design and Standards

Text design and standards stipulate such things as font style, size, and color. The text appearance and resolution on the screen should determine the size and font. Indicate the arrangement—both justification and letter spacing. Also indicate the display treatment (for example: "Bullets appear on the screen, from left to right, one at a time, with a two-second pause before each new bullet and after all bullets are in place").

Activity Six: Prepare the Graphic Design Standards

The graphic design standards include file type, file size, file-naming convention, and color range. Graphics should have a clear benefit to the presentation of the content and hold simplicity of design as their overall characteristic. They should not detract from textual information. Graphics should be similar in size and placement, and any text that is included as call-outs must be readable.

Clarity and readability should not be dependent on color variations. There should not be more than four colors on a screen, and the entire course should use a palette of not more than seven colors. The color use on screens should be consistent. Manage color contrast appropriately: no red on black or blue on orange, and for most audiences minimal use of "hot" colors is best.

Activity Seven: Decide on Animation and Special Effects

Determine whether to use animation and special effects. They are good for capturing the user's attention and are effective if used to signal instructional events, such as the beginning or end of a sequence of instruction. They're also appropriate when you have to illustrate a moving object that is not easily photographed, as with the movement of oil through a diesel engine. Animation and special effects should be used to support the learning objectives. Development software options are a good place to start in determining standards. Most software used to develop web applications or CBT—Authorware®, for example—provide a number of options for special effects, such as how a screen is displayed or how the program moves to the next frame. Existing options act like a menu of choices. Review them, and choose two or three. Use effects sparingly and consistently, in support of project goals.

FROM OUR EXPERIENCE

It is easy to be enamored with the options and capabilities of today's multimedia development software. Without standards in place, projects can easily become sidetracked in a constant design and development mode ("Just one more bell or whistle" or "Before we wrap up, why don't we try presenting it with this approach?"). This can undermine project timelines and goals. Sticking to the agreed-on decisions is important because the cost of a redo seldom justifies the added benefit. Unless design decisions have an impact on the effectiveness of the product, it is best to record the suggestions, look over all the should-haves, would-haves, and could-haves, and, when appropriate, apply them to the design standards of the next project.

SUMMARY

The most effective multimedia has a simple interface design and is consistent in

- Writing style and grammar
- Interaction and feedback presentation
- Topography, graphics, colors, video, audio, animation, and special effects

Planning and decision making in the form of standards support consistent presentation of multimedia elements. Standards can serve as benchmarks, ensuring that effective and efficient development can occur. The next chapter presents information on how to structure and group content so that it is well organized, covers the objectives, and is written to the appropriate level of skill and knowledge.

Content Structure

Now that we have detailed the project, schedule, roles, and responsibilities of project team members and the media specifications, it's time to consider the nature of the multimedia itself. That is, if your solution includes courses, you group instruction into concepts or lessons and apply an instructional strategy.

Regardless of the unit of instruction, content should be logically grouped and structured consistently. In conjunction with the user interface, this gives students an effective learning environment where they can access information or learn comfortably.

RELATED THEORY

The structure should follow principles of learning that have been determined to be effective in presenting and learning information.

Certain principles of learning operate in any educational media. Here is a list of sixteen principles of learning that we have synthesized from the research literature on how people learn. We have editorialized to explain how each principle applies to the multimedia design.

Principle One: Use Review in Learning

Students learn more when lessons begin with a review of previous material.

Application to Multimedia. Begin multimedia lessons with a review of relevant information presented in previous lessons. The review should highlight main

129

points that relate to what students are going to learn in the current lesson. If the chosen medium has a menu with navigation controlled by the user, or if the material is not presented in any particular order, then begin with a review of relevant prerequisites to the learning. Example: a lesson on troubleshooting a kiln might include

- An audio statement: "From operating the kiln, you may recall that the pilot light is normally blue."
- Supporting text: Remember: The Pilot Light Is Normally Blue.
- A photo of the pilot light.
- A legend indicating the topic title: Checking the Pilot Light.

Principle Two: Include Introductions and Specified Objectives

Students learn more when lessons and activities are introduced and learning objectives are specified.

Application to Multimedia. Design the beginning of your multimedia lessons to include a statement of lesson objectives put in terms appropriate to the learner, explaining what the student is expected to know or do. Example: a multimedia topic on sanitation might present the objectives on screen along with these elements:

- An audio statement: "This section introduces the procedure to mix and use sanitizing solution. When you've completed it, you will be able to use sanitizing solution to maintain the workroom to OSHA standards."
- Supporting text: Mixing and Using Sanitizing Solutions.
- Photo: a photo of the ingredients.
- Hypertext link: a graphic of a stack of paper titled "OSHA Standards" that links to a text-file copy of the standards.

Principle Three: Be Sure Verbal Content Is Effective

Students learn more when verbal content is precise and presented fluently.

Application to Multimedia. Lessons must present material in very clear, precise language and move (transition) logically from one segment to the next, avoiding unnecessary interruption or digression. Examples:

- An audio prompt to move forward to the next screen, which consistently comes up at the conclusion of a set of screen interactions

- Designing consistent presentation of audio sequences that are timed to the text they support

Principle Four: Use Examples and Demonstrations

Students learn more when relevant examples and demonstrations illustrate concepts and skills.

Application to Multimedia. Lessons must include visual examples of the concept that the student can view to see what he or she is to conceptualize. Examples and demonstrations should be sufficient in number and increasingly complex for the student to discriminate the finer points of the concept.

Example: A multimedia lesson on how to inventory the assets allocated to an office includes a graphic menu of the inventory process. The menu allows users to click on the step in the process to learn about the step and rationale for doing it. The graphical depiction of the process helps users conceptualize the entire inventory process.

Principle Five: Build in Student Success

Students learn more when they are able to handle tasks and questions with a high rate of success.

Application to Multimedia. Design multimedia lessons that ensure success for students who learn at different rates by incorporating supplemental materials, reviews, and summaries.

Example: A multimedia lesson on fiber-optic specifications contains a series of exercises on planning an installation. A button labeled "Look Up Specs" allows users who are not familiar with the specifications to check for information as they are completing the exercises.

Principle Six: Tailor Course to Audience

Students learn more when lessons and instructional activities are presented through concepts and language that are understandable and appropriate to the intended audience.

Application to Multimedia. Develop materials that are based on students' abilities, ascertaining this from audience analysis. Materials must be written at the appropriate audience level, and language should not interfere with the concepts to be learned. Unfamiliar terms must be defined, and students must be taught to incorporate them into their working vocabulary.

Example: a multimedia lesson on the controls used to account for supplies received in a restaurant is designed and written in quite different ways for two particular audiences:

1. Kitchen stewards with Spanish as their primary language. The stewards are mostly male and between eighteen and twenty-five, with no formal education, not computer literate, and having little exposure to accounting terminology. This audience requires a very simple interface, a glossary, and a theme appropriate to their gender and age group. In addition, audio and graphics, not text, are the primary means to depict the content.

2. Restaurant accountants with English as their primary language. The accountants are mostly females between thirty-six and fifty-four, with at least some college education, who use computers daily and are familiar with accounting terminology. This audience requires less audio and graphics, would not benefit from a glossary, and would benefit from a more complex navigation structure allowing more user control.

Principle Seven: Keep Pace Brisk, with Variations

Students learn more when lessons are presented at a brisk pace and when instruction slows to accommodate students' understanding but avoids unnecessary slowdowns.

Application to Multimedia. Effective lessons move at a pace geared to individual rates of learning, moving rapidly for students who grasp information quickly, offering greater depth for those who wish to delve further, and additional explanation for those who have difficulty grasping information. Most frames should be timed so that users do not spend more than three to five seconds before additional elements are added to the screen, or there is an option to move forward, or there is an interaction with the screen content in some form.

Example: A lesson on medical terminology for hospital administrative assistants uses an on-screen crossword puzzle, dictionary, and "Hints" button to teach the meanings of common medical terms at a pace appropriate to the learner.

Principle Eight: Include Smooth Transitions

Students learn more when transitions between lessons are made efficiently and smoothly.

Application to Multimedia. Students need to be reminded (cued) when a shift occurs from one topic to the next or from one activity to the next. This can be handled visually with a standard graphic or screen used to signal the transition; it may include a summary and information about upcoming content.

Example: A web-based lesson on a new plant maintenance software program uses a standard animation and a question to signify that a user is at the end of a topic and is ready to move on to the next topic.

Principle Nine: Use Clear Assignments and Directions

Students learn more when clear and concise assignments and directions are given.

Application to Multimedia. Direction for navigation and interaction must be clearly and carefully explained in unambiguous terms. Most multimedia screens have a prompt box located at the bottom of the screen that gives direction. Care must be taken to keep the user from getting into a loop or stuck because the directions for proceeding are not clear. Here are some standard prompts:

- Click Forward to continue.

- Match the _____ with the _____.

- Type the _____ in the _____.

- Click on the _____ to _____.

- Sorry, that's not correct. Try again. (Then give the user the answer after the next try.)

- That's correct. Good job!

- Yes! That's the right answer.

- That's not correct. The answer is _____.

Example: A distance-learning videoconference always displays the call-in phone and fax numbers whenever a question is posed to the audience.

Principle Ten: Maintain Proper Standards

Students learn more when clear, firm, and reasonable standards are maintained.

Application to Multimedia. Students strive to reach reasonable expectations for knowledge or performance. Standards that are not clearly understood, not adhered to, or too high or too low cause the learners not to challenge themselves to reach the standards.

Example: A self-paced multimedia lesson on English composition implemented without testing or record-keeping functionality may not be successful in a high school environment where students are not generally self-motivated.

Principle Eleven: Monitor, Circulate, and Check Work

Students learn more efficiently when instructors circulate during classroom assignments to check student performance.

Application to Multimedia. Students tend to stay on task when learning is monitored. Automated response, capturing test scores and reporting results, tracking, and feedback cause students to be careful when answering questions.

Example: In a CBT chemistry lesson, the computer is able to check responses to procedures used to perform experiments and immediately correct any errors.

Principle Twelve: Ask One Question at a Time

Students learn more when questions are posed one at a time.

Application to Multimedia. Automated media can deliver questions in any sequence desired. Questions should be posed one at a time and be important and relevant. Students need time to formulate answers.

Example:

Question 1: Add the following equation and record the sum in the space at the right.

$$2 + 7 + 9 + 14 + 11 =$$

Question 2: Add the following equation and record the sum in the space at the right.

$$6 + 7 + 3 + 19 + 4 =$$

Question 3: Add the following equation and record the sum in the space at the right.

$$1 + 7 + 8 + 6 =$$

See how much more difficult it is to answer this question asked by a teacher in rapid succession.

"What is $2 + 7 + 9 + 14 + 11 = ?$ What is $6 + 7 + 3 + 19 + 4 = ?$ What is $1 + 7 + 8 + 6 = ?$" This rapid succession of questions with no time for a student to respond creates confusion. Which question should the students answer first?

Principle Thirteen: Work in Feedback

Students learn more when instructional feedback on the correctness of their work is offered.

Application to Multimedia. Praise learners for correct answers, and give information about incorrect answers. A simple "Incorrect" is insufficient for students to learn from their mistakes. Instead, provide context-specific feedback such as, "No, that's incorrect because. . . . Try again."

Example: CBT on the procedure for entering a check into a banking software program provides feedback after each step, allowing students to be sure that they are performing each step correctly before going to the next step.

Principle Fourteen: Follow Feedback with Appropriate Technique

Students learn more when sustaining feedback is offered after an incorrect response (or no response) by probing, repeating the question, giving a clue, or allowing more time.

Application to Multimedia. Students should have more than one chance to answer a question, be given clues about why an input is right or wrong, and receive hints to stimulate their thinking toward getting the correct answer. If students give partial answers, another question or some feedback can require them to further their initial response.

Example: In a learn-to-type CBT, if a student types a sentence incorrectly, the program indicates which keys were pressed incorrectly and repeats the sentence, illustrating the keystrokes with an animation.

Principle Fifteen: Material Should Motivate

Students learn more effectively when the material motivates them.

Application to Multimedia. Lessons must be designed to create and hold the student's interest. Topics and information must be relevant to the learner and demonstrate the reason he or she needs to know the material. Frequent interaction, correct pacing, and a theme and interface design that appeal to the audience are important components in creating and holding attention.

Example: A military, sports, or hunting theme may not be the most appropriate choice for a lesson aimed at an audience of young girls. A Barbie theme would be equally unappealing for those in the business world.

Principle Sixteen: Connect Material to the Real World

Students learn more effectively when the concepts taught are closely related to the real world.

Application to Multimedia. Lessons should practice something closely simulating the actual conditions under which the task has to be performed. Simulation practice must be included in materials, rather than just imparting information. Even showing and telling is not enough; students must *do*. This is what makes multimedia such a powerful tool for training on software applications. A multimedia environment can be a realistic simulation of the one where the work is to take place.

Example: A lesson on business processes might use the image of keeping a copy machine stocked rather than one of keeping a tackle box stocked. A business theme (for example, a delivery truck) rather than a fun arcade theme would add credibility to the content.

Forman (2003) has added eleven learning principles that both synthesize and add to those listed above. They are

1. Tell stories. Stories are a natural form of learning. All of our learning is context-based around some experience. That experience is best related through a story.

2. Play games. Gaming uses multiple senses, can involve higher-level thinking, show the value goals and rules, and show outcomes.

3. Explore and experiment. Learning is best accomplished through "doing" something rather than being "told about" something.

4. Use pictures. Make visual representations central to learning rather than as models to represent heavily text-based courses.

5. Have a coach. Most significant learning does not result from formal education settings but rather by being mentored.

6. Learn with others. Collaborative learning environments (live or virtual) provides sharing opportunities where questions are answered and ideas are clarified.

7. Focus on what is important. Determine what is really critical to know and focus on that rather than try to teach everything.

8. Take recess. Take time to reflect on what is learned. It takes time to process new information. Constant bombarding creates information overload and reduces retention.

9. Have lunch. Create and encourage casual and informal settings where ideas are discussed and exchanged.

10. Be passionate. Have genuine excitement and interest in learning. Being emotional about your own learning or the learning of others is critical.

11. Keep learning. Information is outdated at a rate as fast as the rate at which it is created. Continuous learning is imperative to keep stagnation from setting in.

Motivation Is Everything

All of these principles fall into four categories:

1. Acquisition (acquiring knowledge)
2. Transfer (using knowledge)
3. Motivation (the need to possess knowledge)
4. Reinforcement (encouragement to possess knowledge)

The most central concept to learning is motivation.

ACTUAL EXAMPLES OF APPLICATION OF PRINCIPLES OF LEARNING

One of the best ways to gain experience in applying instructional design principles to multimedia is to talk with experienced designers about how the principles apply to successful multimedia projects that they have designed or completed. This section describes actual examples of solutions and how various principles of learning discussed in the section above were applied in each solution.

Example 1

A financial organization was implementing a new, large-scale Enterprise Resource Planning (ERP) system. The project evaluated and examined how management might remove obstacles from the path of successfully implementing the ERP.

The following principles of learning were applied to the solution in the following way:

Principle 7. Keep Pace Brisk, with Variations

Principle 12. Ask One Question at a Time

One component of the training was a series of "weblets." These were very brief (3- to 5-minute) slices of what would as a whole constitute a full web-based training. Each weblet illustrated a transaction and provided a brief practice and feedback for the transaction. This kept the pace quick and presented the information in manageable chunks.

Example 2

An external vendor was employed to develop a solution for delivering information on a company's logistics and finance packages to sales associates for an enterprise resource package (ERP) similar to SAP and PeopleSoft®.

The following principles of learning were applied to this solution in the following way:

Principle 6. Tailor Course to Audience

In the case of salespeople, the training was to help them understand the software product, so they could explain its features and capabilities in sales situations to potential customers. The terms used were not overly technical so that the associates could convey the information to potential customers in a way the customers could easily understand. The training also offered information on how to identify and sell to potential customers.

The company also wanted to create a virtual campus—web-based training that would be accessible to customers who purchased the software. After a rewrite of the existing paper-based instruction, the vendor designed a solution of final web-based training. The end product contained several courses. Each course consisted of modules, and each module consisted of several lessons. Lessons contained eight to twelve screens. The lessons included embedded questions and/or exercises for the users (associates and customers) to complete.

Example 3

An employee relations/labor relations (ER/LR) section of a company developed a self-paced, print-based, modular training course for entry-level LR specialists.

Although the training had been revised, these revisions did not keep pace with the changes in the agency, nor did they occur within a well-defined instructional design framework. This was an unsatisfactory situation for ER/LR because its lifeblood is the credibility and expertise of its LR specialists. Without an effective training and development program to distribute knowledge and cultivate new-hire LR specialist expertise, the credibility and value of ER/LR became suspect.

The solution included the implementation of an electronic performance support system (EPSS), including web-based training (WBT), located centrally and maintained on the company's WAN. The WBT and EPSS were then downloaded to the service center LAN servers. The LR specialists and coaches access and run the WBT and EPSS over the network on their desktop computers using Microsoft Internet Explorer.

The following principles of learning were applied to this solution in the following way:

Principle 2. Include Introductions and Specified Objectives

Principle 4. Use Examples and Demonstrations

Principle 5. Build in Student Success

The overall course has terminal objectives, and each lesson within the curriculum has enabling objectives. The objectives are very specific and outcome based. That is, they clearly state the task as it will be performed in real life, the tools the student will use in real life, and the conditions under which they will perform the task.

The ER/LR specialist's job is centered around cases. The success of the LR specialists hinges on their ability to collect data, form a profile of the situation, and compare against past cases. Because of this necessity to discriminate effectively, the WBT contained numerous examples and non-examples throughout the training to sharpen the ability to discriminate within the context of these cases. Users were given feedback at each step in which they were required to discriminate to refine their interpretation of the cases.

The curriculum was developed on case types or groupings. The cases were arranged from simple to complex. That is, the conditions for the first cases were very simple, and later the conditions were much more difficult to reconcile.

Example 4

A company developed, sold, and implemented a product that links otherwise incompatible messaging systems. The company had established a sales-flow process, which defined the sales and implementation processes, but the sales executives were unfamiliar with the process. In addition, their knowledge of the product was incomplete due to its complexity. The result of these factors was poor communication and coordination among customers, sales executives, and technical functions, as well as faulty expectations regarding product capabilities. This produced customer dissatisfaction and created a burden on the post-implementation technical support functions.

A vendor designed and developed a web-based training course for sales executives. The vendor conducted a needs assessment and front-end analysis to identify the existing gaps in training and performance. Then, based on the results, the team formulated an instructional theory and approach that were integrated within the graphic user interface for the course.

The following principles of learning were applied to this solution in the following way:

Principle 6. Tailor Course to Audience

The purpose of the course was to provide product knowledge to account executives. The information was layered in such a way that the top layer consisted of one-sentence descriptions of the product that could be carried around like pocket change and pulled out when needed to describe a particular feature or benefit of the product. In addition, the one-sentence descriptors were accompanied by a mnemonic tool to allow account executives to remember the descriptors more easily. Beneath that were two more layers that provided more in-depth explanations of the product.

Example 5

An association that serves industries engaged in a similar business provides education, tracks industry trends, and conducts industry research for association members. The association wanted to provide a computer-based educational tool for sales representatives, customer service representatives, and trainees to learn about sales techniques and products within the industry. This computer-based educational tool would replace a video-based training course and would be available to association members. The audience for the training was inside and outside salespeople, and also the customer service staff. This client wanted students to achieve 100 percent mastery of the subject material. Students who passed the tests would be "certified." A grade of 90 percent was required on the master final test. Students were not very familiar with computers. Those involved in the development of the training say it had "awesome" online help for navigation, which helped the unfamiliar students feel comfortable with computer-based training more quickly.

The following principles of learning were applied to this solution in the following ways:

Principle 6. Tailor Course to Audience

Principle 16. Connect Material to the Real World

Based on the audience taking the training, the reading level was adjusted to approximately seventh grade level to facilitate learning.

The training included product training, sales training, techniques of getting sales leads, and other practical information. For example, if a certain type of product was required for a specific situation, the students would have to know that and respond appropriately.

The training included sales lead sources such as company code listings, reference books, and Internet websites. Sales kits were distributed for field use.

LEARNING AND INSTRUCTIONAL DELIVERY STRATEGIES

The media analysis you perform may lead you to conclude that the most effective implementation is a blended solution. Think of, say, a complex scientific concept being covered by a lecture, followed by a practice lab, then CBT examples, and including job aids to support transfer to the work environment.

There are two major learning strategies common to any medium, including multimedia: *deductive* and *inductive*. In the former, students draw general conclusions from specific information. The instruction presents the specific pieces of information from which students draw their general conclusions and apply them to broader situations. The inductive strategy requires students to draw specific conclusions from general information. The instruction allows them to achieve the desired conclusion by establishing the situation and allowing them to gather the necessary information.

Both inductive and deductive processes require students to "prove" their conclusions are correct; the difference is that the processes begin from opposite ends of the spectrum. Both objectivists and constructivists use these strategies.

The major instructional delivery strategies follow.

Lecture or Linear Presentation

The linear interaction is limited to simple statements or actions from the learner (yes, no, click Forward). This strategy is often used to introduce a course that embraces a number of delivery methods. For example, you may have to present some information before a classroom discussion or chat, follow it with a live demonstration or CBT, then conduct a group or individual open exploration, and end with a demonstration.

Lecture, Recitation, Interaction

Information is presented in a lesson, interspersed with questions or interaction. Questions require more than yes-or-no response; students must make a choice among alternatives. The general style is deductive. This is most often used in lecture, CBT, or interactive distance broadcasting.

Lecture and Discussion

This involves presenting information and then discussion questions that require response and interaction among students. Discussion can occur at numerous points during the lecture, or distance-learning session, or online chat, or after an initial presentation of information. The presentation may be as minimal as raising an issue and allowing the group to explore it thoroughly, eliciting divergent views on the issue. An instructor may or may not keep track of discussion points and summarize at the end of the session.

Lecture and Demonstration

Demonstration adds to lecture and recitation the dimension of actually showing concepts to students, using operational models.

Guided Learning, Open Exploration

In this strategy, learning situations are created and structured; students must then explore, raise, and answer their own questions. Information is provided as students discover it is missing and realize they need it. This strategy requires that instructors who are in the classroom, online, or in a distance broadcast session be highly knowledgeable about the subject matter, to answer unrehearsed and unanticipated questions with genuinely valuable information. In a scenario-based multimedia or CBT session, comprehensive reference material and help resources must be readily available. Inductively, this type of lesson poses another question to a first question that gives students a clue as to where to search for the answer but does not give them the answer. Deductively, it supplies the information that moves the student on to the next step or phase.

Brainstorming

Brainstorming is a technique that can be used within exploration. It is easily accommodated in a distance broadcast session or online chat session. It brings out all possible ideas on a topic, which can later be evaluated in some manner and validated as to their worth or pertinence. Brainstorming itself does not make these judgments. Because adult learners often want to impose judgment on their ideas immediately, they don't express their own ideas and may not be accepting of others' ideas. Thus, brainstorming might not work well unless the rules are established before beginning a session. Here are some rules for brainstorming:

- The purpose is to generate as many ideas as possible.
- All ideas are acceptable.
- No criticism of an idea is permitted.
- You can add to, build on, or give the complete opposite of any idea presented.
- Everyone should participate.
- All ideas are listed for everyone to see.
- Don't stop as soon as the initial ideas stop flowing; some ideas take longer to percolate in the mind.
- Point out any violation of these rules.

Games

Don't overlook the advantages of games. But then again, don't use gaming just for the sake of gaming. We are a generation that has grown up on television and is accustomed to being entertained, and this appetite has crossed over into education and training; students now expect to be entertained.

Carefully constructed situational games are appropriate to all media and can have some very positive effects. They can drive home a point that would be rejected or have less effect if just stated. Also, if people enjoy learning, they tend to retain the information longer.

Role Playing

Acting out situations is a very effective method for practicing skills that are being learned. Role plays reinforce; they are an opportunity for the students to receive feedback on how the skill is performed. Role plays are appropriate to all media; a CBT or WBT with an audio recording and playback capability can be used to role play answers to customer service questions.

Simulation

Simulations are high-end role plays, distinguished by being performed in, or as near to, the actual work situation as possible. Simulations are appropriate in all media, but multimedia simulations of software or human interaction situations are a particularly effective design choice.

Performance Support

Performance support is distinguished by information that is readily available via one or two keystrokes, a phone call, or a glance at a job aid or reference manual. This strategy is particularly appropriate for information that is continually updated, overly complex, or necessary to support or enhance performance.

PROCESS

There are three activities in the process of defining lessons:

1. Break the content into units.
2. Map the information.
3. Select SCORM-compliant vendors for custom developed and/or off-the-shelf solutions.

CONTENT STRUCTURE PROCEDURE

Follow these activities:

Activity One: Break the Content into Units

Step one: Categorize the content into six major information types:

1. Concepts (ideas or definitions)
2. Processes (systems of related ideas)
3. Procedures (steps within a process)
4. Principles (guiding forces, mission, values)
5. Facts (single pieces of information)
6. Systems (physical entities with operational parts)

Step two: Arrange information based on a job task in order, from simple to complex, or by logical content groups.

Activity Two: Map the Information

Step one: Create a lesson outline. Be certain it contains the appropriate instructional or learning events outlined in Table 19.1. Each topic within a lesson should be considered a mini-lesson and follow the same pattern.

Table 19.1
Events of Instruction

Event	Description
Advance organizer	Explains what was previously learned, what will be learned in this lesson, and how both connect with one another and to subsequent learning.
	Includes the purpose of the lesson and its relevance to the course.
	Answers the question, "Why should I learn this?"
Objectives	Tells the students what they will be able to do or will know as a result of completing a lesson. *Note:* present the objectives informally and conversationally. Using second person *you* is appropriate in this case.
Content	The presentation strategies defined by the objectives.

Table 19.1
Events of Instruction, Cont'd.

Event	Description
Guided practice	Student practice is closely monitored to provide immediate and corrective feedback on how they are mastering the content; reinforces the presentation of the content.
Feedback	Positive and corrective feedback interspersed throughout each lesson. Positive feedback tells students that they are correct and what comes next. Positive feedback may also include a statement telling the students why they are correct. Corrective feedback explains why the answer was wrong, reveals what the correct answer is, suggests trying again, or points out other action to take.
Transition	Appears between topics throughout the lesson. Transitions are mini-introductions that explain how what was just learned applies to the next topic.
Summary	Closes a topic and reminds students what they learned.
Independent practice	Practice is done after completing the entire lesson but before formal testing. Independent practice engages students in performing tasks in a manner as close to the actual work environment as possible. Students find out if they have followed the correct steps at the end of the practice. At the end of the entire practice, they receive feedback on the points where there were errors. They may try again.
Test	Measuring the effectiveness of the solution.

Table 19.1
Events of Instruction, Cont'd.

Event	Description
Remediation	Clarifies why knowledge and skills have been incorrectly learned, and presents the information that could be learned in a different presentation. Remediation does not entail repeating the same material in the same way. It might mean an abbreviated form of the initial instruction to help students understand points they might have missed.
Retest	Follows remediation. It is used to determine if the students have now mastered the knowledge or skill. The same test as the first may be used. However, it is better to use a parallel test.

The steps presented in this activity are equally appropriate for all multimedia products. Regardless of whether your multimedia includes a web page, a reference manual, or an online help system, you must group and present the content within a defined structure and logic. The events do not always need to be in the exact order and a lesson may not include all events, depending on whether the approach is inductive or deductive. For example, in an inductive lesson you would not tell the users the objectives. The objectives are what the users are to discover for themselves. If you state the objectives at all, it is to allow the users to determine whether their conclusions were the ones that were intended.

Include these elements in a lesson outline:

- *Lesson title.*
- *Objectives for the lesson:* the terminal objectives and the lesson objectives. List the terminal objectives for the lesson in the words and format in which they are going to be seen on-screen. Remember, this format should be conversational so that the audience can understand the goals and objectives.

- *Lesson length:* determine how long it will take for the student who follows the long path (all of the branching, reviews, tests, and so on) to complete the lesson. Timing is important because each lesson contributes to the overall course, whose length is predetermined by analysis or project requirements.
- *Lesson weight:* proportion of the content of each lesson in the course. The weight of the lesson is determined by its importance with respect to the content of the entire course and the length of the lesson compared to the overall length of the course. The weight of each lesson determines how many questions to apportion in a final test; it also affects the overall grading procedure. A process for weighting lessons is covered in Part Four, Multimedia Evaluation.
- *The lesson introduction:* write the introduction just as you want it in the lesson.
- *Presentation strategy:* detail what presentation strategy is to be used, and tell the developer how to write it, along with the information you intend to present.
- *The testing strategy:* how to test and track student scores. This topic is covered in the fourth part of this book, Multimedia Evaluation. Remember to include all questions for lessons, units, and the course when you write the lesson outline.
- *The lesson summary:* follow the same steps you did for the introduction.
- A list of *the media* to be used in the lesson.
- A list of *the resources* required to complete the lesson. These may be instructional tools that supplement the lesson (user's guide, student manual, course administrator guide). Include any resources that the student needs to complete the lesson.

Concept mapping is another method for organizing material for presentation. Mapping is much freer in structure than outlining, and it allows more creativity. It lets you consider all ideas before beginning to organize content.

Concept mapping is superior to outlining or flowcharting if you are using the constructivist perspective to develop your solution. Your resulting interface will allow the users to navigate the solution using their own path.

See Figure 19.1 for an example of how information is organized in a concept map.

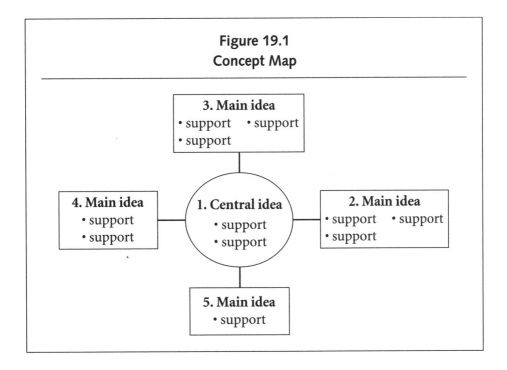

Figure 19.1
Concept Map

3. Main idea
• support   • support
• support

4. Main idea
• support
• support

1. Central idea
• support
• support

2. Main idea
• support   • support
• support

5. Main idea
• support

Here's how concept mapping works:

1. Brainstorm a list all of the phrases that state the main ideas included in the concept, process, system, and so on you are addressing. You may not use all of these ideas in the materials, but let the ideas flow.

2. Choose the central idea, and write one or two sentences that encapsulate the idea.

3. Consider all of the main ideas listed in the first step of the concept mapping, and see which ones go together. At this point, you may determine that some of the phrases listed as main ideas are really supporting ideas.

4. Put the central idea in the middle of the map.

5. Order the main and supporting ideas.

6. Recheck the map to be sure it's logical to you.

7. Explain the map to someone else, and take suggestions on improvements.

8. Make final revisions to the map.

9. Begin developing the lesson.

Step two: After completing the lesson outline or concept map, create a course flowchart or map.

A course flowchart can be developed on any flowcharting software application. Experiment with several such packages before deciding on one, because some are easier to use than others. Figure 19.2 is an example of a high-level course flowchart.

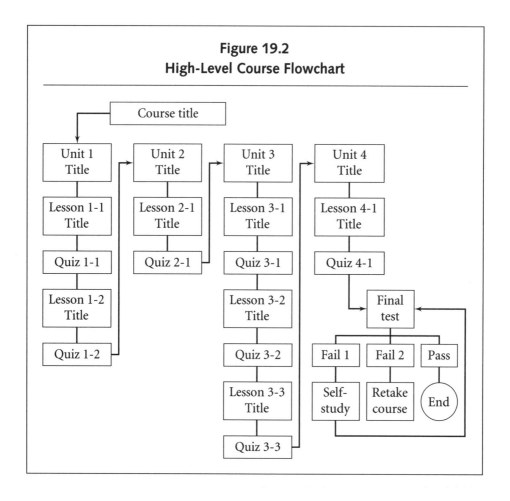

Figure 19.2
High-Level Course Flowchart

Detailed lesson flowcharts show the branching within individual lessons. Figure 19.3 is an example of a detailed lesson flowchart.

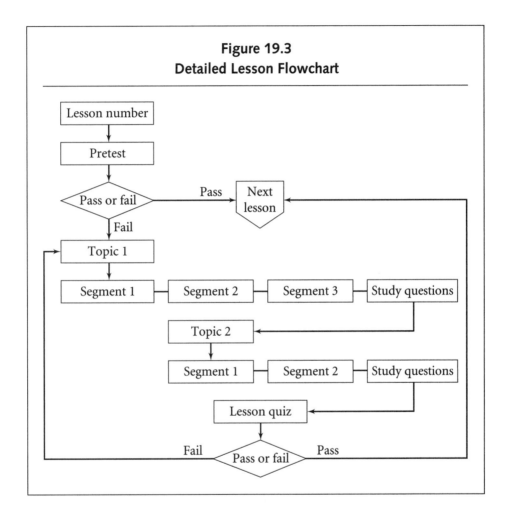

Figure 19.3
Detailed Lesson Flowchart

Activity Three: Select SCORM-Compliant Vendors for Custom-Developed or Off-the-Shelf Solutions

Step one: Ask for the vendor's definition of a reusable content object. There are varying degrees of granularity (size of the pieces of content) for content objects. The best level of granularity is a piece of content that might fit into numerous courses or places in the same course but can still complete a concept on its own. Groupings of content objects form *reusable information objects* (RIO).

Step two: Ask which LMS the vendor has successfully run courseware through. Many vendors will claim their courseware and software are SCORM-compliant. The real proof is in determining which LMS they have actually been successful in running their courseware through. The best vendor to deal with is a company that actually has LANs with all the major LMS on them to test courseware before they deliver it. While this might be expensive for the vendor, it shows a commitment to ensure successful implementation for the customer.

Step three: Ask for the vendor's customer list. Call previous customers to determine how successful the vendor was in delivering courseware that ran through the LMS you are using. Ask questions about the level of technical support, the number of tries to implement the courseware, and any delays in implementing courseware.

FROM OUR EXPERIENCE

Inexperienced multimedia instructional designers and design teams tend to arrange content and use design strategies according to their own preferences and experience. This limits the creativity and effectiveness applied to the design. We have two low-cost suggestions for countering this problem.

The first is that one of the most useful techniques for gaining insight and ideas is to check out similar products by way of the web, by visiting vendors at trade shows, or by experimenting with off-the-shelf offerings. Note what works well or not so well and how these insights can be applied to your own design project. Don't discount children's educational multimedia titles; they contain some of the best (and occasionally some of the worst) examples of simple interfaces and innovative ID strategies.

The second suggestion is to use brainstorming in searching for novel approaches to meeting your design goals. Include non–instructional designers and design team members who have a flair for creativity and can provide fresh ideas and approaches. Design sessions are often some of the most enjoyable and invigorating activities associated with multimedia projects.

SUMMARY

Applying the principles of instruction, along with a sound instructional strategy, allows you to order the content for instructional effectiveness. Involving as many team members as is practical boosts morale, builds consensus, and improves the quality of the design.

chapter TWENTY

Configuration Control

The course design specification now describes the project, schedule, roles and responsibilities of project team members, and media specifications, and it breaks the information into logical chunks. As a final planning step, you need to establish the configuration control (CC) plan for developing course materials. Configuration control is the project's quality-control process.

PROCESS

There's just one activity in the process of configuration management: establishing a CC plan.

CONFIGURATION CONTROL PROCEDURE

Follow this activity:

Activity One: Establish a Configuration Control (CC) Plan

Develop a CC process that regulates the version of the materials under design, development, or review. If numerous people are working on the same material, then each team member must have access to the same configured version of the materials.

You can make CC as complicated or as simple as you wish. Complicated procedures slow down the project but afford more control. An important point is that a process is only as good as the people who use it. The team members must commit to following the procedures in the process to ensure uniformity. There is a sample CC plan in the following section.

A master hard copy and an electronic copy of each version of the materials under development or review always remain archived. In that way, if electronic disks are corrupted or hard drives fail while in use, the only changes lost are the most recent. Plus, you have the hard-copy comments from the last version. It might be annoying to have to rework the storyboards or program files, but at least the work is recoverable rather than lost forever.

Continue the CC steps until there is no need to return the lesson materials to the project team and the materials can be stored as the final version. The material is resurrected when entering the development stage of the project and turned over to the development team, who then make their contributions.

All project members must provide version copies of their electronic files to the configuration control designee for security. The designee is responsible for dispensing the correct version of the materials.

SAMPLE CONFIGURATION CONTROL PLAN

This configuration control plan outlines the steps and the roles used to maintain version control. In this plan, the course developer, script writer, or any design team member can be substituted for "author." The most important element of any CC plan is the configuration control gatekeeper (CCG), whose responsibility it is to manage the review cycle.

Step One (Author's Responsibility)

Deliver the material to be reviewed to the CCG.

    A. The electronic disk version should have a label indicating
- The name of the document
- The version of the document
- The original author
- The date of the version

    B. The hard copy version of the document should have the same information that is on the disk, with the version number and date printed in the footer.

Step Two (CCG's Responsibility)

Prepare the material for routing through the review cycle.

A. Make a duplicate of the material (electronic or hard copy).
B. Label the original of the material "Master Version 1" and the copy "Copy Version 1."
C. File the Master 1 of the material and circulate the Copy 1 for review.
D. Attach a routing sheet to each document that is put into review. The routing sheet should contain:
   - The name of the document
   - The version of the document
   - A place for reviewers to sign their names and the date they complete the review
   - A place for final sign off if the document needs no changes
E. Deliver the material to the first reviewer in the review cycle.

Step Three (Reviewers' Responsibility)

Complete one entire review cycle before the document goes back to the author for changes. The review forms are in the Design Tools section of Appendix E.

Step Four (Last Reviewer's Responsibility)

The last reviewer returns the material to the CCG.

Note that the first review (Step Three) should be the subject-matter expert (SME) review, or technical review. If the content contains significant technical inaccuracies, this reviewer can return the material to the CCG to send it back to the author for changes before completing the review cycle. The technical reviewer is the only one who has this option. The reason for allowing the technical reviewer this choice is simple. If the material does contain significant inaccuracies, it has to go through an entire review cycle again after the author makes the revisions. Therefore, it makes sense to cut down review time and cycles by catching these technical problems immediately.

Step Five (CCG's Responsibility)

Return material to originator.

Step Six (Author's Responsibility)

When the author gets the document back from review, he or she:

A. Opens the electronic document
B. Makes changes to the document
C. Saves it as Version 2
D. Returns the original and Version 2 to the CCG

Step Seven (CCG's Responsibility)

The CCG prepares the material for routing through the second review cycle.

A. Make a duplicate of the revised material (electronic copy or hard copy).
B. Label the original of the material as "Master Version 2" and the copy "Copy Version 2."
C. File the Master 2 of the material and circulate the Copy 2 for review.
D. Attach a routing sheet (same type as in Step Two, part D) to each document that is put into review. The routing sheet should contain:
  - The name of the document
  - The version of the document
  - A place for reviewers to sign their names and the date they completed the review
  - A place for final sign off if the document needs no changes
E. Deliver the material to the first reviewer in the review cycle.

Step Eight (Reviewers' Responsibility)

Complete the second review cycle.

A. It's important to note that the second and subsequent review cycles are only to determine if all changes were made to the reviewer's satisfaction and for final signoff.
B. If all changes were not made, initial that there are still changes to be carried out and pass the materials to the next reviewer.
C. The last reviewer returns the material to the CCG.

Step Nine (CCG's Responsibility)

Return the material to the original author if there are still changes to be made. If all changes have been incorporated and the document is final, the CCG should mark the material "Final Version" and file it.

Step Ten (Author's Responsibility)

If the material must go back to the author again, he or she:

A. Opens the electronic document
B. Makes changes to the document
C. Saves it as Version 3
D. Returns Versions 3 and 2 to the CCG

Cycles continue in this fashion until there are no further changes required.

FROM OUR EXPERIENCE

In general, the more planning done up-front in any project, including planning for configuration control, the more smoothly the project operates; the result is a quality product delivered within budget and on time.

Much work is lost, duplicated, or repeated if CC is not well planned, communicated, and followed. This is especially true in large projects. Multimedia projects have numerous components and many project team members handle them. If there's no one in charge of managing this cycle, integration of these components is confusing, frustrating, and fraught with errors that require rework—often involving long hours.

SUMMARY

Including the project's configuration control process is an important part of the CDS. All project-team members can reference it in their own copy of the document.

part three

Multimedia Development and Implementation

Introduction to Multimedia Development

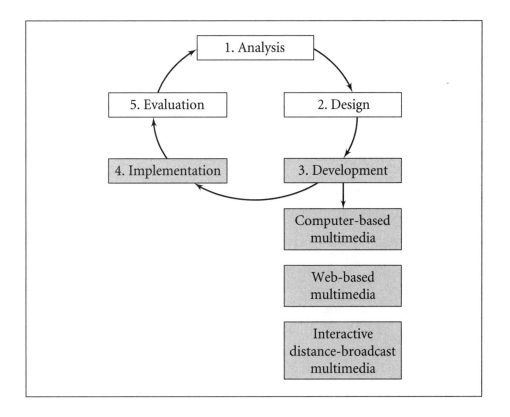

The course design specification (CDS) document is implemented during development. At this point in multimedia projects, more team members become involved. Storyboards are written; video is shot, edited, and logged; audio is recorded, edited, and logged; graphics are created, edited, and logged; and initial versions of web pages are developed, tested, and reviewed.

The larger the project, the more important it is that the development phase be well managed. Team meetings are extremely important during development and are necessary to coordinate the various activities. All project team members must know their roles and responsibilities, understand the project timeline, and fulfill their assigned responsibilities.

Review cycles must be implemented, with each reviewer clearly understanding what to review and how to do it. Records of approvals, decisions, and changes must be maintained. Each media element must be integrated and coordinated, and the unique project production and implementation requirements must be managed.

Whatever the type of multimedia, the basic development principles remain the same:

1. First, establish a framework of development tools, development specifications, and standards.

2. Next, develop the media elements that fit into the framework.

3. Then review and revise the product.

4. Finally, implement the finished product.

Successful multimedia development methodologies tend to include these elements:

- *Design-time prototyping:* creating an early application-system prototype so as to review, test, and approve the interface design, media elements, script, or map. This is an efficient method for rapid development.

- *Evolutionary development:* using each stage of prototyping and development as the basis from which to evolve the next prototype. For this to be successful, design decisions that do not involve the content must be locked in.

- *Use of rapid development tools (RDT):* templates are useful for parallel development projects. They are particularly useful in projects where content is added in an iterative process, as it is made available. Templates are created and used as a framework for content as it is identified. For example, in a software development project we're familiar with, the instructional design, look and feel, and functionality were developed first so the content can be inserted when available. Here is a list of the screens or frames that were developed at the same time the final changes to the software were being finalized:

- Title screen (with music)
- Main menu
- Help screen
- About This Course screen
- Credits screen
- Topic level one: "What is this topic about?" (includes seven screens)

  Title and objective for the topic; how long the topic should take (with animation and music)

  How will it affect my job?

  When will I do the task?

  What do I need to know to perform the task?

  What are the steps I need to take?

  Are there any special hints? Common errors or time-saving tricks

  Summary and transition (with music)

- Topic level two: "How is it done?"

  Title (with animation and music)

  Video sequence of the steps, audio, text

  Summary and transition (with music)

- Topic level three: "Let me try"

  Title (with animation and music)

  Functionality; screen for clicking on an object, with feedback

  Functionality; screen for text entry, with feedback

  Summary and transition (with music)

The topic-level model above is a production prototype that serves as a template for the follow-on development. In development, the prototype is copied and revised. This rapid development ensures that the training can be deployed along with the new software. This development approach is necessary if a change in content or revision is likely. Such screen elements as titles, prompt boxes, buttons, graphics, photos, text display areas, and video windows must be consistently sized and placed for this approach to be fully successful.

Using prototyping methodologies reduces risk, increases consistency between lessons, ensures acceptance from those authorized to approve the project, and uncovers any production problems or issues when they are at a manageable level. Prototyping and rapid development cycles are increasingly important in industries such as telecommunications, where time to market is critical to product success and supporting multimedia must be ready when the product is ready.

In some sectors the rate of change means it's essential to be able to produce ongoing updates and revisions to the courseware. To accomplish this goal, use topic or lesson-level templates, combined with libraries of graphics and photos, all of which allow the designer to change the graphic once and see it updated throughout the multimedia. To design for this type of development approach, consistency is the key.

Commercially available CBT and web-based rapid development tools (RDTs) are available. They contain lesson, interaction, and tracking templates, along with the computer-managed instruction (CMI) program components in which the various text, graphic, and video elements of a program can be inserted. Intellinex (www.intellinex.com), an enterprise of Ernst & Young, produces one such rapid development tool.

Figure 21.1 is a template that permits the course developer to build the components of course (that is, Table of Contents and Body).

Figure 21.2 is the template screen where developers access existing courses. Each course listed includes a status line to identify the state of creation (that is, development and production). The template allows for an automatic search function to find the course to modify. Changing something in one course will change it in every course where it is used if the reusable content objects are created correctly.

There are icons that can be inserted in a course that provide various branching capabilities. Figure 21.3 shows those icons and a description of each.

There are other templates the developer can use to create or modify a course:

- The developer can set the parameters that will permit or deny the users to download the course or require them to take it directly from a LAN. The option to permit the user to download creates two other options—the user can get credit for the course after uploading results *or* the user gets credit upon downloading the course.

- The Insert Question icon permits the developer to insert a passing course score and weight lesson scores for the question. Questions can either be equally or individual weighted. Choosing a calculation option permits all lessons to be weighted equally, automatically weight lesson scores according to the number of questions, or manually weight the scores.

- Implementing efficiencies during the development phase, coupled with using a rapid analysis method (RAM) can significantly decrease project cost.

Efficiencies can be gained by:

- Using rapid prototyping to increase communication and buy-in and to reduce rework. For example, consider the benefit of creating paper-based simulations of a proposed screen interface, or acting out a proposed videoconference sequence.

Figure 21.1
Intellinex Template

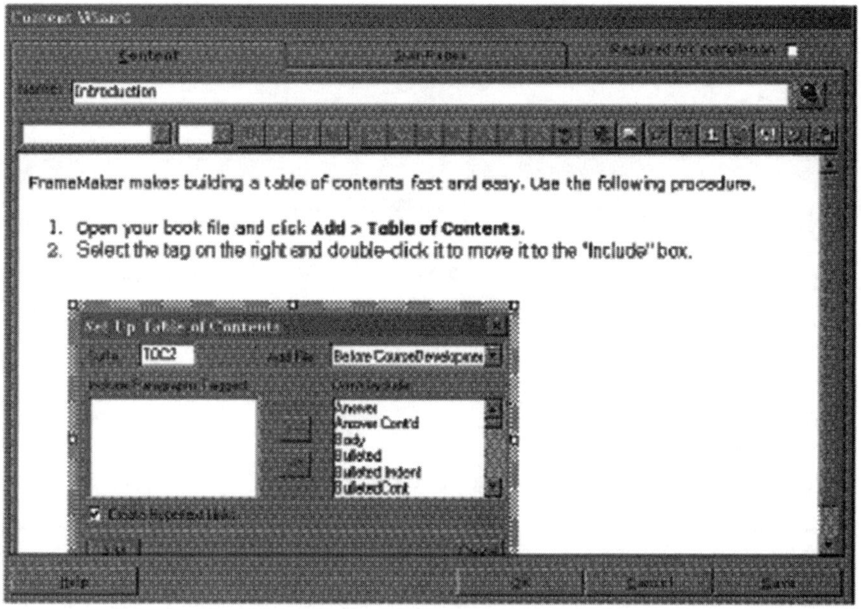

Source: Used with permission of Intellinex, an Ernst & Young enterprise.

Figure 21.2
Intellinex Development Screen

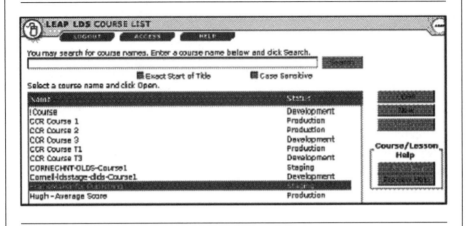

Source: Used with permission of Intellinex, an Ernst & Young enterprise.

Figure 21.3
Intellinex Icons

Icon	Name	Description
	Insert Hyperlink*	Inserts a hyperlink
	Insert Graphic	Inserts a graphic, either in *.jpg* or *.gif* format
	Insert Example	Inserts an example
	Insert Question	Inserts a question
	Insert Glossary Term	Inserts a glossary term
	Change Page	Changes page layout

Source: Used with permission of Intellinex, an Ernst & Young enterprise.

- Leveraging available expertise by teaming with experienced mentors, vendors, or consultants. Previous development experience is invaluable, especially in a first-time multimedia project. Determine who has experience and is willing to act in the coaching role, and make sure he or she is part of the development team.

- Aggressively managing scope creep and timelines. It's always tempting to agree to include "just one more graphic" or "one extra link" that does not actually increase the overall effectiveness of the solution. Keep in mind that you are solving a business need rather than producing a product. Sticking to the planned course design, content, and development timelines ensures that you maintain or even shorten project timelines, and therefore contain costs.

Regardless of the type of multimedia, reducing the time spent in development has some significant benefits:

- Decreased cost by increasing speed to market and return on investment
- Maximizing the shelf life and how long a product can be used by deploying training in conjunction with the product
- Freeing resources for additional development work

E-LEARNING'S IMPACT ON DEVELOPMENT AND IMPLEMENTATION

The web has changed development methodology, and recent enhancements have made even more dramatic advances (Lee, Owens, & Benson, 2002). Of course, SCORM has impacted development as much as it has impacted design, making courses (and even raw media elements) portable between LMSs.

In the new model, solutions might be so well constructed that no one completes them from beginning to end. Today, one of the values of training that is tracked is being able to determine who has completed a course. In the new model, just looking at tracking data could be very discouraging. If users *do* complete the course, it may be because it was *not* well structured.

Multimedia technologies have also necessitated rethinking traditional accepted wisdom about the implementation of solutions. In addition to customary forms of delivery, there is now a variety of choices for distributing solutions, including linking to web pages on corporate intranets, online help systems, databases, wizards, online coaches, and performance-centered tools.

Web delivery can either be synchronous or asynchronous. Synchronous delivery is place-independent, but time-dependent. It has created the virtual classroom where geographically dispersed participants in a learning session can still meet together collaboratively. While the participants in a synchronous session don't have to be physically present at the same location, they must be present at the date and time of the scheduled delivery in order to participate. This design usually uses high-speed transmission because of the bandwidth required to send content and link to numerous end-users. An Internet chat session is another example of a lower-end synchronous delivery method.

Lack of human interaction was one of the major arguments against computer-based training or individualized (asynchronous) web training. That argument is now moot. Participants can even see each other with the use of miniature cameras mounted on computers.

Asynchronous delivery is both time- and place-independent. For example, an online management training course available at the convenience of the individual end-user twenty-four hours a day, seven days a week. Yet another example is a multi-functional web-based support system that is accessed "on demand." Imagine a customer service system that runs on the web. Customers can order via a browser, ask questions via e-mail, and look up information on products and services. They can track their orders. The system will even track customers' purchasing habits and send them personalized messages about specials and suggest related items in addition to what they order. Employers use the same system to train employees to serve customers and to analyze customer data for marketing, service, finance, and manufacturing in order to relate effectively to customers.

Software help systems are used to aid users in tasks and functions related to software. The example that many are familiar with is Microsoft's Help menu and its context-sensitive help assistant. Examples of web solutions abound that provide users with around-the-clock access to information. Designs include linear, media-rich, response-appropriate feedback and interaction, complex testing and remediation strategies, and unstructured learning and exploration. Some of the best design examples are customized products that are very specific to a topic or task. A good example is a telecommunications company's phone customer support website that blends performance support and learning with online marketing and sales. This type of delivery bridges the gap between interface design, business goals, and performance support.

Another example from Northwestern University—a deliberate strategy in redesigning intranet sites—has paid real dividends. The university organized and made accessible 250,000 documents from three hundred servers. Previously, Northwestern lacked a standardized approach, making searching and retrieving information difficult and time-consuming. Improved organization enabled online search capabilities, improved site management by removing old and outdated content and adding relevant content, consolidated pages, and created policies for privacy, security, intellectual property and commerce. The result is quick and easy access to knowledge. Eliminating duplication from department to department and reducing server and provider costs have resulted in significant cost savings.

A positive consequence of this new delivery model is the collaboration available through learning communities that have been enabled by technology. The "Luddites" claimed that computers would cause people to become isolated. Just the opposite is true. The Internet has enabled people to virtually collaborate to share knowledge and improve performance.

A negative consequence of the model is the ability to design e-learning that far surpasses the infrastructure's ability to deliver it. Although bandwidth is increasing, the demand seems to be constantly outstripping capability. At one time, the hardware capabilities were ahead of software. That trend has changed. In this respect, the advances made to rich-media learning environments provided by CD-ROM have taken a step backward and will continue to lag until the infrastructure makes the next dramatic advance.

FROM OUR EXPERIENCE

In a development process, keep the emphasis on the fact that "only the project wins." When the subject of individual preferences arises, we like to use the analogy of an orchestra. If each member of the orchestra decides to individually interpret the music and play in the key of his or her own choice, the result is dissonance and chaos. No one will listen for very long. When everyone works together and plays on the same page, the end result is much better.

The same concept applies to multimedia projects. The CDS is the conductor, keeping project team members on the same page. If you are developing in a medium for the first time, recruit an expert to coach you. It can mean the difference between a successful project and a disaster.

The newest versions of many authoring packages contain templates for authoring. Intellinex, a division of Ernst & Young, distributes one such system for CBT development. Centra's Symposium offers a shell for delivering live, interactive, virtual-classroom (synchronous) or individualized (asynchronous) web-based course delivery. Leading authoring packages—such as Authorware®, Attain®, and Toolbook®—now provide tools for web-based training design. In addition, Toth (2003) lists other currently available authoring software packages, their features, system requirements, current pricing, and distributors.

SUMMARY

Regardless of the type of multimedia, the basic development process is the same. First, establish a framework; then develop the media elements that fit it; next, review and revise the product; and finally, implement the finished product. Multimedia development is most successful if design-time prototyping, evolutionary development, and templates are used.

Common Development Components

Within the multimedia development process, during production there are components common to computer-based, web-based, performance support, and interactive distance broadcast solutions:

- Preproduction and production cycles
- Postproduction quality-review cycles

THE PRODUCTION CYCLE

Table 22.1 encapsulates the development methodology described in this chapter.

Preproduction

Lesson outlines and concept maps become programmed lessons in the development phase. This is an easy concept to express, but it's complex in execution. The responsibility for development is placed in the hands of many people who have to be counted on to do their jobs well and deliver each piece on time.

The *instructional designer* (ID) who outlines the lesson is responsible for organizing and conducting a preproduction meeting. He or she must duplicate the lesson outlines or concept maps that will be used during the meeting and distribute a copy of the set to each team member.

The *author* (programmer) assigned to the project reviews the outlines and maps and comes to the meeting prepared to ask for clarification and make suggestions about the programming. The author should be ready to offer suggestions for standardizing, reducing costly customization and time required for programming.

171

Table 22.1. Development Methodology

| Stage | Media | | |
| | | Interactive | |
	CBT	Distance Learning	Web Site
Preproduction	Create storyboards with review cycles to establish adherence to technical and instructional standards.	Create a script with auditions to establish adherence to visual, audio, and instructional goals.	Map the links in a flowchart, check page design, and review to establish adherence to technical, web, and instructional standards.
Production	Create and assemble media elements according to the storyboards and course-development standards.	Shoot the video; edit and create additional media elements according to the script and course-development standards.	Create and assemble pages according to the map and course web-development standards.
Postproduction and quality review	Perform technical reviews, debug, and test the programmed lessons for adherence to the storyboards and programming standards.	Rehearse and practice the session, adhering to the script and allotted time frames.	Perform technical reviews, debug, and test the web pages for adherence to the map.
Delivery or implementation	Deliver the course.	Conduct the session.	Implement the web page.

The *art director* comes to the meeting prepared to ask for clarification or to make suggestions regarding the graphics. Because graphics can be a time-consuming and costly component of the development phase, the art director should be encouraged to suggest using available clip art, which is prepackaged with various software programs or free or inexpensively obtained from any number of websites (see Figure 22.1). To access these websites, search on "clip art" at www.askjeeves.com, www.google.com, or www.clipart.com.

Figure 22.1
Clip Art Example

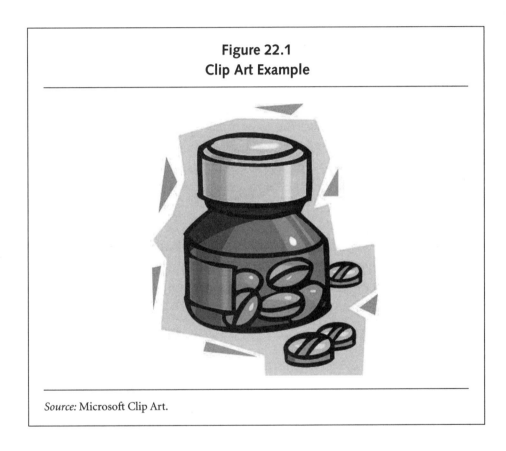

Source: Microsoft Clip Art.

The *audio specialist* manages and sometimes records the audio files. Some manipulation of the file format, such as conversion of tapes to digital format files, is often necessary. The audio specialist comes to the meeting prepared to ask for clarification or to make suggestions regarding the audio and sound effects. The audio specialist ensures that the audio script design:

- Uses double spacing and large font so that the narrator can easily read the phrases. (Avoid using the storyboards for narration, because this is one place where there is no efficiency to be gained. It usually takes too long for the narrator to adjust to all the information on the storyboard and find the narration.)

- Begins each phrase with a corresponding storyboard number (including a pause) so the audio can be easily tracked and converted into sound files.

- Indicates acronyms with hyphens (for example, I-S-D).

- Spells out phonetically any special terminology or hard-to-pronounce words.

The audio specialist should be encouraged to suggest music or sound effects to enhance the presentation of the content. The audio specialist chooses experienced *narrators* (who must be available to redo the narration should revision or additional narration be required).

The *video director* coordinates the video production. He or she reviews the storyboards and video scripts and asks for clarification on the set, cast, shot angles, and special video effects required. This director works in conjunction with the instructional designer and a scriptwriter to prepare the script for production. This involves checking the number of locations, types of shots, lighting, and so on, to effectively manage the crew and ensure resources are available when they are needed. He or she often clarifies script instructions with the instructional designer and scriptwriter.

Video scripts are the blueprints for video production in the same way that storyboards serve as the blueprint for assembling the CBT. Professional video scripts have their own industry-specific nomenclature for giving directions to each member of the video team. Long or complex video sequences or scripts prepared for outside vendors need to be written using this nomenclature. If the video requirements are not presented using the standard script format, it can dramatically increase the cost, the probability of delay and errors, and the time required to communicate the intended results. See the Script Standards section in Appendix C for more information.

The *subject-matter expert* (SME) comes to the meeting prepared to give technical advice and make certain that any changes to the outlines or concept maps do not create technical errors.

A *quality-control representative* attends the meeting to ensure that any changes made at that time conform to the CDS. In addition, if an issue reaches an impasse and discussion continues for too long without a solution in sight, the quality-control representative stops the discussion and makes a final decision.

His or her decision cannot be questioned, for two reasons. First, it puts teams on notice that they had best be able to come to agreement if they want to influence the decision. Second, it prevents an issue from stopping the preproduction meeting, an impasse that ultimately is sure to delay the production schedule.

Production

Here are descriptions of the team members' roles and responsibilities during production.

Authors integrate the elements of the CBT into the interactive models. They enter the text into the framework for each lesson and add the video, graphics, and audio according to the storyboard specifications. The author uses the storyboard with the audio and video files listed as a reference to program the computer to pick up the correct segments and shots and run them at the correct spot in the lesson.

Graphic artists create the graphics and animation sequences and store them according to the file-naming conventions established in the CDS.

Videographers (or a video team) create shot lists, shoot the video sequences, and log them according to the CDS. The *video team* usually consists of the *producer, the director, actors, camera operators, lighting and sound experts, set designers and decorators, costume designers,* and *makeup artists.* The video team is often the largest in terms of the number of people.

It is useful to have a shot list to record the link between each video sequence filmed and the video script. An example is in the Development and Implementation Tools section of Appendix E. It's also often helpful to shoot each sequence from the preferred angle and, if time and budget allow, from a couple of angles. This approach allows options in editing and helps to eliminate reshoots.

After the filming is completed, the video used for multimedia must be converted from videotape to a digital video file format. Be very careful in conducting reviews, editing, and ensuring all video has been shot, particularly if the video must be shipped out to be mastered or digitized. It's extremely important that all of the video and audio be logged accurately so that the author can identify the exact point at which the audio and video begins and ends.

Similarly, establish a relationship with a vendor who is sensitive to schedule requirements. Errors or delays in postproduction can impede completing the project.

It can be expensive to delay implementing a project while the video is returned for remastering or digitizing.

The video and audio are often stored on a CD-ROM that is sometimes called a *check disk*. The check disk, or check files, must be reviewed for four reasons:

1. To be certain that all of the video is on the disk.
2. To be certain that all of the audio is on the disk.
3. To determine that the media is of high quality (free of glitches and so on).
4. To check the video and audio file numbers for the author.

Preventing video reshoots is important because it's expensive to reassemble talent, crew, sets, and costumes. In some cases, the filming circumstances are impossible to reconstruct because people, special events, or equipment may no longer be at your disposal.

Reshoots may be required for three reasons:

1. None of the takes clearly indicates or shows what is required.
2. There is a change to the item (machine, process) that is being depicted.
3. There is an error in the shot or contradiction with the previous video and audio.

If there is no usable video shot for a sequence, use the Reshoot Request form in the Development and Implementation Tools section of Appendix E to request a video reshoot. Fill in each section completely so that the director clearly understands the problem with the old shot and the set-up of the new shot. Of course, the instructional designer and SME should be on the set for all reshoots, just as they were for the originals.

Use the Audio Log in the Development and Implementation Tools section of Appendix E to keep track of each audio segment as the audio is recorded.

Requests for rerecording audio can be for two reasons. Perhaps the audio is incorrect (a word mispronounced, wrong inflection, and so on). Or the audio may need to be changed (as with modification to the machine you are describing).

If the audio requires a rerecord because of the first circumstance, use the Audio Revision and Error List in the Development and Implementation Tools section of Appendix E so the error does not happen again. If the requirement is a complete rerecord, use the Audio Rerecord Form found in the same section.

Overall, the *director*'s job is to be certain everything runs smoothly on the set and in the control room. A very large production might include a *producer,* who is in charge of arranging the entire shoot, and an *assistant director,* who stands in for the director when there are shoots in two places at once.

In multimedia development, the director or a team member having specialized knowledge about video should assemble the video team. It is the director's responsibility to

- Contact local talent agencies to request photos, résumés, and whatever else is needed to choose the talent for auditions
- Audition and choose the actors to perform in the video and to be available for reshoots
- Rehearse the on-screen talent
- Supervise set designers, costumers, and decorators
- Supervise camera operators

Set designers determine what the set looks like and supervise the construction crew in building backdrops or scenery required for the video shoot.

Set decorators gather props and construct the physical look of the scene according to the director's instructions.

Costume designers must find or make the clothing worn by the on-screen talent.

Camera operators film the scene in accordance with the director's instruction.

The *actors* memorize scripts, rehearse, and perform.

Lighting designers and *grips* carefully set the lights to accent the scene.

Sound designers set the microphones to achieve the best audio production and run the recording equipment in the studio, in the control room, and on location. They also convert the taped audio to digital files ready for assembly in the CBT.

The *instructional designer* also serves as technical advisor on the set and helps establish the shots according to the storyboards. His or her responsibility is to ensure the concept is filmed as intended.

The *SMEs* often come to the video set or are on call for technical aspects of the shots. This is necessary to give advice and make certain the execution of the scene is technically correct.

The *art director* supervises photographers and graphic artists and provides the look-and-feel direction for the project. This director is often responsible for locating off-the-shelf clip art or photography to reduce costs and meet project needs. Many multimedia backgrounds and buttons are available in off-the-shelf products.

Photographers take the required shots, either using a digital camera and saving the images directly to disk or shooting the photos and having them scanned or imaged onto a CD-ROM, from which proof sheets can be made.

Graphic artists and *animators* create the graphics and animation sequences and save them to a directory or disk. A sample Graphics Log is provided in the Development and Implementation Tools section of Appendix E.

There are instances when requests for graphics rework may be called for:

- The depiction is unclear—perhaps too small, or the colors of adjacent items interfere, or there are undefined borders between important areas.
- The depiction is proportionally incorrect.
- The animation sequence is incorrect.
- An incorrect standard (such as font size, style, or color) is applied.

Use the Graphics Rework Request in the Development and Implementation Tools section of Appendix E to request graphic changes.

A *system engineer* or *programmer* may appear in projects where the course requires special data links to be programmed. For example, links between applications or other special programming may be required to write training records from the CBT to a training records database, or to access an application or set of files from the CBT. System engineers and programmers troubleshoot development software and files; create models and templates; compile programs; and manage file configuration, back-up, and test platforms.

Postproduction and Quality Reviews

During postproduction, all of the segments of the lesson are reviewed and the final formative evaluation of the courseware is conducted.

Only three reviews are required during postproduction:

1. *Standards review,* to ensure that the standards described in the course specification document are followed throughout the lesson.
2. *Editorial review,* to be sure there are no errors in grammar, spelling, spacing, or punctuation.
3. *Functional review,* to be certain there are no bugs in the programming logic and no glitches in the audio, video, or graphics. A Functional Review Checklist is included in the Development and Implementation Tools section of Appendix E.

The instructional effectiveness of the course was determined by the review during preproduction, so an instructional review is redundant at this point.

Nor do you need a management review; the courseware should meet the requirements based on the review of the storyboards during preproduction.

A technical review is also unnecessary. The SME has reviewed the technical accuracy of the storyboards, participated in the preproduction meeting, been on the set for video shoots, and reviewed the final video and audio with the instructional designer.

Follow these steps to conduct the required reviews of online lessons:

1. The first reviewer should number the Online Review Form pages. (This form is available in the Development and Implementation Tools section of Appendix E.) If more than one page is required for a particular screen of the lesson, subsequent pages should be numbered with an alpha character (for example 1, 1A, 1B, and so on).

2. Blank copies of all the review forms (editorial, standards, and functional) should be included in the packet of lesson review forms. The reviewer assigned to each review should complete the appropriate form.

3. In a large project, it's the author's responsibility to list the lessons on the Review Scheduling Form as each becomes available (see the sample form in Appendix E).

4. The reviewers are responsible for checking the list regularly to confirm that lessons are ready for review.

5. Should the author remove the lesson from review at any time, this fact should be indicated on the schedule with the author's name beside the appropriate time and day.

6. Each reviewer should use a uniquely colored pen to record errors. That way, if questions arise about a comment, the author knows whom to ask.

7. Each reviewer records errors on the same page. This method of recording

   • Helps the author correct all errors on one screen at one time.

   • Speeds up the process because the author only has to review one page of comments. Reviews must contain enough detail so that the author knows exactly what needs to be changed.

8. All reviewers should complete their reviews by running the multimedia on machines with the same configuration (speed, monitor, hard disk space, random access memory (RAM), and so on).

9. All review forms should remain with the configured machine, until the last review is completed.

10. The last reviewer to complete a review and sign the scheduling form should return the online lesson review forms to the author.

11. The author makes changes and reintegrates the files.

After the author corrects the identified changes, there is no need to have each reviewer go through the lesson again. One person should be assigned to validate that the changes have been made, placing a check mark beside each change to confirm that it has been reviewed and corrected.

It is the responsibility of the system engineer or programmer to

1. Coordinate installation of hardware for pilot studies and implementation sites.

2. Coordinate installing the program on LANs or servers.

3. Maintain hardware and the program during testing.

4. Be present at the implementation sites during the first pilot test and initial testing of the program.

5. Troubleshoot problems that arise after initial installation.

SUMMARY

Regardless of your role on the multimedia development team, you participate in or are affected by preproduction and production cycles, postproduction quality-review cycles, and instructional delivery strategies.

Being aware of team member roles, participating fully, and lending your expertise at the team level improves the quality, effectiveness, and viability of your multimedia project.

Developing Computer-Based Learning Environments

When someone says "multimedia," for many in the corporate training world the term signifies a computer-based learning environment. Indeed, the flexibility of computer-based learning environments brings some significant advantages to solving today's business needs. Because a computer-based learning environment can include video, audio, and graphic elements, the forms, processes, and roles and responsibilities presented in Part Three of this book can be adapted to a variety of multimedia projects.

You can speed up development by using software with prebuilt functionality that eliminates the need to program. Menu systems use libraries of functions to create four types of templates:

1. *Screen and lesson shells:* to build course content

2. *Skill assessments:* at the end of a unit or for pretesting

3. *Proficiency exams:* to build and score tests

4. *Course management system:* for tracking students

The screen and lesson shells allow the multimedia author to begin adding content immediately. Standards and style guides are prebuilt into the template and can automatically enter a font type, font size, and overall placement of the content, or they can be fully customized.

Navigation components usually include a menu, forward and backward navigation, a glossary of terms, and a help function.

Skill assessment models usually have prebuilt logic for developing questions of various types (true-false, matching, multiple-choice, short-answer) and giving students feedback. The questions can be formatted creatively—as in matching items by dragging a graphic or text from one column to another—rather than just the typical text questions you would find on a paper-and-pencil test.

A course manager can register students, track their progress through the course (including scores on tests), and produce reports for administrators.

PROCESS

There are four activities in the procedure to develop a computer-based course:

1. Create storyboards.

2. Create and assemble media elements.

3. Perform online reviews.

4. Deliver and implement the course.

COMPUTER-BASED TRAINING DEVELOPMENT PROCEDURE

Follow these activities:

Activity One: Create Storyboards

Use storyboard standards established in the CDS.

Step one: Review the rationale for the treatment of each type of learning outcome as presented in the outline, map, and specifications.

Step two: Translate the rationale to a screen-by-screen outline. It's important to standardize the CBT design so the programming elements can be modeled not only at the screen level but also at a topic or lesson level. Use the CDS elements of lesson construction you developed during design.

The resulting content may be linked and navigated as a series of screens or grouped into functional circles accessed through a menu, as illustrated in Figure 23.1.

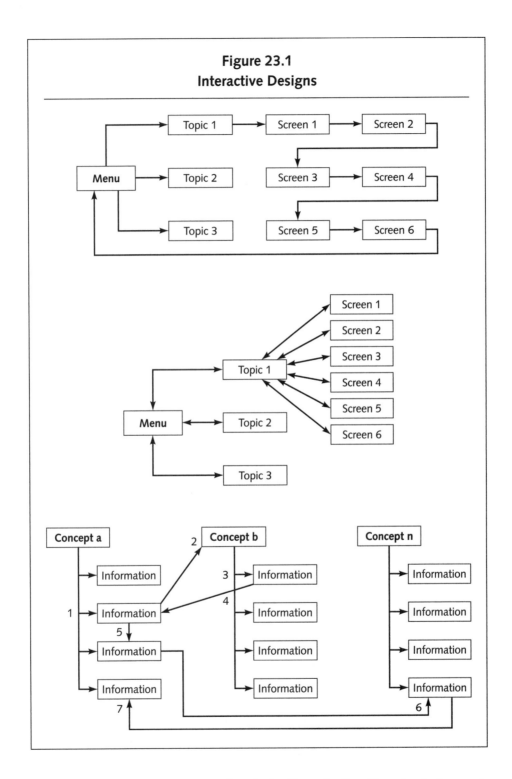

Figure 23.1
Interactive Designs

The first two navigational systems in Figure 23.1 would be a construct you might see if you are developing from an objectivist perspective. The third system would be more indicative of a constructivist perspective. Follow the numbers to see the path that a user might take through the solution this system is designed for.

A major manufacturing company uses one of the best computer-based training programs with the constructivist approach. The program is in performance management. It consists of three diskettes. The first diskette is on Goal Setting, the second on Coaching and Counseling, and the third on Performance Appraisals. Figure 23.2 is a flowchart of the interaction.

The scenarios begin with one screen of the entire system of performance review tools, information from other managers, and access to the employee's personnel file. The next screen is a meeting with the previous manager, who provides you with some information about the team. You, the manager, then must meet with each employee. You begin a discussion with the employee where he or she tells you about his or her situation and goals. At this point you are given several choices. You can choose to respond to the employee and receive feedback about your response. Or you can explore the employee's personnel file, check the performance toolkit, hear stories from managers who have had similar issues with employees.

The entire environment is dynamic. Depending on which options you choose and which employee you are seeking information on, the next screen addresses that situation. Once you decide to respond, you receive video feedback from the employee. When you have followed the correct path and provided the appropriate response at each step, the scenario ends with a satisfied employee.

The entire path through the course is controlled by the users based on the decisions they make. There is never an <Enter> button on the interface for users to "Press Enter to Continue." The course permits full exploration of all available resources to obtain as much information as the user needs to make the appropriate decision.

Step three: Add title frames (also called "splash screens"), main menus, course introductory segments, overall reviews and summaries, pretests and posttests, and credit screens to the content storyboard as indicated in the CDS.

Figure 23.2
Flowchart of Constructivist Course

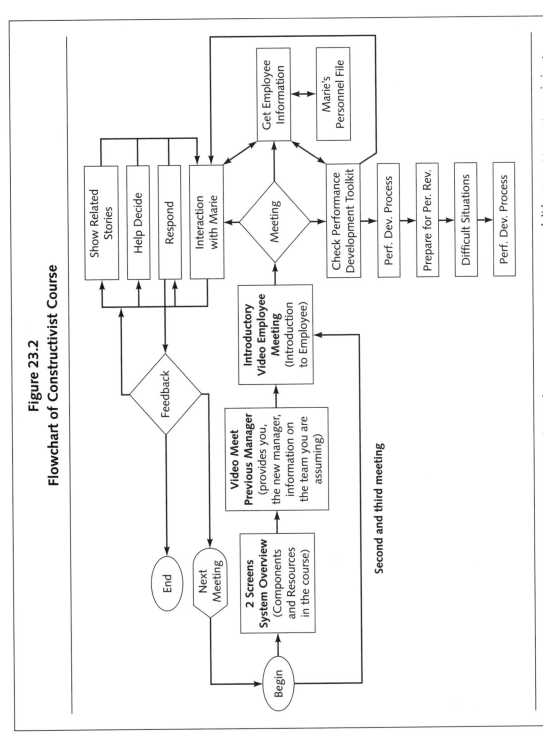

Note: The company that used this courseware has changed its performance management program and did not want to grant permission to use its name. However, we think that the previous description and flowchart adequately demonstrates the constructivist model. Plus, it is a superior example of how management skills can be taught using e-learning.

Each storyboard should include detailed information and directions:

- Date, version, and designer's name and phone number
- Lesson, topic, and frame number
- Graphic description, reference, or rough drawing
- Audio and sound effects, or video sequence and script
- Interaction instructions: which interface buttons are active, type of interaction (text entry, click on, match, move), and so on
- Screen text
- Animation and special effects
- Navigation links and instructions for pagination

We offer an example of a storyboard template in the Development and Implementation Tools section of Appendix E.

Step four: Review and validate the storyboards to be sure they contain correct information and meet specifications.

Step five: QA reviews are conducted on storyboards. Several reviews should be included:

- Editorial
- Standards
- Technical
- Instructional
- Management

Review forms for each of these reviews are in the same section of Appendix E.

Activity Two: Create and Assemble Media Elements

Media elements are created and assembled according to the storyboards and course development specifications.

Step one: Hold a preproduction meeting to review storyboards, audio scripts, and video scripts and to make final determinations about producing the various elements of the project before each of the groups involved begins work. This meeting is the forum to resolve conflict, negotiate differences, and achieve consensus on all aspects of the lesson before beginning production. Although some restraints must be imposed (for reasons of logistics or because of the technical systems used for production), be careful not to stifle creativity and input to the development process.

If it is practical, we suggest that storyboards be distributed well in advance of the meeting—we recommend a minimum of two days—so each member of the preproduction team has the opportunity to thoroughly review the storyboards and bring questions, comments, and suggestions to the meeting. Distributing copies of storyboards a few hours in advance is generally unacceptable. When the storyboards are distributed, the time, place, and date of the preproduction meeting should be announced.

The instructional designer leads the meeting, asking for questions, considering suggestions, and clarifying ID issues. Chapter Twenty-Two details which team members might be included in the preproduction meeting.

Step two: Produce the CBT. The finalized storyboards are known as production baseline storyboards. They establish what is required to produce course components and serve as a test plan for post-development evaluation.

Authors use the storyboard to identify what graphics, video, text, or audio elements they will receive and where each contributed component fits. Each frame of the course is built using the storyboard as the guide that cements the elements together.

Activity Three: Perform Online Reviews

Test, debug, and review the programmed lessons for adherence to the storyboards and programming standards.

Step one: Produce the test CD-ROMs. In preparation for final review, the CD-ROMs must be produced or the final version of the lesson must be loaded to the delivery system (a LAN or one or more correctly configured computers). To be valid, reviews should occur on test computers that are configured exactly like the lowest-common-denominator end-user machine.

Step two: Use the storyboards as a basis for review. The instructional designer, subject-matter expert, and quality-control representative review the CBT navigation, text, graphics, photography, video, and audio to be certain that they all perform and look as intended. Reviews conducted include:

- Editorial
- Functional
- Technical

> These three reviews are the only ones necessary at this point to ensure the course is free from spelling and grammatical errors, that the course has no "bugs," and that all technical components are integrated correctly.

Step three: Record errors, either online or using a numbered set of Online Review Forms (see Appendix E). The numbers on the forms should coincide with storyboard numbers (which now match screen numbers), and there should be a separate page for each storyboard.

Step four: Correct errors.

Step five: Review corrections. Review corrections identified and determine those that will be made and those that will not (either because they fall outside the scope of the original storyboard or cannot be duplicated). Follow the steps outlined in Chapter Twenty-Two to conduct online reviews.

Activity Four: Deliver and Implement the Course

Delivery should be well planned to accommodate the business constraints inherent in the time frame, environment, and audience requirements.

FROM OUR EXPERIENCE

When we talk about multimedia production, we would be remiss in not reminding you to back up your computer files and plan for space to work.

Back up files to the LAN, disk, or zip drive. Most computers have an automatic backup you can set through the program manager function menu. Set this function to back up frequently and "auto save" files. Hard disks do crash, and you can lose significant amounts of work. You don't have to learn this the hard way (as we have). Make backup copies of your work daily.

Plan for file size and space requirements. It is not unusual for the data in a single graphics file or audio segment to total one megabyte or much more. Don't underestimate the amount of space required for CBT working files, storing copies of media elements, moving and backing up files, and storing compiled versions of the program. A good rule of thumb is to reserve ten times the anticipated file size of the finished program.

Let us emphasize once more that video and photo reshoots translate into big money because of the difficulty, and sometimes impossibility, of assembling all of the people and elements to do a scene or segment over again.

Audio studios charge setup fees and hourly rates for studio personnel, so make sure any audio scripts that accompany the storyboards are approved and additional retakes are carefully planned and considered. Plan all retakes to be completed in one session. It's much less costly to plan carefully, involve a subject-matter expert and the instructional designer at the audio session, and do multiple readings the first time.

The project team may require technical-support expertise to configure delivery systems during implementation. The technical-support team members must have a high degree of knowledge and skill in the hardware platform your CBT courseware is to be delivered on.

Success of the pilot test—indeed, the overall success of the project—may depend on the skills of your technical-support group. Even if, for your project, the customer has its own technical-support group, your own technical-support team probably should conduct the initial training of the customer's group.

If everyone does his or her job efficiently and effectively (which storyboarding encourages), much of the mystery is removed about how a seemingly chaotic effort becomes a thing of beauty that is also instructionally sound.

SUMMARY

CBT continues to have a use and market for the foreseeable future. However, it will probably dwindle as newer technologies advance. But then, so will the current technologies as the next breakthrough is developed. Even though classroom training is often less effective than CBT, companies still spend billions on facilitated instruction every year. The move from classroom training to electronic forms is more a matter of economics than education. It is not feasible to continue to train using the classroom model with companies continuing to operate over wide geographic areas and even globally. However, remember, as Part Four on Multimedia Evaluation will emphasize, you may be able to initially justify moving to e-learning on the basis of cost savings from eliminated travel, but eventually you will be asked to demonstrate how it enables people to do their jobs better and the relationship of improved performance to the bottom line.

Developing Internet, Intranet, Web-Based, and Performance Support Learning Environments

The interactive age is here. Those who gain the skills to design for it now are wise. Those who resist gaining skills to develop for the Internet will become obsolete in the near future. The next generation of interactive multimedia will reside on the World Wide Web.

Internet delivery seems to meet many of the requirements of training on demand:

- It's available at the desktop.
- It eliminates the need for travel.
- It's cost-effective compared to conventional delivery media.
- Text-based web interventions can be developed quickly.

Designing training for the web follows the same ID process as any other medium. You must first establish a framework of specifications and standards; then develop the media elements that fit the framework; and finally review, revise, and implement the end product.

When we mention implementation and delivery technology, we are often asked about web technology. Web-based applications use existing technology. Most businesses are in the process of developing or refining an intranet, which constitutes a ready-made distribution channel.

THE INTERNET AND INTRANETS

For many instructional designers, the difference between an intranet and the Internet is a key concept. Simply put, an intranet is an Internet surrounded by a firewall to protect an organization's internal communication network. Because an organization has complete control over its intranet, it manages issues such as network performance and security, which cannot always be controlled in using the public Internet.

Sometimes the terms Internet and World Wide Web (WWW) are used interchangeably. But they are not synonymous. The Internet is the hardware (backbone) and wiring. The WWW is the content referenced by an URL (uniform resource locator).

The intranets of many businesses and educational institutions are much more advanced than the Internet as a whole. The use of Internet technology to deliver course materials is occurring first on corporate and higher education intranets. How courseware is being delivered over intranets today serves as a model for how courses will be delivered over the Internet in the future.

Adoption of the Internet and intranets as delivery media by business and educational institutions has been phenomenal. There are three primary reasons for this:

1. *Universal access.* Anyone can access the web with a web browser and modem connection. Anyone can deliver content anywhere in the world using a web server. The web is based on a few simple technology standards, such as transmission control protocol/Internet protocol (TCP/IP), web server software, and web browser software. This simple technology has allowed the number of intranet and Internet connections to grow exponentially.

2. *Ease of use.* Internet and intranet software is very easy to use. This is opening up adoption to a much broader audience with limited computer experience.

3. *Multimedia content.* Web-based technology support for multimedia (text, graphics, audio, and video) content has enabled delivery of a wide range of interesting content, again opening up the web-based intranet and Internet to a broad audience. Web-based technology support for multimedia allows instructional designers to meet the needs of a technologically savvy audience with varied learning styles.

The costs, skills needed, and technology associated with developing multimedia and video distance-education technologies have been and will continue to be a barrier for many businesses. Two issues exist regarding delivery of content over the web. First, most software tools, including CBT authoring tools, do not produce applications that are based on Internet standards. As a result, web browsers are unable to access these nonstandard applications. To get around the problem posed by applications not being based on web standards, many tool vendors have developed add-on software that extends the browser's capabilities to run nonstandard applications. These web browsers and add-ons are commonly referred to as "plug-ins" for the Netscape Navigator® browser and "Active X" controls for the Microsoft Internet Explorer® browser.

Although there are advantages to being able to access existing applications without having to convert them to Internet standards, there are some significant disadvantages. One of the reasons the web has caught on so quickly is its simplicity. A user only needs a web browser to access web content. Introducing a plug-in requirement adds significant complexity because it is up to the users to make sure that they are running the specific plug-ins required to view the content they need to access. Plug-ins are dependent on the web browser and underlying operating system and, in many situations, must be updated each time the plug-ins change.

Internet technology is evolving rapidly. Using applications based on Internet standards rather than using plug-ins would make the Internet more efficient and put it in a better position to take advantage of new capabilities as they are developed. For example, if a new Internet standard were adopted for video, it would be much easier to integrate video into web-based training without using the extra memory required by plug-ins. As computers are built with ever-increasing amounts of RAM and ROM and as older computers' memories are upgraded, more complex forms of web-based multimedia can be accessed.

The second important issue in delivering content over the web concerns network performance. Many of the Internet's current limitations are related to network capacity or bandwidth (the rate at which information moves across the network).

Generally speaking, internal intranets allow information to move much faster than most public telephone lines do. Information accessed over a company intranet travels at an average rate of 1.25 megabytes per second; information accessed over a telephone line using a modem travels at a rate of .004 megabytes per second. As a result, a web course delivered over a company intranet can use a combination of rich multimedia. But if a course is to be delivered to remote users who must access it using a telephone connection, the course should be limited in its use of high-density media components.

Streaming is a term that refers to a technique developed to get around some of the network limitations for delivering e-learning. This is a technology that essentially breaks a course, application, or file into small pieces and starts delivering the beginning of the application, so that the user can access it, while the remainder of the application continues to be broken up and sent separately. From the user's perspective, the experience is the same as if the application were available and running locally on his or her computer.

However, streaming technology is relatively immature at this point, and there is no prevailing industry standard. As a result, individual vendors have developed their own proprietary software that requires plug-ins.

Until usability catches up with capability, CD-ROM may be a better delivery strategy for multimedia courses if your only alternative is the Internet. The intranet and Internet infrastructure, expertise, and technology must be analyzed to understand the delivery options and successfully deliver multimedia.

DESIGNING FOR THE WEB

Web-based design and development can contain all of the components of computer-based courseware. Successful web development is dependent on (1) the creativity and skill of the course developers, (2) bandwidth, and (3) hardware capabilities.

Hypertext markup language (HTML) is a programming language particularly suited for use on the web. HTML allows sophisticated design and development of web-based courseware. It can incorporate video, audio, animation, graphics, and sophisticated branching. Development can be less expensive than CBT because HTML does not require any particular authoring system and is relatively easy to use. Most designers can master it without extensive training and are productive as soon as HTML commands are mastered. Authoring systems contain the basic structures for integrating HTML components. Authoring shells can be developed that make media input into a program efficient without extensive authoring skills. Instructional designers can easily perform much of the design and development online.

Those who resist using the Internet for training raise the criticism that it is not as interactive and engaging as high-level CBT; it's too linear, they say. However, that's a designer's perspective, not the end user's. Millions of businesses and homes worldwide are connected to the Internet, and people spend countless hours every day online. This indicates that there are plenty of creative ways to engage a user.

For now, online text-based courses, if that's all your infrastructure can handle, are OK as long as we use what we've learned from developing CBT to move forward rapidly. In other words, it should not take another twenty-five years for Internet training to reach the same degree of sophistication that CBT enjoys today. Instruction does not have to suffer using the Internet. It is limited only by the imagination and creativity of those designing instruction (or by inadequate hardware systems delivering the instruction).

Interactivity need not suffer using the Internet. Indeed, it can be enhanced. A chat room incorporated into an asynchronous Internet lesson allows participants to log on at specified times and carry on a dialogue with the instructor and other students. The instructor usually begins by posing a question, issue, or topic. Participants then type in their comments, responses, and additional questions. The entire dialogue is saved in a file for future reference by the instructor and by students.

Another way to enhance interactivity that accommodates learning styles and at the same time addresses bandwidth issues is to develop a solution four ways in the same package:

- Full motion video, audio, text, and graphics
- Stop motion video, audio, text, and graphics
- Still shots with audio, text, and graphics
- Still shots with running text script, text, and graphics

E-mail is an important feature of an asynchronous course. While students study online, they can send an e-mail to the instructor at any point, asking for clarification or proposing comments. The instructor must be continually aware of participants' questions and respond promptly.

Centra's Synchronous Web-Based Solution

Much efficiency can be gained by using existing web design and development software. Software is currently available that organizes synchronous and asynchronous training into a total web distance-learning environment that integrates and simulates classroom, instructor-led, and CBT training. Centra Software, Inc., has created one example of this type of learning environment.

Centra has developed a suite of products called Symposium® that simulate the classroom environment. This virtual classroom consists of a synchronous web-based tool that can also be used as an asynchronous tool by recording the live sessions, a web conference tool, and an eMeeting tool. All of the tools are based on the synchronous web tool but are flexible enough to be used for virtual conferences and virtual meetings.

It is ideal for highly interactive team collaboration, virtual classrooms, sales and product training, online workshops and labs, hands-on technical training, and enterprise software rollouts. Each Centra Symposium event can support up to five hundred simultaneous users in a live, structured environment. Unlike streaming broadcast technology or static web pages, Symposium enables large groups of dispersed employees, partners, and customers to interact, collaborate, and learn—replicating typical classroom interaction—in real-time over intranets, extranets, and the Internet. Symposium provides unprecedented cost savings over traditional teaching and knowledge-sharing methods by using existing corporate computing infrastructure and the Internet.

A demo of Symposium is available on Centra's website, www.centra.com. Figure 24.1 shows the student graphical user interface for Symposium. Figure 24.2 shows the session leader's interface.

Symposium's features virtually emulate everything that can be done in the live classroom. The features include:

Structured, Live Interaction

- Audioconferencing that is integrated into the overall system. This eliminates using teleconferencing that many users of other synchronous software packages use, where the interaction between audio and video is not synchronized well.

- Real-time videoconferencing that enables users to see the session leader or other designated participants within the interface. A unique adaptive video bandwidth feature ensures the highest possible performance over connections as low as 28.8 kbps.

- Choice of languages for participants. Before a session, each end user can individually choose his or her own language of preference from the twelve supported languages. Users can then participate in a live session with others who have different localized client user interfaces.

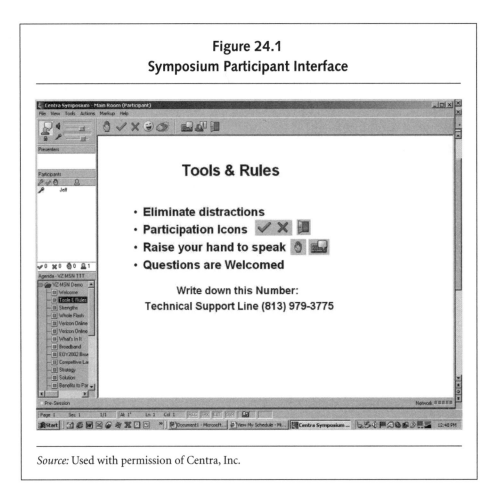

Figure 24.1
Symposium Participant Interface

Source: Used with permission of Centra, Inc.

- Breakout rooms and labs. Session leaders can use multiple breakout rooms for team or individual lab exercises. The leader can "look over the participant's shoulder" and even take control of his or her application.

- Multiple presenters. Centra Symposium supports an unlimited number of co-presenters and subject-matter experts.

- Evaluations and quizzes. These permit a wide choice of questions to be auto-graded and reported on from the database at a later time.

- Surveys. Leaders and presenters can create, display, and collect data from surveys in advance or "on-the-spot."

- Whiteboard. Multi-user, interactive whiteboard markup, including content created in a breakout room, can be saved for later review.

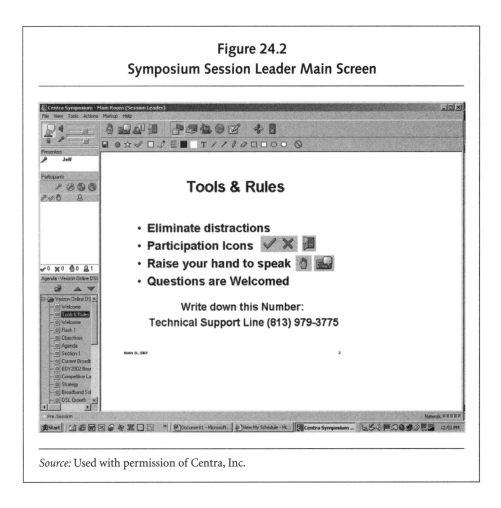

Figure 24.2
Symposium Session Leader Main Screen

Source: Used with permission of Centra, Inc.

- Choreography. The session leader can control which participants have the ability to speak and interact with the collaboration tools.

- Feedback. Participants' ability to indicate they want to be recognized, respond to polling, demonstrate electronic laughter and applause responses, use text chat that only the instructor can see or that everyone can see, and provide anonymous feedback to the instructor and presenters.

- Full-screen content viewing. Instructors can automatically expand the participants' content windows for viewing large shared applications or web pages.

- Peer-to-peer interaction. The leader can choose to open the "floor" to several participants at a time for peer-to-peer interaction and learning.

- Peer-to-peer text chat. Leaders can choose to enable peer-to-peer text chat that permits participants to simply right-mouse-click on another participant's name and send that person a private text chat message.

- Application sharing with mark-up. Instructors and participants can share any Windows application, including their entire desktop or even a remote server, with other participants. Instructors can quickly initiate sharing of a remote participant's application by simply clicking on the participant's name and selecting "Share Application." Participants can then use the mark-up tools directly on the shared application to highlight a specific area or point.

- Web safari. This allows the session leader to take the participants on a synchronized web tour. Participants can see the leader's "pointer" and will automatically scroll when the leader scrolls up and down on a web page.

- Just-in-time import of PowerPoint® with animation. PowerPoint presentations, with any animations or embedded multimedia preserved, can be imported into a Centra Symposium session before or during a live session to create engaging presentations. Then the mark-up tools can be used to emphasize your point.

- Self-paced CBT or WBT integrated into live events. Leaders can import self-paced individualized learning segments during a live event or as prework. This blended learning approach is ideal for enabling class participants to take part in an integrated self-paced exercise.

- Multimedia. This supports prerecorded video clips, audio clips, animated GIFs, and other multimedia content, including Flash®, DHTML®, and JavaScript®.

- Centra Agenda Builder. Agenda Builder® is a sophisticated agenda creation tool for building web-based evaluation forms and assembling event content into a structured, customized format.

- Integrated Knowledge Catalog. This allows users to quickly search and retrieve session recordings and other topical materials on-demand from a menu system.

Real-Time Interactivity

- Rich collaboration tools. Attendees can actively participate in an event by providing immediate, nonverbal feedback via yes/no polling, instant surveys, electronic hand-raising recognition, and public and private text chat. Also, any attendee can speak using voice over IP if given a microphone by a presenter.

- Live application demonstration with mark-up. Conference presenters can show a live, full-screen demonstration of any Windows application to the audience. In addition, presenters can host their own applications or interact with one being shown and use the markup tools to emphasize a point right on the live application.

- Multiple presenters. Up to five presenters can lead or moderate an event, allowing each person to present his or her own content to the audience and use the full set of collaboration tools.

Rich Content and Multimedia

- Rich, multimedia support. To engage your audience, incorporate any browser-rendered content into your online presentation, including Flash, Shockwave®, and JavaScript, in addition to animated GIFs and streamed video and audio-clips.

- Session recording and playback. Events are automatically recorded on the server and can be played back later by users. In addition, with easy-to-use features for recording, editing, and storage, users can create professional, self-paced recordings in other industry standard formats. These recordings can be viewed outside the Centra environment with any standard media player or included as content within a live or self-paced session.

- Low bandwidth requirements symposium. This provides network efficiency and can be accessed by end-users relying solely on dial-up connections.

- 28.8 kbps dialup support. Full product functionality is supported with Centra's thin client web application over a single network connection as low as 28.8 kbps, allowing even users with a slow connection to experience a fully interactive experience.

- Thin client web architecture. At 1 MB, the thin client software installs automatically and quickly, even over a low bandwidth connection, facilitating enterprise-wide deployment.

- Content pre-caching. Events can be configured so that the event content will be automatically pre-cached or delivered to the participant's PC prior to the actual session.

- Satellite servers. To reduce bandwidth requirements across an organization's wide area network (WAN), satellite servers can be deployed in strategic, geographically dispersed locations. Participants in the same event will then automatically receive data and content from their local satellite server. Users will automatically be reconnected to the next best available server if a satellite server goes down during a live session.

Class Management Features

- User authentication. An integrated directory enables single-point user authentication to verify user logins and accounts.

- System capacity management. Automatically managed server capacity prevents users from exceeding available system capacity when scheduling sessions. Only a certain number of users will be permitted to register for an event, not exceeding system connectivity capabilities.

- Event scheduling and enrollment. A robust web-based scheduling and registration interface allows users to browse the event schedule or search for a particular event, self-enroll in events, or be preenrolled by an event manager. Event managers can then send follow-up e-mails that can include attachments and rich text to participants of a particular event. In addition, event creators can choose to make an event publicly accessible or private. And administrators can batch create and delete events.

- Tracking and reporting. All assessment, user, event, and attendance data are tracked and reported. Additional custom reports can easily be generated.

- Content management. Event content is managed and organized to allow the same agenda content to be easily reused in different Symposium events or even on different servers.

- Multiple recording servers. Multiple recording servers can be added to a Centra system to record more than one session at a time.

- Distributed server architecture. Multiple Centra collaboration servers (CCS) can be distributed across the world to optimize bandwidth efficiency and provide additional capacity, yet still be centrally managed from a common web interface.

- Firewall transparency. The unique adaptive connection feature automatically configures Symposium to work through corporate firewalls using the best connection possible.

- Smart client auto-upgrade. The Symposium client application will automatically upgrade itself whenever the Centra server is upgraded or a new patch is installed on the server, dramatically reducing the amount of IT involvement in product upgrades.

- System check. A web-based, self-service system check makes sure each user's system, including audio settings, is properly configured before the live event begins.

- Password reminder. Provides a secure solution for users who forget their login information, reducing the amount of resources required for end user support.

Integration and Customization

- Microsoft Outlook® integration. Schedule a training session and invite participants right from your Microsoft Outlook calendar. The people you invite will receive a standard Outlook calendar invitation that they can accept or decline.

- Application program interface (API) toolkit. This feature makes Symposium SCORM compliant, which provides seamless integration with virtually all of today's leading learning management systems (LMS), web portals, intranets, and eCommerce systems.

- Automatic NT authentication. This allows Internet Explorer users on a corporate Windows NT domain to be automatically logged in to their personal Symposium home page.

- Oracle 8 and SQL 7 database support. Allows existing databases to be used as an eLearning repository.

- System co-branding and customization. Symposium's web-based user interface can be easily customized to meet your needs.

- Active directory integration. Integration with Microsoft's Active directory enables single-point user authentication so there is no need to re-check user logins and accounts.

Security

- User login encryption. This is to prevent access of personal data by unauthorized persons.

- Encryption of live events. Unauthorized users cannot access the event.

- Event password protection. This permits access by only registered users.

- Administrator-set password policies. The feature permits specific and unique sign-on requirements.
- Ability to easily eject an individual participant from session. The instructor can disconnect a user.
- Privilege-based user authentication. This permits different levels of access based on authorization.
- Complete encryption of management interface (HTTPs). The encryption prohibits access to records by unauthorized persons.
- Content encryption. This prohibits access to live or recorded sessions by unauthorized persons.

Asynchronous Learning Solutions

- Session recording and playback. Events can be automatically recorded on the server and played back later by registered or guest users. In addition, with easy-to-use features for recording, editing, and storage, users can create professional, self-paced recordings in other industry standard formats. These recordings can be viewed outside the Centra environment with any standard media player or included as content within a live or self-paced session.
- Self-paced content viewing. Events can be configured to allow enrolled participants access to event content before and after the live session. Of course, pre-recorded courses do not contain the interactivity afforded to the live audience. It does allow users who could not view the live session to obtain the information. Symposium does permit individualized web courses to be delivered through the tool.

TESTING ON THE WEB

There are issues of test security in using any form of web-based training. Usually, testing is possible as long as certain security functions are embedded in the Internet infrastructure. If you do not want tests to be printed and widely distributed, you need to consider security issues. Designing tests taken online with the capability to generate random questions makes it more difficult for students to collaborate on answers. Timing tests can also discourage collaboration. A student who knows the material is less likely to want to devote time from his or her test to taking it for a student who does not know the material. Finally, remember that in web-based applications most students are at remote sites and are not together in the same room. Exchanging answers in such a situation is pretty difficult. Because there is two-way video or audio in synchronous web software, instructors can monitor students remotely to determine whether they are working on their own. Instructors can also use the glimpse function to see how students are progressing through the test.

A web course that we saw included a paper-and-pencil test distributed and taken while a room camera monitored the students. One student collected all completed tests, placed them in an addressed envelope, sealed the envelope, and sent it to the regional training facility.

A test can be useful even if the course does not require certification or is not designed to meet some industry regulations. Students often learn something just from taking the test. Even if they do get an answer from someone else, there is a higher probability they will retain the information.

However, the discussion of how the web has changed our perception of testing in Chapter Fifteen is the best advice we can offer.

PERFORMANCE SUPPORT SYSTEMS

We include the performance support system (PSS) environment with the web-based one because we have found the storyboarding process and the user interface similar to the web with respect to development and interactivity. There are two types of PSS: performance support systems and performance-centered applications. Performance support systems entail online and on-demand access to integrated information, guidance, advice, assistance, and training to enable high-level job performance with little support from people (for example, the automated project management tool from Xegy™ that accompanies this book that you can access through a special URL on the CD-ROM and the Help function in Microsoft Word). Performance-centered applications encompass integrated business information processing with task or job-structuring support and related business knowledge, reference, data, and tools (for example, a bank ATM or an enterprise-wide system that permits electronic submission of all business forms).

Simulation performance support systems are advancing and automating the development of system environments that look and behave like the actual system.

First used in enterprise solution software such as SAP and PeopleSoft, most now support any Windows or web-based applications. Using this approach for web-based performance support has the benefits of program development, delivery, and maintenance costs that are significantly lower than traditional performance support, facilitator-led, or synchronous or asynchronous web courseware.

Employees retain information longer and more thoroughly because they apply new knowledge and skills immediately and almost always at the "moment of need." These systems offer flexible options that are in line with employees' hectic schedules. Individuals can get what they want when they need it twenty-four hours a day, seven days a week, 365 days a year.

Internet web-based delivery means that information is delivered faster, more efficiently, and to larger groups of employees. As with other types of performance support, information can be accessed at any time to refresh an employee's memory.

Content can be created once and distributed immediately. Updates are transparent to the user, that is, content changes simply appear in the program without the user being aware.

There are a number of vendors offering simulation products. The products are similar in their development approach. One such simulation software is On Demand from Global Knowledge Network, Inc. The developer accesses the content that they want to simulate. Then they bring up the On Demand simulation software and turn on a recording function and click through content capturing those portions they want to use. They "turn off" the recording and create a "video" vignette, simulation, training materials, checklists, or knowledge tests that can be immediately published to the web.

Most simulation products provide you with options regarding what you generate, how it will be displayed, and, if text, the type of output file. When comparing products, we suggest that you conduct a test to compare the capabilities of the various products with the software that you are simulating so that you have a realistic view of each simulation product's capabilities. In other words, ask the vendor to do a "proof of concept" for you and create a simulation so you can see how easy or difficult it actually is to use the simulation software.

The following are considerations when purchasing performance support simulation software:

Acquisition
• How much are the license agreement costs and additional end user fees?

Development

- When you turn on the simulation software and begin the video capture, are all mouse clicks and screen captures recorded?
- Is the process for clicking through the software to create a simulation (capturing the simulation) easy?
- After the simulation is created, how much editing is required to remove extra steps or to add callouts or text boxes?
- Most simulation software products provide a variety of interactive modes. For example, On Demand provides See It, Try It, Do It, Know It modes. Determine for yourself whether or not the level of interaction matches your business requirements.
- Does the vendor say the software is AICC and SCORM compliant? If so, have the vendor define what that means and test it with your learning management system to ensure compatibility.
- If the software application or procedures you wish to simulate are complex, determine whether the software provides advanced branching and looping capabilities. These capabilities will allow you to add simulations together and to create decision trees and branches.
- Does it provide testing capabilities?
- Does it require plug-ins in its delivery or testing modes?
- Can documents the simulation software compiles be generated in the required format, for example, Word, PDF, or HTML formats?
- Some simulation software automatically creates and positions call-out text boxes. This feature can speed development and lower costs. Determine if the simulation software requires developers to create and position notes.

Implementation

- Can the simulation be used as both a support and training tool?
- If there are several software applications that you wish to simulate, determine whether the simulation software can be used across multiple applications.

Support

- What are the estimated costs to train developers to use the software?
- What technical support is available from the vendor and how reliable is the support?

- Is there an online user group available where you can find answers to development questions?

Maintenance
- How many upgrades are included in the initial purchase license and what are the costs of ongoing upgrades?
- What maintenance is included in the original contract and what is the cost for ongoing maintenance?

Performance-centered applications are supported by software (such as SAP) that automates and integrates business processes throughout a corporation. Another example of a performance-centered application is an automatic teller machine at a bank, where you can withdraw money, make deposits, check account balances, and make payments.

PROCESS

Our development process is designed for performance support systems. There are five activities in developing web-based products:

1. Determine the type of product and platform.
2. Assemble components.
3. Conduct reviews.
4. Rehearse the presentation.
5. Conduct the session.

WEB DEVELOPMENT PROCEDURE

Follow these activities:

Activity One: Determine the Type of Product and Platform

Step one: In deciding on the type of web application and the platform, determine which of two major types of content structure for the Internet will be used: asynchronous or synchronous.

Asynchronous content is analogous to computer-based courseware delivered to the desktop on demand. The entire content is resident on a LAN or WAN and available through dial-up access and password supplied to students registered for the course.

The interactivity is sometimes different from that of computer-based training. Rather than branching to various instructional paths through menu systems like those built into CBT, interactivity and branching are achieved through using hot links (areas of the screen that, when clicked, jump the user to another place in the program) to other web pages or sites. A system of menus achieves branching to various parts within the course. Whatever the level of interactivity, a button or selection on the main menu should always appear on the screen or be readily available on every page of the course so that users can navigate back to the main menu to make other choices or exit the program.

Synchronous training means all students are online, taking the training at the same time. Interaction is possible between students, with the instructor, and with course materials through various means (including e-mail, chat rooms, telephone, faxes, scheduled conferences, video, online audio, and application sharing).

Lesson plans are constructed in the same manner as for any other instructor-led class. Plans are sequenced and time-based, indicating what happens and when it happens, rather than event-based as with CBT, where the sequence and time frame are user controlled. A lesson plan template for web-based training is in the Development and Implementation Tools section of Appendix E. Lesson plans for web-based training must be much more detailed and scripted than for live classroom training. Instructors must be much more mindful of extending verbal information on what is happening during the lesson (as examples stating that control is being turned over to a student or explaining that the instructor is now launching an application). Instructors must remember, or should assume, that the students are alone at a computer and cannot see everything that is about to happen.

Step two: Choose the development platform, language, editor, or software appropriate to your technical specifications.

Create web-based instruction by choosing one of the following means:

- A web development language, such as HTML. In this case, you need to integrate required audio, video, and animation.
- An HTML editor, consisting of a series of templates containing the necessary coding. Drag-and-drop menus allow authors to immediately begin entering content and view what the page looks like.

- An authoring system that incorporates required plug-ins (such as Attain®, Dreamweaver®, Flash®, or Macromedia's Authorware®).

- A system that incorporates a graphical user interface, such as Symposium, for online training sessions with live instructors in a virtual classroom environment.

Activity Two: Assemble Components

Create storyboards and assemble and link web pages according to the map and CDS. There is an example of a web storyboard in the Development and Implementation Tools section of Appendix E.

Activity Three: Conduct Reviews

Perform QA reviews, debug, and test the web pages for adherence to the map. (Use a machine with a web browser to test the site. Web reviews do not have the same test platform configuration issues that CBT projects normally face. The only requirement is to use the same web browser.) All of the QA reviews used in CBT should be completed. Good record keeping and file and configuration management are required.

If your solution is synchronous web-based, then complete Activity Four. If the solution is asynchronous, go directly to Activity Five. Use the Lesson Plan Template in the Development and Implementation Tools section of the CD-ROM.

Activity Four: Rehearse the Presentation

Rehearse and practice the session, adhering to the script and allotted time frames.

Step one: Have the instructor practice using the technology. Practice is particularly important because you do not want to have any "dead air time" on the monitor. Even during activities that occur at the local site, there should be a message on the screen and some appropriate, nonintrusive music.

Step two: Review clothing considerations with instructors. Blue and off-white are best. Instructors should not wear white; it glares on the camera. Reds bleed. Certain patterns (such as hounds-tooth) make wavy motions on the screen as the person moves. Instructors should not wear jewelry; it may make sounds that are magnified by the microphone. Rings may reflect the studio lighting.

Step three: Instructors follow the outline to perform a dry run with a small group at the broadcast site.

Activity Five: Conduct the Session

In conducting the session, note that maintenance is a bit more difficult for synchronous web-based sessions than it is for classroom instruction. Some additional practice sessions might need to be scheduled to integrate new material.

Step one: (This step starts before session.) Send the teaching assistants (TAs) at the student sites information regarding their roles and responsibilities.

This assumes you are going to use TAs at the sites. If not, the information should be sent directly to the participants.

TAs and participants should also receive copies of the print materials:

- A welcome letter to participants explaining as much about the course content and structure as possible
- Topical outlines delineating the amount of time to be devoted to each topic, or a workbook if appropriate
- A biographical information form for participants to complete and return
- Instructions to complete any local activity, such as creating on-screen messages, before airtime

Step two: Put the site online by using off-the-shelf web server software and a dedicated server, within the structure of your organization's intranet, or by using a commercial web service. Your implementation strategy depends on the level of technology expertise within your organization.

FROM OUR EXPERIENCE

Asynchronous Internet courses are useful even if they are more text based than CBT. What we presently accept as Internet training would likely not be tolerated in CBT. What we have learned about CBT over the last thirty years produces a shorter learning curve to bring Internet training to what we consider state-of-the-art CBT today. LANs with dedicated bandwidth for video and upgrades to computer systems to handle video and audio are probably the largest web-based investments a company makes. Once this investment is made, there is a rapid return on investment if a company delivers a lot of training.

If web applications are delivered via a company intranet, they can pose some special problems for web developers. Intranets usually have a protective "firewall" that prevents access by the general public to information proprietary to the company or organization. Special software on remote computers as well as special passwords are required to access information from outside the company's direct LAN. These requirements may entail coordination with the company's IT group and special programming expertise that is not normally resident among development-team members.

Companies considering using the Internet for training should understand the benefits and obstacles to Internet development and delivery before making a final decision. For example, bandwidth is a common obstacle. Limited bandwidth encumbers transmittal of all components (video, audio, text, and graphics). A certain amount of space is required for the components to flow, and video takes up a lot of space. To pass it through the pipeline, it must be compressed at the sending end and decompressed at the receiving end. Compression and decompression rates differ depending on the modem speed and the available bandwidth. The higher the bandwidth and modem speed, the better the decompression rates. Low decompression rates result in an effect analogous to a badly dubbed foreign film: you hear the audio, but the video doesn't match, and it looks jerky and grainy.

One way to achieve better compression and decompression rates is to have a dedicated video server. These systems are often referred to as "video-on-demand." Rather than send all the video at one time, the video is streamed in small amounts over its own part of the pipeline.

To justify the cost of the dedicated systems and equipment, a company must do a substantial amount of training. Given the typical speed of processors and the memory and storage capability of most corporate computers, video is usually too memory-intensive and takes much too long to download. Many computers do not have video cards. Video cards are available, though, and upgrades to computers can overcome this obstacle. However, upgrades must be cost-effective. Usually there is not enough usable video to make it worthwhile to upgrade a system.

Video and audio hardware issues are rapidly becoming moot points as factories install both audio and video cards in new computers. Consumer demand has driven the computer industry in this area. When the Internet was mostly an e-mail system by which users communicated more rapidly than through regular (snail) mail, there was no need for video and audio. As consumers demanded more enhancements and sophistication in software programs, hardware began to come installed with more components at the point of sale.

Overall, using the Internet is less costly than CBT for maintenance, updates, and changes to courses. Whereas changes to a CBT course often require burning new CD-ROMs and the expense and time that that entails, changes to an Internet course can be made with only minimal time required for the course to be offline. Changes to a CBT course also mean that all copies of the CD-ROM previously distributed are obsolete and may need to be replaced. Unused CDs must be scrapped.

Web-based courses are easily changed as content requires, so programs are offline far less. The turnaround time is only as long as it takes to make the changes to the parts of the content that are obsolete and put the program back online.

Business was also to some extent a driver of Internet enhancements in the 1990s. Virtual teams are rapidly replacing actual teams in a global corporate environment. With reduced profits and more competition, it is too expensive for companies to send large teams to remote sites for extended periods of time.

The Internet, coupled with videoconferencing, has allowed companies to reduce relocation expenses dramatically and still keep project teams in constant contact. Customer contact is maintained in much the same manner. There still may be times when the project team must be at the customer site, but these instances are increasingly shorter in duration and scheduled only at important milestones for the project. The Internet can thus dramatically reduce project costs in a global environment.

Well-constructed templates are invaluable in reducing development time, and therefore costs. Most web authoring systems include templates that are basic structures for integrating all HTML components. Macromedia, a San Francisco company, makes one such authoring system. Its version 5.0 of authorware has produced the Attain® enterprise learning system, a complete suite of software tools for planning, producing, administering, delivering, and reporting results from web-based training.

Attain's planner is a curriculum-building tool used to outline and organize programs. Planner supports a full range of online and traditional learning techniques, and each curriculum component can be tracked. Attain's client administrator permits access to data by course administrators and others who need information about student progress.

Dreamweaver is a visual design tool that generates HTML-based learning applications. It records student results, including scores and answers that can be stored and accessed through an administrator. It permits delivery of highly interactive and easily updated courses over low-bandwidth connections. Dreamweaver also contains "wizards," called "knowledge objects," preprogrammed templates that can be dragged onto the authoring flow line and opened, to which content can be added immediately. The programming is done for the author.

HTML acts somewhat like word processing software, where the author can change the size, style, color, and position of fonts. Simple, non-proportional fonts are best because complicated fonts may be degraded if the computer on the user's end does not have complex fonts resident. Text can be graphical in form, but graphical text can demand a lot of memory and be slow to download. Usually you need to save the memory and downloading for graphics, video, and so on.

Graphics with nearly any file name extension (.BMP, .CGM, .PCX, and so on) can be converted to graphic interchange format (GIF) files for incorporation into web courseware. GIF reduces graphic file sizes but retains up to 256 colors. Microsoft PowerPoint® graphics can also be formatted into GIF files.

Photographs and artwork requiring more than 256 colors can be incorporated into HTML using JPEG (joint photographic expert group) files. JPEG permits near-paper-quality visual output if the end user's computer monitor and display card have the capability to reproduce them. Animation can be created using Macromedia's Shockwave®, which strings together individually created graphic files.

Video is shot and converted to a digital format and accessed by the computer from the file server or the CD-ROM as it is required. The user must have the correct player for the type of video file. Video plug-ins are often available from the web browser.

Audio is recorded as for any other delivery, converted to .WAV or other digital sound files, and stored on the LAN or CD-ROM. The user must have the correct player for the type of audio file. Sound plug-ins are often available from the web browser.

Instructions should include prompt boxes stating the type of plug-in required for the program and the location on the web where the plug-in can be accessed and downloaded.

Branching can occur using hot links within the course, but additionally, hyperlinks can connect to other web pages and Internet sites. Although linking to other sites cuts down on the amount of development required, it presents a maintenance issue. If the developer does not have control over the sites linked to, there may be problems as sites are removed from the Internet, URLs (universal resource locators) change, or content may change. If you control the websites you link to, this issue is less of a problem.

SUMMARY

Designing training for the web follows the same ID process as with any other medium:

- A framework of templates, specifications, and standards is used.
- Media elements that fit into the framework are inserted.
- Review and revision cycles ensure quality.

In implementing the finished product, take into account web limitations and considerations during development. In the final analysis, we believe that companies that are not putting the infrastructure in place for Internet training development and delivery will be left in the dust.

Developing Interactive Distance Broadcast Environments

Distance learning is a generic term for any training that is delivered from one central location to multiple, remote sites simultaneously. Distance learning may take the form of satellite broadcast or video teleconferencing or a combination of phone and video strategies. We use the term *interactive distance broadcast* (IDB) training to be inclusive of all types of distance learning, whether by satellite or over telephone lines.

Interactive distance learning is somewhat of a misnomer, since often it's neither "interactive" nor involving much "learning" in the instructional sense—unless you consider "online lecture" and "learning" to be the same. However, it does travel over a distance. For all of its promise, often all that is seen is a talking head with an occasional break for some sort of graphic. Although there are many capabilities in IDB for interaction between the talking head and the listener at the remote site—say, through fax, telephone, or even keypads that permit people to buzz in with questions—they are still often under-utilized. There is much unfulfilled potential for combining this medium with other communications media and innovative designs. Figure 25.1 shows one type of keypad produced by ONETOUCH Systems, Inc., which has good interaction capabilities.

There are many design, development, delivery, and maintenance issues to consider with interactive distance broadcast systems. Many of the considerations are

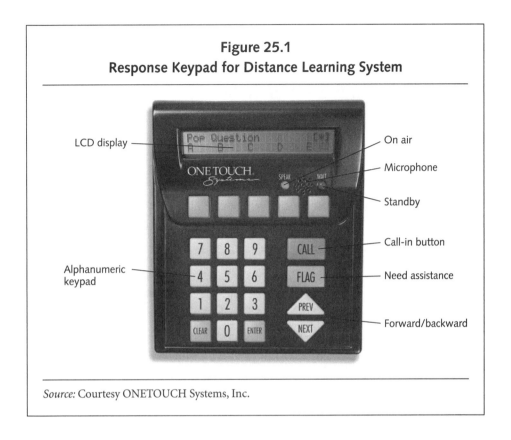

Figure 25.1
Response Keypad for Distance Learning System

LCD display

On air

Microphone

Standby

Call-in button

Alphanumeric keypad

Need assistance

Forward/backward

Source: Courtesy ONETOUCH Systems, Inc.

the same as for classroom learning environments. However, the number of sites does add other considerations, such as coordination and scheduling issues across time zones.

The concerns for video and audio production are much the same as those covered in Chapter Twenty-Two.

PROCESS

There are four activities in the procedure of developing an IDB course:

1. Develop script and materials.

2. Shoot and edit video.

3. Rehearse the presentation.

4. Broadcast the session.

DISTANCE BROADCAST ENVIRONMENT PROCEDURE

Follow these activities:

Activity One: Develop Script and Materials

To develop the script and materials, use the delivery and instructional strategies determined in the design phase (see Part Two).

Keep these points in mind while creating the materials for the IDB:

- Overheads should have no more than thirty characters per line, with a maximum of nine lines per image. You must match the aspect of the camera, which has a ratio of three high to four wide. Do not use extremely vertical images or portrait-view paper.

- Keep text in the "safe zone." Remember that a television monitor is wider and shorter than an 8 1/2-inch by 11-inch sheet of paper, and leave margins of at least an inch to accommodate a border on all sides.

- Minimize the need to write on blank overheads or on flip charts. For the best use of visuals, prepare them ahead of time and test them in advance to see how they look on camera. If you must write while on camera:

    Use manuscript print instead of cursive.

    Use medium-thick, dark markers.

- When you use flip charts:

    Use inexpensive off-white or light blue paper.

    Paper lined in light blue keeps on-screen writing from running uphill.

    Cut the paper to fit the on-screen format.

    Anchor paper so it does not move around.

- When you create slides, use large-size print and simple fonts. Titles should be 30 point or greater. Use no less than 20 points for bullets. Bold face makes text legible.

- When you use handouts:

    Do not have a lot of text on a handout.

    Fax, make handouts available online, or send the materials to participants before the session.

- In storyboarding the session:

    Consider opening with an activity to break free of the idea that participants are watching television. Something as simple as asking a question and having participants respond using the keypad is enough to get the point across. Use the Lesson Plan Template in the Development and Implementation Tools section of the CD-ROM.

    Keep formal lecture periods short. Avoid the "talking head."

Activity Two: Shoot and Edit Video

Shoot the video, edit it, and test additional media elements according to the script and course-development standards. It's a good idea to have a detailed outline indicating when supplemental media such as video, overheads, and so on are to be inserted in the course. It's also important to list when exercises occur and what specific questions to ask.

Activity Three: Rehearse the Presentation

Rehearse and practice the session, adhering to the script and allotted time frames.

Step one: Have the instructor practice using the technology. Practice is particularly important because you do not want to have any "dead" air time on the monitor. Even during activities that occur at the local site, there should be a message on the screen and some appropriate, non-intrusive music.

Step two: Review clothing considerations with instructors. Blue and off-white are best. Instructors should not wear white; it glares on the camera. Reds bleed. Certain patterns (such as hounds-tooth) make wavy motions on the screen as the person moves. Instructors should not wear jewelry; it may make sounds that are magnified by the microphone. Rings may reflect the studio lighting.

Step three: Instructors follow the outline to perform a dry run with a small group at the broadcast site.

Activity Four: Broadcast the Session

Note that maintenance is a bit more difficult for IDB than for classroom instruction. Some additional practice sessions might need to be scheduled to integrate new material.

Send the teaching assistants (TAs) at the student sites information regarding their roles and responsibilities. (This is done before the session.)

> This assumes you are going to use TAs at the sites. If not, the information should be sent directly to the participants.

TAs and participants should also receive copies of the print materials:

- A welcome letter to participants explaining as much about the course content and structure as possible
- Topical outlines delineating the amount of time to be devoted to each topic, or a workbook if appropriate
- A biographical information form for participants to complete and return
- Instructions to complete any local activity, such as creating on-screen messages, before airtime

FROM OUR EXPERIENCE

When used correctly, IDB can create the atmosphere of a small class while delivering instruction to a large number of people at one time.

If a satellite is used, cost is a significant factor. The costs to uplink to a satellite and downlink to remote locations can be significant (in the thousands of dollars for one hour of broadcast time). However, cost is becoming less of a factor for other forms of interactive distance learning. Barron (1999), in an issue of the journal *Technical Training* called "Interactive Distance Learning: Special Report," addresses technological advances and the increasing feasibility of distance education.

Video teleconferencing is less expensive because it uses telephone lines and television technology. However, this also requires a significant investment. There are many good commercial production houses capable of providing a turnkey solution that includes cameras, televisions, wiring, instructor stations, student stations, and instructor training.

There is justification for having two-way video as well as audio. A student with a question might display his or her work to the instructor, who can then give corrective feedback. Two-way video adds another dimension to student-instructor interaction and personalization of the training.

The return on investment for interactive distance broadcasting should be justified by analysis, as discussed in Part One. But media analysis is only the beginning. It then depends on the creativity and imagination of the instructional designers to have IDB reach its full potential.

The design and development options vary widely, depending on available hardware. IDB often consists of one-way video and two-way audio. The students can see and hear the instructor; the instructor can hear the students. Depending on the course design, this arrangement may still permit a great deal of interaction. If it's designed to be interactive, it will be. If designed as a lecture, it will be. The same considerations, including physical room arrangement, apply to IDB as well as classroom environments.

Design and development time is often longer than for classroom training. Much more thought and detail must be included in instructor manuals regarding when to

- Display graphics
- Ask questions
- Switch cameras
- Move from camera to overhead or video

Time must also be included in the schedule for practice sessions so the instructor can become familiar and comfortable with the materials and the equipment. Pilot sessions for the training, desirable for most media, are almost mandatory for IDB.

If you are delivering over a great and varied distance, time zones are a big consideration. For example, if you're transmitting live in New York at 12:00 noon, it's 12:00 midnight in Singapore. It is inevitable that someone will have to be inconvenienced, but try to set start times that best fit the majority.

Instruction can also be arranged around breaks. For example, an instructor begins a session with a group at 9:00 A.M. Central time. At 11:00 A.M. Central, the instructor assigns an activity that lasts ninety minutes. The participants in the Central time zone complete the assignment and then go to lunch from 12:30 till 1:30 P.M. A group in the Pacific time zone thus begins this session at 7:00 A.M. Pacific time (9:00 A.M. Central time). The Pacific group works on the activity at 9:00 A.M. Pacific and goes to lunch from 10:30 A.M. to 11:30 A.M. The entire group comes back at what is 1:30 A.M. Central or 11:30 A.M. Pacific.

Larger time-zone differences require more complicated arrangements. There is also always a taping and playback option, but this takes away interactivity with the instructor. However, the presentation can be stopped to answer questions and complete activities if TAs are at the student sites.

SUMMARY

The essence of interactive distance broadcast training is well-orchestrated, instructor-led training. Design should focus on well-conceived interactions and integrated media. Implementation requires an instructor who is always aware of the audience, the technology, and the content.

If creatively designed, video and audio teleconferencing over television and telephone lines have great potential to obtain and maintain interactivity. These forms of delivery may be the most underrated and overlooked media available today. The technology is relatively inexpensive compared to using satellite broadcast and is easier to use.

Multimedia Evaluation

Introduction to Multimedia Evaluation

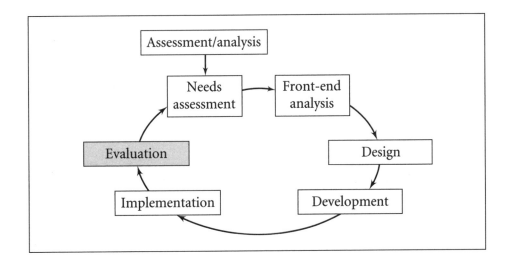

Congratulations! You've just made your delivery date, after many long hours and much hard work. The solution is now installed and it's being used. "What a relief," you say—but it's only for a few seconds. Suddenly you're called in to your manager's office and given another assignment (as a reward for a job well done). Actually, what you need is a month off to recover from this one!

You really do derive a certain satisfaction from a job well done. But if you ever had the time to reflect on what's been done, you might want to know if what you developed is truly effective in teaching the skills needed to do the job the solution was developed for.

You have given feedback in the course to reinforce the learning of the students so they can improve. Well, just as feedback keeps students on track, feedback on your design and the effectiveness of the solution helps you improve the next project.

But if this requirement isn't in the contract and you're on to the next project, then you put feedback in the back of your mind. We want to bring those thoughts to the foreground and have them nag you a bit.

If you have completed all of the activities during assessment, analysis, design, and development, then *formative evaluation*—which is all about quality—is completed. Now you are ready for *summative evaluation,* to judge the effectiveness of the solution.

Evaluation is typically what we do worst. The causes of poor measurement stem from lack of knowledge or lack of attention, or both. Knowing what to measure and how to do it to target the data that yields relevant information is a process requiring careful thought by persons with highly specialized skills. Your evaluation design may be very sound, but something as simple as choosing the wrong measure of what you are trying to prove may cause you to find significant levels of learning where there is none, or no learning where there actually is some.

Part Four of this book explains summative evaluation from four perspectives: establishing an evaluation strategy, developing an evaluation plan, developing accurate measurement instruments such as tests and observation instruments, and applying appropriate statistical measures to the instruments for the purpose of analyzing results.

Donald Kirkpatrick (1994) identified four levels of evaluation. We have summarized the four levels in Table 26.1, labeling them slightly differently from how Kirkpatrick does. (His levels are reaction, learning, behavior, and results.)

The four levels of evaluation are highly interdependent. For example, it's important to determine the positive reaction to a course before starting to measure improved performance. The same goes for determining improved performance before measuring ROI.

<table>
<tr><td colspan="3" align="center">**Table 26.1**
Levels of Evaluation</td></tr>
</table>

Level 1	Reaction	Measures participant's response to the activity in the form of impressions about the relevance of the activity in enabling them to fulfill the duties of their jobs
Level 2	Knowledge	Measures increased level of achievement of the content and skills intended by the activity
Level 3	Performance	Measures change in behavior or attitude as a result of using the knowledge and skills of the activity transferred to the job over a period of time
Level 4	Impact	Measures the impact on the business in the form of return on investment (ROI) from the activity

Certain skills are outside the scope of this book. Therefore, we don't cover statistics, statistical analysis, interpretation, or conducting research studies. There is, however, an Evaluation Glossary at the end of Appendix D to clarify some of the technical terms used in evaluation.

E-LEARNING'S IMPACT ON EVALUATION

One area that is a particular challenge in the web environment is testing. In the traditional model, tests could be used to judge the knowledge gained from a training event. In the virtual environment, the model must change. Unless tests are monitored in a secure testing environment, there can be no certainty about who is taking the test and whose knowledge is being evaluated. The model that needs to emerge is that tests no longer evaluate knowledge gains. Tests should only be used as self-assessments to provide feedback to the learners about their own progress. Level 3 testing (observing and monitoring performance on the job) is the level where developers must look to determine the knowledge gained. If students can do the job now and you know they couldn't before or if you can observe the improved results, the training must have had some impact.

Even certification must be rethought. Courses can no longer be used to certify competency unless they are administered in a testing environment that is monitored. Other options to testing are observation forms signed by the employee's manger, customer, or someone who is on-site and able to make accurate judgments or review the end result.

Rather than track scores, designs must incorporate tracking such things as time in a module or segment, time on an activity, time on test, time on a screen, frequency of access, frequently asked questions or help desk queries, error rates, number and types of requests for additional information or coaching, and level of participation. None of these items alone can provide valuable information but, used together, they can provide indicators of impact. Since the purpose of e-learning is to reach a distributed audience, it often is not feasible to send observers to the field, but it is possible to monitor results.

FROM OUR EXPERIENCE

During the 1980s and early 1990s, instructional designers and developers hoped that customers wouldn't ask for evaluation. Since the late 1990s, they have tried to convince customers they don't need it when they ask for it. ASTD's *State of the Industry Report* (2002) found that very few companies use the upper two levels of evaluation to measure the success of training or other solutions.

Yet, customers are increasingly more sophisticated about evaluation and are asking for evaluation. Therefore, the days are rapidly coming to an end when developers can abdicate responsibility for the effectiveness of the solutions they create. Development groups that are not willing to stand behind their products are subliminally telling customers they don't have confidence in what they are doing.

Purpose of Evaluation

Subjective criteria continue to be used to evaluate the worth of individuals. Students go through school making decisions about life choices based on grades derived from invalid measures.

The trend carries over into adult education and training. Many businesses use evaluations to determine salary increases, promotion, and employees' career paths according to criteria just as subjective as those used by teachers in schools.

Meanwhile, little or none of this evaluation is held up to the scrutiny of criterion-referenced and norm-referenced measurement principles to establish congruence between the amount of knowledge gained (indicated by test scores) and one's ability to perform the job better. In essence, evaluation is failing people rather than people failing evaluations.

Much has been written about applying Kirkpatrick's four levels of evaluation (1994). Borg and Gall (1996), Shrock, Coscarelli, and Eyres (1996), Campbell and Stanley (1963), Phillips (1997) and Martuza (1977) are leaders in the field of measurement, evaluation, and testing, whose perspectives form the backbone of Kirkpatrick's levels. The model presented here synthesizes the work of all of these experts.

The model is based on the principle that the level of evaluation must be connected primarily to the purpose and intended use of the results of the evaluation.

PROCESS

Assessing the appropriate amount of evaluation required involves one activity: determining the purpose of the solution. Table 27.1 shows the variables of the decision-making process; each is explained in the steps of this activity.

Table 27.1
Evaluation Matrix

Measurement Variable	Purpose	Low Validity		Test Item Validity		High Validity
		Face Validity	Content Validity	Distractor Analysis	Correlation	Predictive Validity
Organizational needs	Return on investment	▓	▓	▓	▓	▓
	Improved workforce	▓	▓	▓	▓	▓
	Regulatory requirements	▓	▓	▓	▓	▓
	EEOC requirements	▓	▓	▓	▓	▓
Individual needs	Promotion	▓	▓	▓	▓	▓
	Professional development	▓	▓	▓	▓	▓
	Improved performance	▓	▓	▓		
	Increased knowledge	▓	▓	▓		
	Self-improvement	▓				

▓ indicates level of validity required.

PURPOSE OF EVALUATION PROCEDURE

Follow this activity:

Activity One: Determine the Purpose of the Solution

Step one: Determine whether the measurement variables are organizational or individual.

If the variables are organizational goals, determine whether the organization is getting a return on investment that justifies the amount of money spent on developing and implementing the solution. To determine this:

- Collect data on the cost of the solution the customer was delivering before implementation of the new solution, and compare that information to data collected over a period of time after the new solution is implemented.

- If there are no data available about the previous solution, collect as much information as you can on costs of the previous solution while you are developing the new solution. Using the information gathered before the new solution is implemented and comparing it to data gathered for a period of several months after, you can predict the effectiveness of the solution over yet other extended periods of time. Actual data plus your predictions determine how long it will take for the intervention to pay for itself.

Determine whether or not the solution results in an improved workforce to accomplish the organizational goals. An improved workforce with higher levels of skill can get the job done better, faster, and more economically. Both speed and economy can be investigated separately, but increased speed at a sacrifice of improved performance is usually not a desirable outcome.

Determine also whether the solution produces employees who are aware of government regulatory requirements, such as those imposed by the banking industry regulatory body, the Securities and Exchange Commission (SEC), the airline industry's Federal Aviation Administration (FAA), and the Occupational Safety and Health Administration (OSHA) in manufacturing.

Is the level of validity required by the regulations satisfied if the employees are simply aware of the regulations? Or must they be able to perform a skill or task as a result? The answer to this question determines the level of validity that the solution must achieve.

Finally, find out whether the solution complies with EEOC guidelines (Equal Employment Opportunity Commission, 1978) on fair employment practices and nondiscrimination.

Step two: Identify the measurement variables that are individual rather than organizational.

With variables designed to measure individual traits, you must be able to prove that the traits accurately predict individual performance and that the solution used to impart knowledge and skills is valid. This is particularly important if the training is part of a career ladder required for an employee to advance in a company, or if the training is incorporated into a performance appraisal.

Does the solution provide the skills necessary for employees to successfully complete the job into which they will be promoted?

Can you predict that employees' professional development will increase as a result of successfully completing the developmental activities? The activities might include training, but could also be much broader in scope.

Does the training predict improved performance from successful completion? If so, it can therefore be incorporated into a development plan for the purpose of granting merit pay increases.

Determine whether increased performance has occurred after the training. These skills may be documented in the form of a performance appraisal. This information lets the employer know that the training is effective in having employees better prepared to do their jobs.

Note that performance appraisals should not be used as the basis for granting merit increases or incentive compensation. Merit and incentives should be attached to professional development plans that have goals with associated accomplishments and timelines attached.

Determine whether the training results in increased knowledge and skills based on a standard measurement. Again, note that training designed to increase knowledge need only document that those who complete such training comprehend or understand the information offered by the training. There is no condition or implication of being able to perform better based on the content.

Finally, does the training result in self-improvement on the basis of the individual's own perceptions? Courses designed for self-improvement purposes require only that those who take the course believe that they have more knowledge or skills as a result of taking the training.

Step three: Determine whether the solution will be used commercially. Commercial products to be used off the shelf have their own unique qualities and require specific mention. Because many products targeted for commercial use are developed by training-and-development companies that then resell them, the producer cannot be certain how the product will be used. Therefore it's imperative that commercially developed products (1) be validated to the highest level (predictive validity); (2) specify the level of validity in the course documentation; or (3) translate the level of validity into terms that explain how and what the solution can be used for.

FROM OUR EXPERIENCE

Careful consideration of the purpose for which a solution is being developed is the first step toward accurate evaluation. We find both extremes; either the mention of the word evaluation sends people fleeing from the room or else they decide to kill a fly with a wrecking ball. Too little and too much evaluation are both wasteful.

Evaluation requires time and resources that translate into lengthened project schedules and increased cost. Be certain the expense is worth the cost and time.

SUMMARY

You now know the purpose of evaluation and whether your solution should be measured on an organizational or an individual level. Knowing the purpose of evaluation, you can now develop an evaluation strategy for your organization and evaluation plans for each project you decide to evaluate.

Evaluation Strategy

Y ou need to begin with a clear plan in mind of what your organization's evaluation strategy is going to be. What level of evaluations are you going to use and how will you measure them? What will your resources be to provide guidance about how to build evaluation into each solution developed?

Figure 28.1 shows the four components of an overall strategy. The much larger component is an overall *learning strategy*. A learning strategy lays out an organization's overall philosophy about what it wants to achieve by providing learning to its employees.

A second component is an *e-learning strategy* that is a subset of the learning strategy. The e-learning strategy outlines what technology the company needs to invest in, or is willing to invest in, to deliver learning. The e-learning strategy uncovers the technology infrastructure capabilities that will be used to fully implement the learning strategy, as well as what talent and skills will have to be acquired or developed to implement e-learning.

The *evaluation strategy* is the third component. It outlines how the other two components will be measured and against what criteria (such as improved performance or return-on-investment). Component four is an *evaluation plan* (covered in Chapter Twenty-Nine) that is developed for each individual project within the learning strategy.

The learning strategy and e-learning strategy are beyond the scope of this book. We recommend William Horton's series of books published by ASTD (see the ASTD bookstore at www.astd.org). What we will provide here is a process and tools for developing an evaluation strategy.

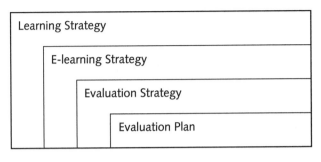

**Figure 28.1
Components of a Learning Strategy**

Learning Strategy

E-learning Strategy

Evaluation Strategy

Evaluation Plan

PROCESS

There are three activities to complete to form an evaluation strategy:

1. Write an introduction regarding the philosophy, purpose, and need for an evaluation strategy.

2. Determine the requirements to evaluate the results.

3. Determine what your sources of information will be from which you draw your strategy.

EVALUATION STRATEGY PROCEDURE

Follow these activities:

Activity One: Write an Introduction

What is the rationale or reason for the need for an evaluation strategy? What are the components?

Activity Two: Determine the Evaluation Requirements

Consider the following:

- How to implement the evaluation strategy
- What to measure
- How to measure it

- How data will be validated
- How data will be collected, analyzed, and used
- System that will be used to analyze the data

Activity Three: Determine Sources

Compile a list of resources for expertise (books, journals, vendors, and/or conferences) that everyone must become knowledgeable about.

Appendix E includes an Evaluation Strategy Form; a completed example for a company called Training and Consulting Softek is found in Appendix D.

SUMMARY

An overall strategy that everyone understands and follows is critical to performing quality evaluations. A strategy allows developers to build evaluation into every solution. The next chapter, Evaluation Plan, shows how to make decisions for each solution based on the overall strategy.

Evaluation Plan

Each project needs an evaluation plan that outlines exactly how and to what level the project will be evaluated. An evaluation plan should be developed at the end of the analysis phase or at the beginning of the design phase so that all project team members can build the evaluation into each component of the project as it progresses. A template for an evaluation plan can be found in the Evaluation Tools section of Appendix E.

PROCESS

Complete the following activities for an evaluation plan:

1. Complete the problem statement section.
2. Complete the solution section.
3. Complete the objectives section.
4. Complete the components of the evaluation plan for each level at which you will evaluate the project.
5. Complete the executive summary.

EVALUATION PLAN PROCEDURE

Follow these activities:

Activity One: Complete the Problem Statement Section

Step one: Clearly state the rationale for addressing this issue. What problem is it causing for the organization? This might be the gap that was discovered at the end of assessment.

Step two: Describe the gap between the present and the desired state. Describe the desired state.

Activity Two: Complete the Solution Section

Describe the solution (from the analysis stage) for bridging the gap.

Activity Three: Complete the Objectives Section

State the desired performance outcomes. What will be improved when the solution is implemented?

Activity Four: Complete the Pertinent Components of the Evaluation Plan

Complete the plan for each level at which you will evaluate the project. Here are the varying levels and the questions that must be answered:

Level 1: Reaction

- Survey construction—the content of the survey

  What parts of the solution do you want information about?

  Are there supplemental materials for which you want to determine usefulness and quality?

  Are these activities viewed as valuable to the content?

  Do you want to gather information on the quality and performance of facilitators or onsite assistants?

  When will the surveys be administered? Only at the end or after certain parts of the solution have been viewed?

  Will there be experimental and control groups, and will the groups be administered a different or the same survey?

  Do you need demographic information?

  Do you want to match demographics to certain types of responses on the survey to determine whether certain participants have different reactions to certain aspects of the solution than others?

- Data collection—the methods and systems that will be used to collect data

  Will the surveys be online, paper-based, or scannable forms?

  How will data from the survey be captured?

  What type of measurement scale will be used?

  Where and how will data be stored and retrieved and by whom?

- Data analysis—the types of information needed from the data and the systems that will be used

  Which responses will be compared to other responses to determine the significance of data? (For example, you might compare demographic information to the content to determine how people of varying ages, gender, or ethnic background react to it.)

  How will responses be tabulated (averaged, summed, levels of significance)?

- Expected results—the changes in reaction to the content, the solution, and so forth, that you want to see before and after the solution is viewed

  What are acceptable levels of change?

  Are different results expected from varying demographic groups?

- Reporting results—format and use of the information

  How will the information be reported and distributed and by whom?

  Will reports be paper or electronic?

  Will there be a meeting to review results? If so, who will coordinate that meeting and how will it be conducted?

  How will questions be handled and decisions from the meetings implemented?

Level 2: Knowledge

- Test construction—the form of the testing instruments

  Will there be a test?

  How many forms of the test will there be?

  When will tests be administered?

How will tests be weighted?

Do you need to collect demographic information? If so, what information?

Will you use experimental and control groups?

Will both groups receive the same test?

Will the tests be pre and/or post?

Will the tests be prescriptive or diagnostic?

Will the tests be online or paper-based?

What type of questions will be used, and why is that form the best for measuring the knowledge gained from this solution?

- Data collection—how data will be collected

Will the data be automatically transferred to an electronic database or will paper tests have to be mailed to a central location?

If mailing, who is responsible for sending and who will receive them?

Will data be hand-entered into a system and what will that system be?

- Data analysis—the information desired from the tests

Are you looking for trends of improvement and/or cutoff scores?

If you are running a pilot test, are you conducting distractor analysis and determining the standard error of measurement and standard deviation?

What statistical test are you using to measure data? Is the statistical test appropriate for this test instrument?

- Expected results—the improvement you want to see

How much improvement do you expect to find?

Do you expect to find varying results from different demographic groups?

- Reporting results—format and use of the information

How will the information be reported and distributed and by whom? Will reports be paper or electronic?

Will there be a meeting to review results? If so, who will coordinate that meeting and how will it be conducted?

How will questions be handled and decisions from the meetings implemented?

Level 3: Performance

- Observation study construction—the form of the observation study

  What will be the format of the observation instruments?

  How are the instruments validated?

  Will you conduct inter-rater agreement? How and when?

  When will the observations take place?

  How will observations be conducted?

  How will observations be weighted?

  Do you need to collect demographic information? If so, what information?

  Will you observe performers before and/or after the solution is viewed?

  At what time period after participants view or complete the solution will the observation take place?

  Will you use experimental and control groups?

  Will both the experimental and control groups receive the same observation and at the same time?

  Will you observe the same group before and after using the solution?

  What type of observation will be used, and why is that form the best for measuring successful performance?

- Data collection—the way the observation will be made

  Will the observations be direct, through hidden cameras, by videotape, or by looking at the end result that the solution was designed to change?

  Who will make the observations and what are their qualifications?

  How will observers be trained?

  What will be the interaction between the observer and the performer?

  What type of instructions and information do observers provide the performer, if any?

- Data analysis—the information desired from the observation

    Are you looking for trends of improvement and/or minimal performance?

    What statistical test are you using to measure results?

    Is the statistical measure appropriate for this instrument?

- Expected results—the improvement you want to see

    How much improvement do you expect to find?

    Do you expect to find varying results from different demographic groups?

- Reporting results—format and use of the information

    How will the information be reported and distributed and by whom?
    Will they be paper or electronic?

    What were the anticipated results?

    What were the unanticipated results? What occurred that may have caused these results?

    Will there be a meeting to review results? If so, who will coordinate that meeting and how will it be conducted?

    How will questions be handled and decisions from the meetings be implemented?

Level 4: Impact

- Study construction—the form of the study

    What calculations will go into the ROI formula?

    What elements of cost will be included? Which will be excluded and WHY?

    What variables may intervene that you cannot control in your study? How will you account for them in your results?

    Will you gather data on the costs associated with lost opportunity, productivity, and so on, for comparison before and after the solution is implemented?

- Data collection—sources of data

  What data is available and where can it be located?

  Who will collect the data and how?

  How accurate is the data? How will you compensate for incomplete or inaccurate data?

- Data analysis—how the data will be calculated

  Use the formula for ROI in Chapter Thirteen.

- Expected results—the improvement you want to see

  How much ROI did you expect to find based on the cost-benefit analysis you conducted? Were the CBA and ROI close? If not, what unanticipated factors caused the disparity?

- Reporting results—format and use of the information

  How will the information be reported and distributed and by whom? Will the report be paper or electronic?

  What were the anticipated results?

  What were the unanticipated results? What occurred that may have caused these results?

  Will there be a meeting to review results? If so, who will coordinate that meeting and how will it be conducted?

  How will questions be handled and decisions from the meetings implemented?

Activity Five: Complete the Executive Summary

Step one: Briefly state the problem. This statement should be a brief summarization of the problem statement section.

Step two: Briefly describe the solution. This statement should be a brief summarization of the solution section.

Figure 29.1 is a flowchart of the evaluation plan process.

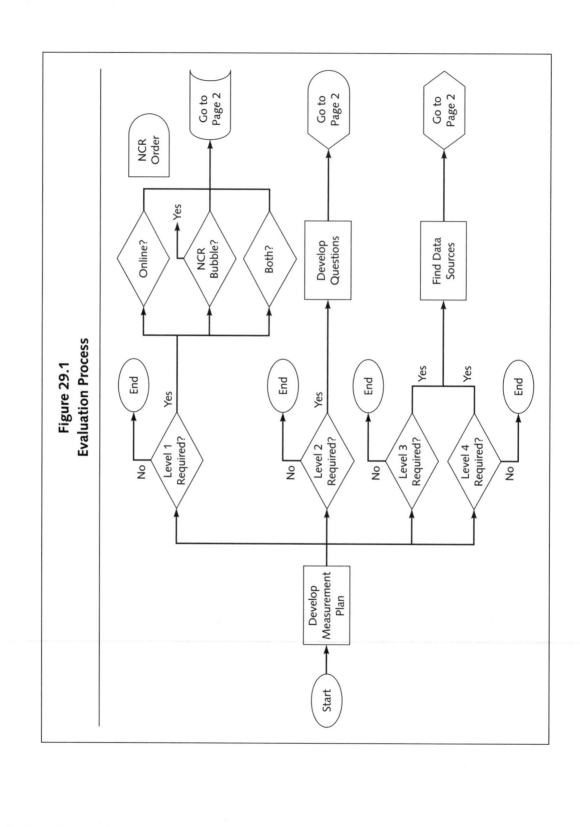

Figure 29.1
Evaluation Process

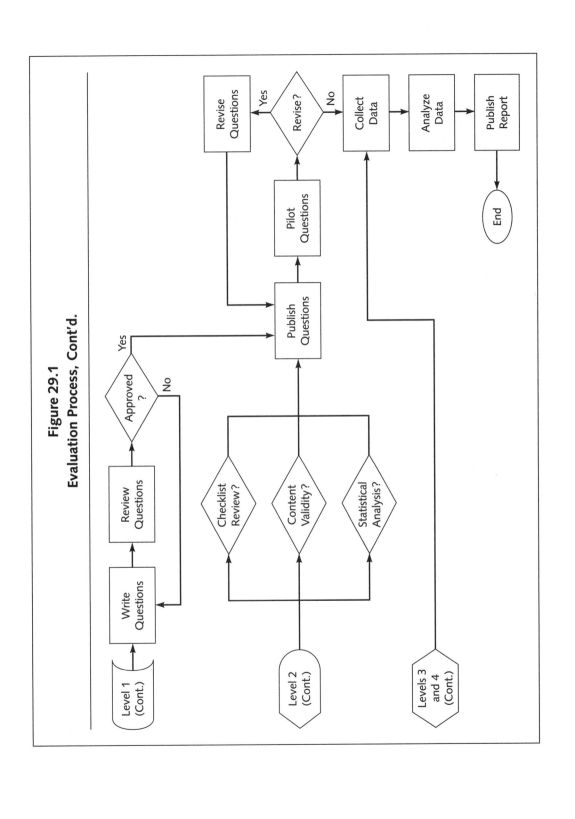

**Figure 29.1
Evaluation Process, Cont'd.**

FROM OUR EXPERIENCE

Don't try to measure every project at the highest level. Set measurement targets. For example, if you are an internal training group or corporate university and maintain a certain number of curricula, you might set a goal of having 100 percent of all your offerings include a Level 1 evaluation within ten months. You may decide to have 75 percent of your offerings attached to a Level 2 knowledge test within twelve months (but only those offerings where a knowledge test makes sense). You may decide to evaluate 25 percent of your offerings with a Level 3 evaluation within the next twelve months and conduct two Level 4 evaluations within the next year.

Be certain that you choose solutions that are corporate initiatives for the Level 4 evaluation, as these fit into the corporate goals and will receive the most recognition when you show a positive ROI.

SUMMARY

Chapters Twenty-Eight and Twenty-Nine outlined how to develop an evaluation strategy and an evaluation plan. The remaining chapters explain how to construct the components of an evaluation plan. Information in these chapters will include specifically how to develop a survey, a test, an observation, or an impact study and how to analyze the data that go into the evaluation plan.

chapter THIRTY

Measures of Validity

Now that you have determined why you want to evaluate, you can construct the instruments to assess that purpose. But before you construct the instruments, you must determine how to estimate whether they actually measure what they are designed to measure. Proper measurement is the test of validity. Test validity is established though statistical testing.

RELATED THEORY

Face validity establishes that a course teaches what it is intended to teach. Face validity is relatively easy to establish, but should be attempted before too much development is completed because experts may have suggestions to change and improve the product. We recommend that face validity be established during the first stages of the development phase, when the content is organized.

Content validity of the course material is established through the technical content review cycles conducted during development, so you need to establish test item content validity during evaluation, if it was not established during the development phase, when you were incorporating the measurement instruments into the solution. Test questions are harder to change after they are online than when they are on paper, so establish content validity immediately after questions are written.

Inter-rater agreement is established through practice by having evaluators view the same performance task (either live or on videotape) and rate the tasks using the validated checklist. You can use a norm-referenced statistical test here to determine inter-rater agreement—a t-test of statistical significance. If you establish an inter-rater correlation coefficient of +.90 or higher, you have a high degree of inter-rater agreement (+.95 is excellent); again, the criticality of what the raters are observing determines the degree of inter-rater agreement you need. Higher levels of agreement take more training and longer to achieve. However, evaluators should be retrained regularly if their evaluations occur over an extended period of time because the number of students they observe over time can affect their judgment.

PROCESS

Lee, Roadman, and Mamone (1990) recommend a process for establishing validity that has three activities:

1. Determine the level and type of validity required.
2. Determine when to validate measurement instruments.
3. Document your decisions.

MEASURES OF VALIDITY PROCEDURE

Follow these activities:

Activity One: Determine the Level and Type of Validity Required

The type of validity required for the intended use of the product can be found using Table 29.1. Types of validity are defined in Table 30.1.

Activity Two: Determine When to Validate Measurement Instruments

Examples of the various validity requirements and the corresponding phase of the instructional design process are found in Table 30.1.

Activity Three: Document Your Decisions

Document your decisions on the Test Item Validity tool found on the CD-ROM under Evaluation Tools and include it in the test plan section of the course design specification that you created during the design phase.

Table 30.1

Types of Validity and When They Are Established

Type of Validity	Level of Validity	How to Accomplish It	Importance	Phase
Face validity	Low	Formative evaluation, where experts review the course materials and validate that the course content approximates what a course on this subject should teach	Minimum validity required to establish that a course teaches what it intends to teach or that a test measures what it claims to measure	Design or development
Content validity	Low	Formative evaluation, where experts review the course materials and validate that there is congruence between the objectives, content, and test items	Minimum validity required if the course is used for certification of competence in a subject	Design
Concurrent validity	Medium	Quantitative summative evaluation, measure of the similarities between two tests	Establishes test item validity	Evaluation

Table 30.1

Types of Validity and When They Are Established, Cont'd.

Type of Validity	Level of Validity	How to Accomplish It	Importance	Phase
Construct validity	Medium	Quantitative summative evaluation, measure of relationship between scores on a test and job performance	Establishes positive relationship between test questions and the actual job performed	Evaluation
Test item validity	Medium	Quantitative formative or summative evaluation, measure of the relationship between individual questions and the overall test	Gives a high degree of confidence that test items accurately measure skills	Design evaluation
Predictive validity	High	Quantitative summative evaluation, measure of the ability of a test to predict future success in a skill area	Establishes validity of a test and ensures that a test positively correlates with the job performance it claims to measure (short-term); establishes reliability of a test or course (long-term)	Evaluation
Inter-rater agreement	High	Quantitative formative or summative evaluation, measure of the ability of raters to agree on successful performance of a task	Establishes the confidence level that independent observations are consistent among raters	Assessment and analysis or evaluation

FROM OUR EXPERIENCE

You can measure the reaction (Kirkpatrick's level 1 evaluation) to a course by using surveys (sometimes referred to as "smile sheets"). If you are going to use reaction surveys, tailor each to the objectives for the solution. A specific question such as, "Did the course teach you to interact more effectively with co-workers?" generates substantially better information than the question, "Did the course meet your expectations?" In the second question, you don't know what information you are getting because you don't know what the respondent's expectations were! Table 30.2 compares the type of survey questions found on "smile sheets" and on objectives-based surveys.

Table 30.2
Comparison of Survey Question Types

Smile Sheets	Objectives-Based Surveys
Did the course meet your expectations?	Did the course keep your attention and interest?
How would you rate the instructor?	Was the instructor able to answer questions to your satisfaction?
Did the course meet the stated objectives?	Do you feel you know how to register a customer for our services?
Were the activities valuable?	Did the role-playing activity on handling difficult customers provide information you can use on the job?
Were the course materials valuable?	Did the participant handbook contain information that added value to the class?
Was the room comfortable?	The temperature in the room was (a) too warm, (b) just right, (c) too cold

Knowledge tests require differing levels of validity, depending on the intended use of the test. Performance tests require methods for validity similar to those for knowledge tests, and the level is also dependent on the intended use. However, there are usually no alternate possible responses to choose from in a performance test. Rather, there is a checklist of the skills that must be performed, and an evaluator must check that the skill was performed correctly.

To establish test-item validity during development, use a panel of judges with subject-matter expertise. There should be a minimum of four judges, each given a Test Specification Form (see Appendix D, where a completed form is also included).

Do a frequency count on the number of judges who respond that any given question meets the criterion. If you are using five judges, the criterion should be 80 percent (four of the five judges answer yes), 75 percent with four judges. If the level of knowledge required is extremely critical, you may choose 100 percent for the criterion, regardless of how many judges you use. (For instance, the criteria for the knowledge level of a brain surgeon would be much higher than for someone learning team-management skills.)

Each question that achieves the criterion level is considered to have content validity. Those questions that do not meet the criterion must be returned to the test writer for revision. He or she uses judges' comments to determine why an item was rejected. Rewritten questions must go through judging again. This process continues until all test questions reach the desired criterion level.

Although content validity is best determined using judges, various forms of statistical tests can also determine validity. *Point-biserial correlation* tells you if those who are the masters of the training are performing the skills consistently. The *difficulty index* can be used for those performance items that produce low or no positive correlation.

Any type of correlation involves very careful assessment and analysis of the tasks that the students who take the course are trained on. An assessment has to establish that enough people who are already masters have been observed, interviewed, and rated to establish the criteria for successful completion. You must use SMEs who are highly trained in inter-rater observation skills to perform the assessment and establish all levels of validation below predictive validity. Whether the tests are objective (based on knowledge acquired) or performance (based on ability to accomplish the skill), predictive validity must be established. You don't need to use both judging and statistical methods to determine content validity.

Once an analysis establishes the required skills and level of proficiency, you can use performance validation procedures to determine that all students are trained to the required level. You must then follow the students into the actual workplace and evaluate them at pre-established points over time, using the same evaluation instrument, to establish that adequate levels of proficiency are maintained. Predictive validity studies typically take place over an extended period of time. If your customer is really dedicated to improving individual performance and output, he or she will continue to collect data on employee proficiency on the job.

SUMMARY

Now that you have decided the type and level of validity that must be built into your test for the effectiveness of your solution, you can begin to develop the testing instruments.

Instrument Development

Tests, questionnaires, and surveys must all be developed according to the overall evaluation strategy, the evaluation plan, and the type and level of validity required. All measurement instruments must attain the degree of validity required to offer any degree of certainty about the effectiveness of your solution.

Interview instruments, as with questionnaires and surveys, must at least have content validity to be useful. Beyond this, certain other conditions are conducive to good results, such as the interpersonal skills of interviewers.

Surveys present some difficulties. Enough must be returned to consider the resulting sample adequate. It is very optimistic to expect a 50 percent return rate on surveys. Here is a way to ensure that you do obtain the total number of responses you need. When choosing subjects who are to receive surveys, keep the 50 percent return rate in mind and use the method for determining sample size and random selection discussed in the Direct-Interview Instructions section of Appendix D. Proceed as follows:

1. Obtain a certain number of names (for example, five hundred).
2. Select a sample size of 10 percent of the population (in the example, this means you need fifty responses).
3. Anticipating a 50 percent return rate, double the number of names (a total of one hundred).
4. Derive a random sample of names of people who receive the survey (or a total of one hundred in this example).

5. Re-send the survey to nonrespondents if you don't receive the fifty responses you need on the first try.

6. If you still do not get the required number after the second time, repeat from step 3 with a *different* group.

7. Use all responses (the fifty required is a minimum; more than that is better).

PROCESS

Six activities are necessary to complete a measurement plan:

1. Select the types of measurements.

2. Develop the measurement instruments.

3. Calculate the length of each instrument.

4. Calculate the weight of each item.

5. Decide when the instrument should be administered.

6. Document decisions in the evaluation plan.

INSTRUMENT DEVELOPMENT PROCEDURE

Follow these activities:

Activity One: Select the Types of Measurements

Step one: Determine what to measure using the terminal objectives created during objective analysis. If the objective involves students doing something, your instrument should measure skills; if students only need to demonstrate that they know something, a knowledge-based measure is appropriate. Decide how performance measures are to be constructed.

Step two: Determine whether measures need to be norm-referenced (NR) or criterion-referenced (CR).

Norm-referenced measures estimate characteristics and capabilities of people compared to the general population. *Criterion-referenced* measures estimate characteristics and capabilities of people compared to a standard. For example, the reading level of adults in the general population would be a norm-referenced characteristic. The leadership capabilities of all managers compared to exceptional managers would require CR measures.

Step three: Determine whether the measures are qualitative or quantitative. Although they use data, qualitative measures of validity handle the data with a method that requires professional judgment; quantitative measures rely heavily on standardized methods of interpreting statistics (although some people argue that there is judgment involved in the interpretation, with which we agree).

The trick is knowing which statistical tests to use and how to interpret the data you receive. Here are some common statistical measures of validity, with an explanation of when to use them and how to use them.

Quantitative Measures

Quantitative measures consist of the following:

1. Correlations
2. Difficulty indices
3. Item analysis
4. Tests of significance

Correlations. Correlations establish the relationship between two variables. The result is a number between -1.0 and $+1.0$. Numbers closer to $+1.0$ indicate a high positive correlation, and those closer to -1.0 indicate a high negative correlation. The higher the positive correlation, the better the test item. But what about questions that receive 0.00? You must then use a difficulty index to determine whether to include or exclude the item.

Here is an example of how correlation works and its value. A company we worked for developed an interactive video basic mathematics course. The course used a pretest and a posttest to measure the students' increase in knowledge and skills. During the pretest, students could test out of certain modules by answering selected questions correctly; they were channeled into other modules if they incorrectly answered these selected questions. If the students failed the diagnostic pretest, they had yet another chance once they entered a module of instruction, through another mastery test. If students scored 90 percent on the mastery test, they could at that point skip the module or choose to continue through it anyway.

But management wanted to know whether or not the test measured the skills generally determined by experts to be required by students who have mastered basic mathematics skills. They needed an answer to the question, "Does this test have a high degree of predictive validity?" The testing team began by administering a test they had developed internally to groups of college freshmen (about one hundred) determined by college placement tests to be in need of remedial mathematics to succeed in their college courses. The testing team also found that the mathematics test from a national high school equivalency exam had been well documented as having a high degree of validity and reliability. The team also administered this test to the same group of students.

Comparing the scores on the course test and the standardized test, the testing team determined that there was a high degree of correlation between the two tests. As a result, management could declare that students who passed the posttest in the interactive video course had the mathematical knowledge and skills of students who have graduated from high school.

Difficulty index. But what about the questions that score with no correlation (0.00)? You must look at an index of the level of difficulty for that question. If all students get the question right or if all get it wrong, then the question is probably a poor question and needs to be rewritten. Compare questions with 0.00 correlation to your frequency tables.

How high should positive correlation be for a question to be considered valid? A sufficient level of positive correlation for each question should be +.80, again based on the criticality of the knowledge (say, brain surgeon versus management trainee). Low positive correlations require distractor analysis and frequency counts. No correlation below +.50 should be considered valid.

Item analysis. This determines whether the individual test items and the overall test are valid. Item analysis establishes the validity of test questions by determining that those who performed best on the overall test also got a particular item correct.

To perform an item analysis, you must have two independent variables that can be compared in some way to make the determination about how good your test questions are. There are a number of statistical tests that establish this for NR measures and others for CR measures.

Tests of significance. Tests of significance are used when you want to determine whether the results from running your data on your sample group are typical or not typical of the total population from which the random sample was drawn.

Qualitative Measures

More qualitative measures include the following:

1. Distractor analysis
2. Frequency counts

Distractor analysis. Analyzing the answers that students give to a test is known as distractor analysis. In this analysis, you must look for any questions that receive a low positive or negative correlation using quantitative methods and determine whether one particular distractor (possible answer) draws the better students away from the correct answer. Find out which distractor is causing the problem, and then determine why it might be doing so. Rewrite the distractor (and any others for that question that need clarity), administer the test again, and perform the same correlation analyses. Frequency analysis also reveals this information.

If you are fortunate enough to have access to the students who answered the question incorrectly, ask them why they chose their particular answer. This is a very good source of feedback. If those students are not available, use only the data from distractor analysis.

Frequency counts. Although frequency counts are a quantitative measure, they require judgment to determine the cutoff for success or failure. Frequencies are easy to generate even if you don't use a statistical package; just count the number of responses based on some standard (say, correct or incorrect). However, a statistical package generates the data much faster, especially for a large number of cases.

Step four: Determine whether you will administer measures before and/or after using your solution. If both before and after, will you use the same measure or use parallel forms of instruments? If you are developing parallel forms, use the following instructions and the Parallel Test Item Bank Construction Form in the Evaluation Tools section of Appendix E.

Follow these steps to develop parallel tests and establish parallel test validity:

1. Provide a set of numbered objectives, a set of numbered test questions, and the Parallel Test Item Bank Construction Form to a panel of SME judges, who will determine the parallelism. Have the number of each terminal objective marked in the "Terminal Objective Number" column before you give the form to the judges.

2. List the weight of each terminal objective in the second column of the form.

3. List the item numbers for the test items that match each of the terminal objectives in columns 3, 4, 5, and 6 (all labeled "Test Item Number").

4. Provide directions for developing parallel test item banks to each judge and ask them to complete and return the form.

5. When all the forms have been returned, check to see that all judges have signed off. If they have, create the parallel test. If they have not, revise the problematic items and ask the panel to review them again.

6. Repeat steps 3, 4, and 5 until all judges have signed off.

Activity Two: Develop the Measurement Instruments

Depending on the question types you decide to construct, use one or more of these forms from the Evaluation Tools section of Appendix E:

- Matching Question Checklist
- Multiple-Choice Question Checklist
- True/False Question Checklist
- Completion (Short-Answer) Question Checklist
- Simulation/Role Play/Performance Test Checklist
- Essay Question Checklist

See the instructions for developing questionnaires, surveys, and interview instruments in Appendix D to construct these types of measurement instrument.

Phillips and Phillips (2003) present a method to use if the group that will use the solution has a performance management system in place. Their system advocates using action plans (Level 3, Performance) to hold employees accountable for their own development. They convincingly detail how you can even use these action plans for measuring ROI.

Activity Three: Calculate the Length of Each Instrument

Step one: Calculate the number of questions. Suppose you have fifty terminal objectives and you decide you should ask two questions per objective as a standard. This means you have a test with one hundred questions. Remember, the students must have an adequate opportunity to demonstrate attainment of the knowledge or skill. Multiple questions or multiple attempts per objective on a criterion-referenced test increase the probability of demonstrating attainment.

Step two: Calculate the time respondents need to complete the instrument. How long it takes depends on the nature of the questions. Objective questions vary depending on the type (true/false, matching, multiple-choice), how long the question stem is, and how many distractors are included. Note that a good rule of thumb is to allow thirty seconds for each multiple-choice question that has four distractors. Don't forget that you have to leave time in the test for students to read the directions or for them to be explained. For example, if you (1) have fifty objectives, (2) write two questions per objective, and (3) allow thirty seconds per question, plus about ten minutes to read and understand instructions, this means you need to allow sixty minutes for test completion:

$$(50 \text{ objectives} \times 2 \text{ questions per objective} \times .5 \text{ minutes per question})$$
$$+ 10 \text{ minutes} = 60 \text{ minutes}$$

Activity Four: Calculate the Weight of Each Item

Determine the amount of content in each part of the solution. Not all parts of a solution carry equal weight; in a five-hour training course, if one section takes two hours to cover, then it has more weight in the course than a section that takes half an hour. The number of questions for each terminal objective should be based on the relative weight of the content.

If the two-hour section of the course contains six of the terminal objectives, your job is simple. If two questions per terminal objective is your standard, you simply put twelve questions from that section on the total test.

But suppose you have one terminal objective for this two-hour section. As an alternative to the formula of so many questions per terminal objective, you can calculate the length of delivery time for the section in proportion to the entire course and construct enough questions to match proportionally.

If you administer a performance test where students have multiple chances to complete the task successfully, you can perform a frequency count to determine how many attempts were required for most (whatever standard you want to use, such as 80 percent) of the students to accomplish the task. If the number is low, that task is valid. If 80 percent of the students require four tries to accomplish certain tasks, you had better check those items; they are probably not valid.

Activity Five: Decide When the Instrument(s) Should Be Administered

Determine whether measures should be interspersed in the course or whether there should only be one comprehensive test at the end of the course. If measures are interspersed, determine how many will be needed. Use the information in Table 31.1 to determine the placement of measures.

Table 31.1
Question Types

Type	Location	Level	Purpose	Frequency
Embedded (Study)	Within a lesson	Basic knowledge and understanding	Check basic knowledge of concept(s) taught in the lesson	Interspersed throughout a lesson
Quiz	At the end of each lesson or periodically after several lessons	Knowledge of information within a lesson Application	Test students' grasp of concepts *Note:* Questions should test only the major concepts from the objective(s) that the lesson covers.	End of a lesson or group of lessons *Note:* At least one question should be asked on each major topic.
Test	Interim and end of course	Application Evaluation	Test students' knowledge or performance by integrating information from throughout the course	As required *Note:* Test pool should contain at least one question from each lesson objective.

Activity Six: Document Decision in the Evaluation Plan

See Chapter Twenty-Nine.

FROM OUR EXPERIENCE

Instructional designers find that one of their greatest knowledge gaps is understanding what type of measure to develop. An NR measure only requires a sample of questions from among the objectives. However, a CR measure requires multiple questions for every objective. Whereas NR measures are designed to sample overall knowledge, CR measures are designed to ensure that a population possesses the skill being trained and that those tested have ample opportunity to demonstrate their knowledge or skill. Table 31.2 will help you determine whether or not your statistical test can be applied to NR or CR measures.

Setting a pass-fail level differs for NR and CR measures. On an NR measure, a 50 to 67 percent score may be considered passing because most people who take the test score around the midpoint. On a CR measure, the pass-fail score is determined by the criticality of the skill the test-taker will be performing; thus CR passing scores are usually higher because scores tend to cluster around the upper end of the scoring range. Indeed, they should if the solution is effective. The most important thing to remember is that a test score is not absolute; it is a point within a range (standard error of measurement). That means if the mean score is 80 and the standard error of measurement is ± 2, then there is no difference between a score as low as 78 and as high as 82.

Coscarelli and Schrock (2003) state that "A comprehensive CRT [criterion-referenced test] often measures a number of discrete tasks that may not represent a single unifying ability or competence. Thus CRTs theoretically violate the two most essential assumptions of classic NRT [norm-referenced test]. . ." (p. 74).

For example, a CRT on operating equipment will have questions on safety, hydraulics, and steering, among others. To try to use norm-referenced statistical measures on these types of tests yields invalid results because an operator taking this test may know more about hydraulics than safety, so deriving an overall score would be misleading.

Coscarelli and Schrock also state that CRTs are designed to have more closely clustered scores at the upper end of the scoring range. If a CRT yields a standard bell curve, there is something that is invalid. Either the course does not match the test items or the content is not well presented.

Table 31.2
Appropriate Statistical Measures

Test Name	Purpose	Application Type[a] A	B	C	D	Sample Requirements
Biserial	One continuous, one dichotomy	√	√	√		Representative sample size
Chi-square	One continuous, one dichotomy		√		√	Representative sample size
Kendall's tau	Two continuous variables	√		√		$n < 10$
Kuder Richardson (KR-20)	Measure of equal difficulty	√	√	√		Representative sample size
Mann Whitney	Compare unequal groups	√	√		√	Representative sample size
Pearson Product Moment (Pearson r)	Two continuous variables	√		√		Representative sample size
Phi coefficient (Φ)	Two true dichotomies			√		Representative sample size
Point-biserial	One continuous, one true dichotomy		√	√		Representative sample size
Rank difference	Two continuous variables	√		√		$n < 30$
Analysis of variance (ANOVA)	Significance between more than two means	√	√		√	Representative sample size
t-test	Significance between two means	√			√	Representative sample size

[a]A = Norm-Referenced; B = Criterion-Referenced; C = Correlation; D = Significance

Generally, if you are developing a product so that a specific group learns a specific set of skills, you are probably developing a criterion-referenced test (CRT). Off-the-shelf products usually require CRTs unless the subject is general knowledge on some skill that any person using the product should have, such as basic mathematics, reading, and so on. However, the test must be established to the standard for the group using the product and taking the test.

Artificially imposed restrictions placed on the test before you complete all the activities in this chapter are not a good idea. Here are examples of artificially imposed restrictions:

- Predetermined test format (that is, objective, questionnaire, survey)
- Predetermined number of questions
- Predetermined time for test administration
- Predetermined ratio of class time to test time

You cannot determine the instrument format before completion of front-end analysis, and you cannot determine the number of measurement items until you have written your objectives. Time and ratios cannot be determined until you decide on an instrument format and the number of questions.

Of course, there are certain limitations to the amount of time that can be spent on testing, but let situation and objective analysis shape this decision rather than arbitrary choice. Once you see the number of objectives and the conditions under which the product will be used or delivered, you may decide the format needs to be changed because there is a better method of evaluation.

In our opinion, transfer of skills to the workplace is the only justifiable reason for expending resources on a project. If employees simply have to know or be aware of something, give them a book, pamphlet, or other resource and have them read it. "But people don't take responsibility for gaining knowledge themselves," some say. "If I give them a book, it won't be read." To our minds, if that's the case, then you had best expend your resources in other areas of employee development, such as creating self-motivated employees who are lifelong learners.

We are not saying that employers should not extend learning opportunities to employees. However, evaluation should not stop at the knowledge level. The value of knowledge can only be measured through the resulting performance.

Students who complete the course must be observed regularly over time to determine whether they are using the skills taught during the training. If you can determine that they are, then determine what cost savings can be directly attributed to using the skills.

For either knowledge or performance measures, you have to consider whether or not to pre-assess and post-assess. For example, a new training course should always contain a pre-assessment if there is a post-assessment, for purposes of establishing validity of the instrument. Your goal is to determine if there are significantly higher results on the posttest. If the results are significant, this demonstrates that the course has taught what it was intended to teach.

After you administer the instrument often enough to establish validity and reliability of results, you can discontinue pre-assessing. But if any portion of the course changes, you should revise the instruments, re-administer them to pilot groups of students, and reestablish validity and reliability.

For either objective or performance instruments, if students can test out of a course or particular units of a course based on pretest scores, then this is a valid reason for using the pretest or posttest. If only posttests are administered, there is no evidence that the students learn as a result of taking the course. They might know the material beforehand, in which case they should not have to sit though the course. Another explanation might be that the test is flawed by being so easy or so poorly constructed that students can guess the answers without knowing the content.

If the content is highly technical or presents a new concept, process, or procedure, and you are certain (from information gathered during analysis) that all students are beginning at the same level, pre-assessment may be unnecessary. If other forms of information were provided to certain students in the past or if their work experience afforded some of them higher levels of knowledge than others have, a pretest and posttest might be in order. If there is no evidence of wide diversity in prerequisite skills, don't waste your time. It might be nice to know, but it's not necessary.

Knowledge-based assessments are sometimes unnecessary if performance measures are administered after offering the information. The logic is that if a student can do something correctly, you can assume he or she has the knowledge. However, you might spend a lot of time and resources developing and administering performance measures only to achieve poor results among the students. It may be that they did not gain the knowledge. If so, you must then search for the reasons for low performance. Knowledge assessment at the end of the content portion of the course would be useful in detecting the source. Perhaps certain concepts, procedures, or processes were not emphasized in the content or were taught incorrectly.

Backtracking is expensive and delays how soon the customer can begin fully implementing the program. You must develop instruments, validate them, pre-assess and post-assess, score and analyze, and then reconstruct the performance project.

In our experience, another question that always arises when survey research is involved is, "How many people should be surveyed?"

Sampling some populations is difficult, and there is always a tendency to cut corners. Some professionals and customers point to some of the major rating providers (such as the Harris polling organization), who sample a very small segment of the population and still achieve highly reliable results.

But professional rating corporations spend a great amount of money up-front, using very sophisticated computer systems to continuously narrow and subdivide regions of the territory they plan to survey and the populations of those areas. They use and rely on systems that have been in place for many years and employ methodologies for which reliability has been continually refined.

If your organization is in that lofty minority and has such sophisticated sampling equipment, then use it to choose a sample size. If your organization does not have the equipment and methodologies, then use the rule of 10 percent of the population and be satisfied with a 60 to 70 percent return rate from that 10 percent.

Yes, it takes time; yes, it takes money. But do you and your stakeholders want accurate information? If accuracy is not a concern, then just guess and save the money! Guessing is just as accurate as sampling five people from among a population of one thousand.

SUMMARY

You now know what measurement instruments are required, how to construct them, and how to incorporate your decisions into an evaluation plan. Now instruments will be distributed and completed and returned. You have to analyze and interpret the data and make some sense out of it.

Collecting and Analyzing Data

Plan your evaluation thoroughly before you run it. Some things are recoverable because they are in the data and you only need to analyze them differently; but some things might not be recoverable unless you run the entire evaluation project again—costing time, money, and a delay in final implementation.

Although this book is not intended to deal with statistics, we include some basic information on types of tests, their purpose, and the underlying meaning of the results obtained from each one. Knowing what data to gather, however, requires someone with a background in statistical methodologies. After interpreting the statistical findings, anyone with good problem-solving skills can determine what the data mean.

PROCESS

There are five activities required in data collection and analysis:

1. Set up the database.
2. Develop an evaluation plan.
3. Collect and compile the data.
4. Interpret the data.
5. Document your findings.

COLLECTING AND ANALYZING DATA PROCEDURE

Follow these activities:

Activity One: Set Up the Database

Use the statistical software package you have chosen to set up the database to capture information or transfer information from other sources. For example, if you have set up the database in a CBT course, it is sometimes possible to capture the data in another format (say, ASCII text delimited in some way, perhaps with commas) and import them into the statistical package. Data transfer requires planning well in advance—as far back as when you choose the statistical tool and the development and delivery software.

Activity Two: Develop an Evaluation Plan

Once a project is selected and decisions are made as a result of assessment and analysis, an evaluation plan should be developed (see Chapter Twenty-Nine). The plan specifies how the evaluation is designed and conducted (including identification of time frames, data collection, and analysis methods) and the reporting mechanisms for any and all evaluation activities associated with a project.

The same considerations are required to evaluate performance and impact as are called for in developing tests:

- Number of participants and the amount of data to be collected
- Types of sampling method
- Confidentiality
- Costs

There are additional considerations when measuring performance. The first is use of a control group, that is, a set of preselected participants or data as similar as possible to those in the experimental group. The experimental group is involved in the intervention; the control group is not. The two groups should be equivalent in job settings, skills, abilities, and demographic characteristics. For more information on using experimental and control groups, refer to Campbell and Stanley (1963).

The second consideration is influence outside the scope of the evaluation. External variables include, among other things, organizational changes such as seasonal variations that have a negative impact on business. Internal factors such as new leadership, transfer of participants, budget cuts, and changing organizational goals can affect results. Effective control of these influences increases your confidence in the accuracy of the results, reduces the need for elaborate performance assessment designs, and may reduce the number of required participants in the population or the sample.

Activity Three: Collect and Compile the Data

Capture data from the measurement instruments. Capture as many responses as possible, at least through the end of the pilot test.

Activity Four: Interpret the Data

Step one: Interpret the data against the goals for the evaluation and determine whether the results match the goals or not.

Step two: Make decisions. If the goals match the results, you might decide to do a full-scale implementation of the solution and (1) continue to collect data for consistent results; (2) discontinue collecting data; or (3) wait for a certain period of time and then conduct another evaluation.

If the results do not match the goals, the possible decisions might be to

- Revise the course
- Revise the measurement instruments and tests
- Rerun the study with or without revisions
- Choose another representative sample and rerun the evaluation
- Discard the product

Activity Five: Document Your Findings

Record your findings in the Evaluation Report. A template for completing it can be found in Appendix D and in the Evaluation section of the CD-ROM.

FROM OUR EXPERIENCE

You need a good statistical package to analyze the raw data. We've used SPSS (formerly known as Statistical Package for the Social Sciences), produced by SPSS in Chicago. The Windows version is particularly easy to use, and the documentation is excellent.

SUMMARY

At the completion of these activities, you have the information to determine whether or not your solution is effective in terms of the customer's need (established during needs assessment). All of the activities and steps you complete during every phase of the project contribute to the results you achieve. If you pay careful attention to each activity and each step, and if you plan carefully, you will no doubt achieve the desired result: your solution solves the problem or issue.

APPENDIX A:
PROJECT MANAGEMENT
AND XEGY™ CASE STUDIES

INSTRUCTIONAL DESIGN PROJECT MANAGEMENT TOOL
PHASE: ASSESSMENT AND ANALYSIS

Assessment

☐ Activity 1 Determine the present condition.
    ☐ Step 1 Identify required knowledge and skills.
    ☐ Step 2 Identify the job-related knowledge and skill areas used to select performers.
    ☐ Step 3 Check for discrepancies between steps 1 and 2.
    ☐ Step 4 Check for environmental causes in steps 1 and 2.
    ☐ Step 5 Document task performance affected by environmental factors.
    ☐ Step 6 Review all results and identify areas of need.
    ☐ Step 7 Gather data from employees.
    ☐ Step 8 Review results and identify areas of need.
☐ Activity 2 Define the job.
☐ Activity 3 Rank the goals in order of importance.
☐ Activity 4 Identify discrepancies.
☐ Activity 5 Determine positive areas.
☐ Activity 6 Set priorities for action.
    ☐ Step 1 List all possible solutions suggested and the impact of not providing the solution.
    ☐ Step 2 Define the impact of each solution in terms of time, money, and customer satisfaction.
    ☐ Step 3 Make recommendations, keeping in mind the job goals, desired results, and other relevant factors.

Front-End Analysis: Audience

☐ Activity 1 Analyze demographics and special requirements.
    ☐ Step 1 Verify the audience using job task information.
    ☐ Step 2 Confirm the number of individuals who are targeted and their general education and background.
    ☐ Step 3 Analyze information about audience language, tone, and use of humor.
    ☐ Step 4 Note any physical, ergonomic, or environmental requirements.
☐ Activity 2 Determine attitudes toward content.
    ☐ Step 1 Determine any misconceptions or misinformation that might exist.

☐ Step 2 Determine negative and positive attitudes.
☐ Step 3 Determine special terminology or vocabulary.
☐ Activity 3 Analyze the language skills of the audience.
☐ Activity 4 Document the results.

Front-End Analysis: Technology

☐ Activity 1 Analyze available communication technology.
☐ Activity 2 Analyze the technology available for reference or performance support.
    ☐ Step 1 Determine online reference availability and capability.
    ☐ Step 2 Determine performance support availability and capability.
☐ Activity 3 Analyze the technology available for testing and assessment.
    ☐ Step 1 Determine electronic testing and assessment requirements.
    ☐ Step 2 Define security issues.
☐ Activity 4 Analyze the technology for distribution.
    ☐ Step 1 Determine how materials are ordered and distributed.
    ☐ Step 2 Determine FTP (file transfer protocol) availability and capability.
☐ Activity 5 Analyze the technology for delivery.
    ☐ Step 1 Determine availability and capability of dedicated audio and video servers.
    ☐ Step 2 Determine multimedia PC availability and capability.
    ☐ Step 3 Determine video teleconferencing or educational TV availability and capability.
☐ Activity 6 Analyze the expertise.
☐ Activity 7 Document the results.

Front-End Analysis: Situation

☐ Activity 1 Analyze the job environment.
☐ Activity 2 Analyze delivery environment.
☐ Activity 3 Document the results.

Front-End Analysis: Task

☐ Activity 1 Define the position title.
☐ Activity 2 Identify all job-related duties.
☐ Activity 3 Identify all tasks.

- ☐ Step 1 Confirm or identify primary tasks.
- ☐ Step 2 Confirm that each task stands alone.
- ☐ Step 3 Confirm the knowledge, skills, and attitudes (KSA) required.
- ☐ Activity 4 Order the tasks.
- ☐ Activity 5 Document the results.

Front-End Analysis: Critical Incident

- ☐ Activity 1 Determine the critical tasks.
- ☐ Activity 2 Determine important but nonessential tasks.
- ☐ Activity 3 Determine the tasks you will deselect.
- ☐ Activity 4 Document the results.

Front-End Analysis: Issue

- ☐ Activity 1 Collect data from audience, technology, situational, task, and critical incident analyses.
- ☐ Activity 2 Place the data into the appropriate category of the Issue Analysis Form.
  - ☐ Step 1 Discuss the appropriate categorization of each issue into one of the three categories.
  - ☐ Step 2 Determine any interdependencies between issues at the different levels.
  - ☐ Step 3 Complete the Issue Analysis Form.

Front-End Analysis: Objectives

- ☐ Activity 1 Decide on domains.
- ☐ Activity 2 Decide on level.
- ☐ Activity 3 Write goal statement.
- ☐ Activity 4 Write performance objectives.
- ☐ Activity 5 Engage in a group discussion.
  - ☐ Step 1 Review objectives to validate relevance to job tasks.
  - ☐ Step 2 Rewrite objectives as necessary.
- ☐ Activity 6 Separate terminal objectives from performance objectives.
- ☐ Activity 7 Separate lesson objectives from performance objectives.

Front-End Analysis: Media

- [ ] Activity 1 Rate each of the factors on the Media Analysis Rating Form. Rate each factor on a scale of 1 to 5 regarding importance to the issue.
- [ ] Activity 2 Summarize ratings.
  - [ ] Step 1 List high-ranked media.
  - [ ] Step 2 List low-ranked media.
  - [ ] Step 3 Determine the difference: subtract low occurrences from high occurrences.
  - [ ] Step 4 Determine weight: divide the difference by all occurrences.
- [ ] Activity 3 Place the resulting media in a hierarchy from the highest percentage to the lowest.
- [ ] Activity 4 Analyze advantages and limitations of each type of media.
  - [ ] Step 1 Analyze cost of delivery.
  - [ ] Step 2 Consider delivery factors.
  - [ ] Step 3 Consider maintenance factors.
- [ ] Activity 5 Compare results and decide on the media.
- [ ] Activity 6 Match objectives with the most appropriate media.
- [ ] Activity 7 Document the results.

Front-End Analysis: Extant Data

- [ ] Activity 1 Identify likely sources of information.
- [ ] Activity 2 Collect information and existing course materials.
- [ ] Activity 3 Compare information.
  - [ ] Step 1 Rate the appropriateness and usability of materials.
  - [ ] Step 2 Determine whether materials availability matches the time constraints of the project.
  - [ ] Step 3 Determine the cost of the materials; compare to project budget.
- [ ] Activity 4 Make a Buy-or-Build Decision
  - [ ] Step 1 Place and X in the Yes or No column to answer each question.
  - [ ] Step 2 Total the number of Xs in each column.
- [ ] Activity 5 Evaluate the off-the-shelf solutions.
  - [ ] Step 1 Complete the information at the top of the form.
  - [ ] Step 2 Rate each category on the Courseware Evaluation Tool.
  - [ ] Step 3 Record overall comments at the end of the tool.
  - [ ] Step 4 Select the overall rating for the solution.
- [ ] Activity 6 Document your decision.

Front-End Analysis: Cost

- ☐ Activity 1   Conduct a cost-benefit analysis (CBA).
  - ☐ Step 1   Calculate the anticipated total cost of the project.
  - ☐ Step 2   Calculate the total benefit to the organization.
  - ☐ Step 3   Divide the total cost by the total benefit.
  - ☐ Step 4   Express cost-benefit as a ratio.
- ☐ Activity 2   Determine the return on investment (ROI).
  - ☐ Step 1   Determine the total net value.
  - ☐ Step 2   Divide total net value by total cost
  - ☐ Step 3   Multiply by 100 for a percentage.
- ☐ Activity 3   Document the results.

Front-End Analysis: Rapid Analysis Method

- ☐ Activity 1   Prepare for the analysis.
  - ☐ Step 1   Determine focus of the assessment.
  - ☐ Step 2   Conduct kickoff meeting.
  - ☐ Step 3   Assign tasks.
- ☐ Activity 2   Ask primary questions.
  - ☐ Step 1   Ask target groups the five primary questions; add follow-on questions as required.
  - ☐ Step 2   Identify inconsistencies.
- ☐ Activity 3   Listen and record responses.
  - ☐ Step 1   Listen to the responses.
  - ☐ Step 2   Categorize responses into the five response categories.
- ☐ Activity 4   Observe actual performance.
  - ☐ Step 1   Watch tasks being performed.
  - ☐ Step 2   Reconcile gaps between verbal responses and actual performance.
- ☐ Activity 5   Report results.

PHASE: DESIGN

Project Schedule

- ☐ Activity 1   Document general project information.
- ☐ Activity 2   List project deliverables.
- ☐ Activity 3   Schedule project activities.

Project Team

☐ Activity 1 List team roles.
☐ Activity 2 List project tasks.
☐ Activity 3 Assign roles and responsibilities.

Media Specifications

☐ Activity 1 Define the look and feel of the theme.
   ☐ Step 1 Brainstorm a list of themes.
   ☐ Step 2 Complete a mock-up.
   ☐ Step 3 Decide on theme.
☐ Activity 2 Define the interface and functionality.
☐ Activity 3 Define the interaction and feedback standards.
☐ Activity 4 Define the video and audio treatments.
☐ Activity 5 Indicate text design and standards.
☐ Activity 6 Prepare the graphic design standards.
☐ Activity 7 Decide on animation and special effects.

Content Structure

☐ Activity 1 Break the content into units.
   ☐ Step 1 Break it into six major categories.
   ☐ Step 2 Group information based in job and task order.
☐ Activity 2 Map the information.
   ☐ Step 1 Create a lesson outline or map.
   ☐ Step 2 Create a course flowchart.
☐ Activity 2 Determine SCORM compliance.
   ☐ Step 1 Define a reusable content object.
   ☐ Step 2 Ask which LMS the courseware will successfully run through.
   ☐ Step 3 Ask for the vendor's customer list if using content provider and LMS provider.

Configuration Control and Review Cycles

☐ Activity 1 Establish a configuration control (CC) plan.
   ☐ Step 1 (Author's responsibility)
   ☐ Step 2 (CCG's responsibility)
   ☐ Step 3 (Reviewer's responsibility)
   ☐ Step 4 (Last reviewer's responsibility)

☐ Step 5 (CCG's responsibility)
☐ Step 6 (Author's responsibility)
☐ Step 7 (CCG's responsibility)
☐ Step 8 (Reviewer's responsibility)
☐ Step 9 (CCG's responsibility)

PHASE: DEVELOPMENT AND IMPLEMENTATION

Developing Computer-Based Learning Environments

☐ Activity 1 Create storyboards.
  ☐ Step 1 Review the instructional rationale for the treatment of each learning outcome.
  ☐ Step 2 Translate rationale into a screen-level outline.
  ☐ Step 3 Add up-front components.
  ☐ Step 4 Review and validate storyboards.
  ☐ Step 5 Conduct quality-assurance (QA) reviews.
☐ Activity 2 Create and assemble media elements.
  ☐ Step 1 Conduct preproduction meeting.
  ☐ Step 2 Produce the CBT.
☐ Activity 3 Perform online reviews.
  ☐ Step 1 Produce test CD-ROMs.
  ☐ Step 2 Use storyboards as the basis for review.
  ☐ Step 3 Record errors.
  ☐ Step 4 Correct errors.
  ☐ Step 5 Review corrections.
☐ Activity 4 Deliver and implement the course.

Developing Internet, Intranet, Web-Based, and Performance Support Learning Environments

☐ Activity 1 Determine the type of product and platform.
  ☐ Step 1 Determine whether learning is to be synchronous or asynchronous.
  ☐ Step 2 Choose the platform most appropriate for the technical specifications.
☐ Activity 2 Assemble components.
☐ Activity 3 Conduct reviews.

- ☐ Activity 4   Rehearse the presentation.
  - ☐ Step 1   Practice with technology.
  - ☐ Step 2   Review clothing considerations.
  - ☐ Step 3   Perform dry run of presentation.
- ☐ Activity 5   Conduct the session.
  - ☐ Step 1   Give assistants (or participants) information on roles and responsibilities.
  - ☐ Step 2   Implement the site.

Developing Interactive Distance Broadcast Environments

- ☐ Activity 1   Develop script and materials.
- ☐ Activity 2   Shoot and edit video.
- ☐ Activity 3   Rehearse the presentation.
  - ☐ Step 1   Practice with technology.
  - ☐ Step 2   Review clothing considerations.
  - ☐ Step 3   Perform dry run of presentation.
- ☐ Activity 4   Broadcast the session. Give assistants (or participants) information on roles and responsibilities.

PHASE: EVALUATION
Purpose of Evaluation

- ☐ Activity 1   Determine the purpose of the solution.
  - ☐ Step 1   Determine whether measurement variables are organizational.
  - ☐ Step 2   Declare remaining measurement variables to be individual.
  - ☐ Step 3   Determine whether the solution will be used commercially.

Evaluation Strategy

- ☐ Activity 1   Write an introduction regarding the philosophy, purpose, and need for evaluation.
- ☐ Activity 2   Determine how to measure each level of evaluation.
- ☐ Activity 3   Determine what your sources of information will be.

Evaluation Plan

- ☐ Activity 1   Complete the problem statement section
  - ☐ Step 1   Clearly state the rational for addressing this issue.
  - ☐ Step 2   Describe the gap between the present and the desired state.

☐ Activity 2   Complete the solution section.
☐ Activity 3   Complete the objectives section.
☐ Activity 4   Complete the components of the Evaluation Plan.
☐ Activity 5   Complete the Executive Summary
    ☐ Step 1   Briefly state the problem.
    ☐ Step 2   Briefly describe the solution.

Measures of Validity

☐ Activity 1   Determine level and type of validity required.
☐ Activity 2   Determine when to validate measurement instruments.
☐ Activity 3   Document your decisions.

Instrument Development

☐ Activity 1   Select the types of measurements.
    ☐ Step 1   Determine what to measure.
    ☐ Step 2   Differentiate norm-referenced and criterion-referenced measures.
    ☐ Step 3   Differentiate qualitative or quantitative measures.
    ☐ Step 4   Determine use of pretesting and/or posttesting.
☐ Activity 2   Develop the measurement instruments.
☐ Activity 3   Calculate the length of each instrument.
    ☐ Step 1   Calculate number of questions.
    ☐ Step 2   Calculate instrument completion time.
☐ Activity 4   Calculate the weight of each item.
☐ Activity 5   Decide when the instrument(s) should be administered.
☐ Activity 6   Document decisions in the evaluation plan.

Collecting and Analyzing Data

☐ Activity 1   Set up the database.
☐ Activity 2   Develop an evaluation plan.
☐ Activity 3   Collect and compile the data.
☐ Activity 4   Interpret the data.
    ☐ Step 1   Analyze data according to evaluation goals.
    ☐ Step 2   Make decisions.
☐ Activity 5   Document your findings.

CASE STUDY 1: EMPLOYEE DEVELOPMENT

Situation

One of the most powerful programs in Real Learning Company's (RLI) Performance Master Suite is Performer®, a one-day course designed to help employees assess engagement and alignment on the job and to facilitate manager/employee discussions about performance. The program assists organizations in developing a common language for human performance management throughout the entire organization, not just at the management ranks.

The following two issues drove RLI to deliver Performer as a blended solution on the Xegy™ platform:

1. A need for self-reflection
2. A need to reach a large audience with an efficient and effective delivery method and in a timely manner

Intervention

RLI used Xegy™ to

- Rapidly prototype the design to include both synchronous and asynchronous sessions to accommodate self-discovery and collaborative discovery
- Create multiple short interactive activities to allow each employee to work through the course in time segments of as little as fifteen minutes
- Deliver short video clips (for any connection speed) of a master facilitator giving instructions throughout the process and reinforcing concepts learned
- Create interactive opportunities to compare manager and employee perceptions and journal responses (for example, exploring motivators, values, job goals, talents, and required skills)
- Present reports and analysis of manager and employee perceptions and feedback
- Structure a developmental planning meeting where the employee takes ownership
- Track completion of activities to ensure success

Outcomes

- Development took less than a month to complete.

Figure A.1
Real Learning Xegy™ Application

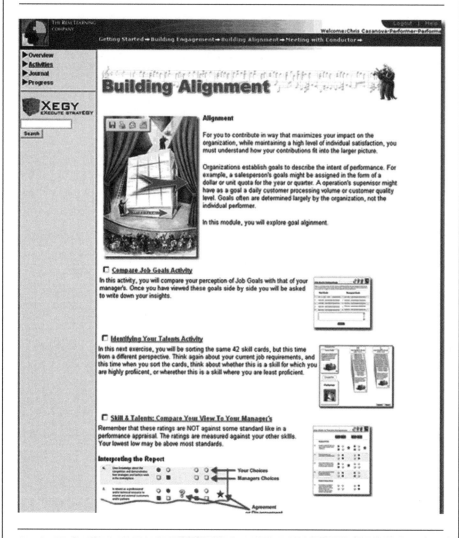

Source: Used with permission from Real Learning Company and Granite Technologies.

- Employees can complete activities from their desks at their convenience and speed.
- The employee is empowered during developmental discussion meetings.

Lessons Learned

- A blended approach using synchronous and asynchronous sessions reduces the amount of required classroom time.
- Video and audio can be produced in a way that accommodates dial-up connection and creates a richer learning environment.

CASE STUDY 2: GOVERNMENT AGENCY

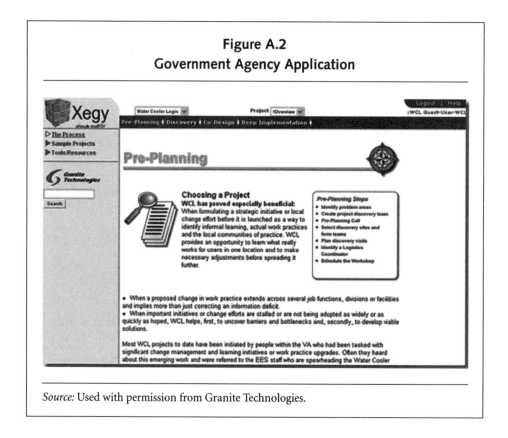

Figure A.2
Government Agency Application

Source: Used with permission from Granite Technologies.

Situation

A major government agency exists to serve the 25 million citizens and their families in 163 facilities across the county. In an effort to continuously improve the level and quality of services provided, employees of the agency have always served on ad hoc task forces to address processes, systems, and issues that can be improved. As with any change initiative in a large organization, these task forces take up a great deal of time and resources. And sustained results are often elusive.

The agency has developed an organic change process called Water Cooler Logic (WCL) over the past four years to create and sustain productive change. The process is local and addresses not only the content (procedures and information) but also the context (environment) and community (culture) in which the current work practice is applied. WCL has been used to improve transfer, waiting times and delays, safety of customers, and new employee orientation.

Scalability became a limiting factor. WCL is organic and involves people with different backgrounds discovering and designing interventions based on unique influences. Champions were critical to transfer the process to each task force through extensive consulting and support throughout the project. The process was so effective that more people needed to be able to engage in WCL.

Intervention

The WCL team used Xegy™ for several purposes:

- To communicate the WCL process in clear understandable steps to a broader audience
- To deliver tools, resources, and job aids within the context of the process
- As a place for WCL teams to capture their observations, documents, and notes
- To archive project information and successes for reference

Outcomes

There is no data available on the outcomes of this program as of the printing of this book.

Lessons Learned

Human nature seeks balance. For every attempt to over-prescribe and document detailed steps and rules, there is an equal and opposite reaction to find the exception and break those rules.

When creating a performance support or process management intervention, it is critical to determine the useful level of detail in each phase for successful guidance and support. Sometimes a suggestion is appropriate and other times forced completion is. The key is to look at the value of innovation and the price of non-conformance to that particular activity.

CASE STUDY 3: PHARMACEUTICAL SALES

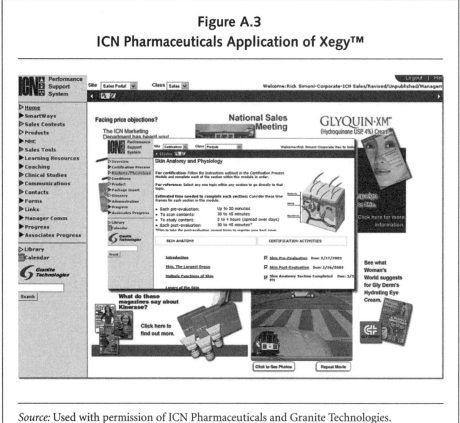

Figure A.3
ICN Pharmaceuticals Application of Xegy™

Source: Used with permission of ICN Pharmaceuticals and Granite Technologies.

Situation

A medium-sized pharmaceutical company was preparing to grow the salesforce significantly in order to add new product lines for a competitive product about to gain FDA approval. The goal was to

- Create a replicable process for product certification
- Increase the competence of the salesforce on existing products
- Strengthen competitive positioning through sales representation
- Increase the speed to profit for new product rollouts

Intervention

Xegy™ provided the foundational framework to

- Deliver product training and competitive strategies consistently
- Track progress and performance through certification
- Gather and disseminate success strategies from high performers
- Access other systems such as prescribing data, job aids, and contact databases
- Provide audio clips of doctors about product-related issues

Outcomes

The original product training, assessment systems, and the Xegy™ delivery platform were developed in less than three months. The IT-free platform allowed the pharmaceutical team to manage and contribute directly.

At the time this book was published, one product had been rolled out to the entire salesforce as a beta test. The results were

- 100 percent compliance in completing certification at a 95 percent accuracy rate within the specified timeframe
- Sales representatives see animations and demonstrations; hear doctors speak from their perspectives about products and treatments; spend less time searching for information and forms; and take charge of their own learning

Lessons Learned

- The scope of product certification should be expanded beyond traditional learning to include all elements relevant to selling the product.
- Systems can and should be used to clear the obstacles and enable sales representatives to make sales.
- A salesforce with limited experience in technology can adapt quickly to systems that support sales.

APPENDIX B:
ASSESSMENT AND ANALYSIS

ACTION VERB LIST

This list presents action verbs for use during objectives analysis. Once you decide on the type of learned capability for the objective, these verbs can be used to match the learned capability with the appropriate action for the objective.

Learned Capability	Verb	Definition
Discrimination	alter	to change
	arrange	to mentally order or classify in categories
	circle	to indicate understanding by encircling
	describe	to characterize qualities
	discover	to detect the true character
	divide	to separate into two or more parts or groups
	isolate	to set apart
	point	to make known or visible
	segregate	to separate or set apart from
	separate	to set apart
	set apart	to reserve to a particular use
	show	to point out a difference
	sort	to mentally group on the basis of common characteristics
	split	to mentally divide into parts or portions
	write (or) type	to put in print
Concrete concept	arrange	to place in an orderly manner; to classify into categories
	call	to make a request
	catalogue	to classify material
	combine	to synthesize in order to form a whole
	connect	to make a mental connection
	describe	to represent or give an account
	duplicate	to produce something equal to
	gather	to bring together or collect
	group	to form a complete unit from two or more parts; to classify; to mentally join or fasten together

Learned Capability	Verb	Definition
Concrete concept (cont'd.)	index	to list items in order to lead to a fact or conclusion
	inspect	to observe or take note of
	itemize	to detail or particularize
	join	to put together to form a unit
	label	to describe or designate
	link	to mentally connect
	mark	to distinguish a trait or quality
	match	to equate
	name	to label; to mention explicitly
	narrate	to relate in detail
	place	to distribute in an orderly manner
	point	to indicate; to assign
	repeat	to summarize principle points
	select	to choose by preference from a number or group
	sort	to arrange in groups according to predetermined specifications
	tell	to relate or give an account of
	unite	to coordinate or blend
Defined concept	alphabetize	to arrange alphabetically
	arrange	to put in order
	change	to modify or make fit
	evaluate	to appraise the worth of
	file	to arrange in order according to specified characteristics
	group	to combine according to certain specifications
	index	to classify according to certain characteristics
	list	to place in a specified category to inventory traits, preferences, attitudes, interests, or abilities that evaluate characteristics or skills

Learned Capability	Verb	Definition
Defined concept (cont'd.)	measure	to make determinations based on standard criteria
	order	to systematize
	organize	to form into a coherent unit
	pigeonhole	to assign to a category or classify
	rank	to make an orderly arrangement
	rate	to assign a value; to estimate
	record	to make a chronicle of
	score	to assign a value to
	sort	to distribute into groups according to specified characteristics
	survey	to examine a condition or appraise
	weigh	to consider carefully or evaluate
	write (or) type	to put in print
Rule	announce	to make known or proclaim
	categorize	to separate according to specified characteristics
	coach	to instruct beforehand
	corroborate	to support with evidence
	define	to fix or mark limits
	depict	to portray or make meaning from
	describe	to represent or give an account
	disclose	to uncover or make known; to reveal
	display	to exhibit or make evident
	divulge	to make public, unveil, or reveal
	explain	to tell, educate, or train
	expose	to portray, reveal, or draw forth
	extricate	to untangle or straighten; to pull from
	locate	to find; to place in a location or category
	organize	to arrange or form into a coherent unit; to integrate
	paint	to make a representation or give an example
	place	to situate or locate

Learned Capability	Verb	Definition
Rule (cont'd.)	present	to show
	proclaim	to give an outward indication of
	prove	to authenticate
	relate	to tell
	reveal	to divulge or make known
	separate	to break up or detach
	show	to demonstrate clearly or make clear
	summarize	to state concisely
	teach	to instruct or train
	tell	to give an account of
	tutor	to coach or guide, usually in a particular subject
	unfold	to open to view; to reveal
	verify	to establish truth, accuracy, or reality; to confirm
Problem solving	acquire	to come to have possession of
	arrive	to appear; to reach a predetermined or undetermined conclusion
	assemble	to fit together
	build	to construct or form
	collect	to bring together into one body or place
	complete	to finish
	compose	to form by putting together
	construct	to arrange parts or elements; to build
	convince	to persuade by argument; establish belief
	create	to produce or bring about by a course of action
	deduce	to derive from
	design	to conceive and plan
	develop	to expound; to make clear by degrees or in detail
	devise	to plan to obtain or bring about
	effect	to bring about, or cause to take place
	eliminate	to exclude based on specified criteria

Learned Capability	Verb	Definition
Problem solving (cont'd.)	enact	to set up, establish, or constitute
	enlist	to secure the support and aid of; employ
	equalize	to make like in quality or quantity
	erect	to put together by fitting materials; build
	establish	to set up or constitute
	excite	to stimulate to action
	exhibit	to present to view
	finish	to complete
	formulate	to form systematically
	give	to furnish what is needed
	inaugurate	to bring about the beginning
	incite	to move to action
	include	to incorporate according to specified criteria
	initiate	to cause the beginning of; set in motion
	introduce	to bring into play; institute
	invent	to originate, find, begin
	launch	to set in motion; initiate
	make	to create or cause to exist, occur, or appear
	originate	to author or cause to exist
	plot	to devise or plan to bring about
	present	to offer to view; show
	produce	to make, yield, render, or bring to bear
	show	to cause or permit to be seen; exhibit
	stimulate	to arouse to action
	supply	to furnish what is needed; give
Cognitive strategy	accede to	to give in to a request or demand
	accept	to regard as having a certain meaning; understand
	admit	to allow or permit; provide for
	advocate	to plead in favor of
	affirm	to validate
	agree	to settle on by common consent; admit; concede

Learned Capability	Verb	Definition
Cognitive strategy (cont'd.)	allow	to permit, admit, consent, say, or state
	approve	to give formal or official sanction
	arrange	to place or distribute in an orderly manner
	authorize	to establish by authority
	champion	to uphold; support
	clarify	to make understandable
	comply	to accept tacitly or overtly
	concede	to accept as true, valid or accurate
	confirm	to give approval to; ratify
	contain	to have within; hold; compromise; include
	corroborate	to support with evidence or authority; confirm
	defend	to protect or maintain a position
	define	to fix or mark limits
	describe	to represent or give an account
	embrace	to include
	employ	to make use of
	enact	to establish by legal and authoritative action
	encompass	to enclose, envelop, or include
	endorse	to express approval publicly
	endure	to remain firm or unyielding
	engage	to attract and hold
	espouse	to give verbal support
	exercise	to make effective; use; exert
	exhaust	to use up or consume entirely
	expend	to make use for a specific purpose
	explain	to make known; to make plain and understandable
	implement	to put into effect, carry out, or accomplish

Learned Capability	Verb	Definition
Cognitive strategy (cont'd.)	incorporate	to unite or work into something that already exists so as to form an indistinguishable whole
	incur	to contract
	legislate	to enact by laws
	list	to enumerate
	manipulate	to manage or use skillfully
	narrate	to tell in detail
	operate	to perform a function; to produce an appropriate effect
	permit	to make possible
	prove	to test the truth or validity of
	ratify	to formally approve and sanction; confirm
	recite	to repeat or read aloud
	recount	to relate in detail; narrate
	rehearse	to present an account of; repeat; narrate; relate or enumerate
	relate	to give an account of; tell
	report	to give an account of
	sanction	to make valid or binding
	simplify	to make more intelligible
	substantiate	to establish by proof or evidence; verify
	support	to substantiate
	uphold	to support against an opponent
	use	to put into action
	validate	to confirm, support, or corroborate
	verify	to confirm or substantiate in law by oath
Verbal information	acknowledge	to make known or take notice
	advance	to move forward
	affirm	to state positively; validate or confirm
	agree	to be consistent or in harmony with
	allege	to assert without proof

Learned Capability	Verb	Definition
Verbal information (cont'd.)	announce	to make known publicly; proclaim
	argue	to contend or disagree in words; dispute
	articulate	to express
	assert	to state or declare positively
	attest	to establish or verify the usage of
	characterize	to describe a quality
	charge	to command or instruct
	clarify	to make understandable
	comment	to explain or interpret
	communicate	to make known
	confess	to tell or make known
	confirm	to approve or ratify
	contend	to maintain or assert
	contribute	to supply information
	decipher	to convert into intelligible form
	declare	to make known formally or explicitly
	decode	to decipher
	define	to explain the meaning of
	delineate	to describe in detail
	describe	to represent or give an account of
	explain	to make known; to make understandable
	expound	to set forth; state
	express	to represent, state, depict, or delineate
	interpret	to explain or tell the meaning of
	justify	to prove to be just, right, or reasonable
	narrate	to tell in detail
	notify	to give notice
	offer	to present for acceptance
	portray	to describe in words
	profess	to declare or admit openly or freely
	propose	to set forth
	rationalize	to bring into accord with reason or cause something to seem reasonable
	recount	to relate in detail or narrate

Learned Capability	Verb	Definition
Verbal information (cont'd.)	speak	to talk
	tell	to state or relate
	utter	to speak
	summarize	to describe briefly and succinctly
	verbalize	to express in words
	vocalize	to speak
	voice	to express in words
Motor/ psychomotor skill	attach	to fasten to
	administer	to manage or supervise the use of
	aid	to help
	arrange	to order
	bring about	to cause to take place
	bring on	to cause to appear
	carry out	to achieve
	clean	to remove or eradicate; strip or empty
	complete	to finish
	conduct	to lead
	deal	to distribute
	deliver	to convey
	demonstrate	to show
	direct	to show or point out
	discharge	to unload
	dismiss	to permit or cause to leave
	dispense	to deal out in portions
	display	to make evident
	distribute	to expend by proportion
	do	to bring to pass or carry out
	donate	to give
	dramatize	to present with heightened action
	emerge	to come forth
	empty	to remove the contents of
	endow	to bestow upon or furnish with
	equip	to furnish
	establish	to physically erect

Learned Capability	Verb	Definition
Motor/ psychomotor skill (cont'd.)	excrete	to sift out; discharge
	finish	to bring to an end
	force	to cause to happen
	free	to rid of restraints
	give	to yield, grant, or bestow
	impersonate	to assume the character of or act like another
	implement	to carry out; accomplish
	inflict	to impose or perpetrate
	liberate	to set free
	make	to create or construct
	organize	to arrange
	pass	to move ahead of
	perform	to act out or dramatize
	play	to engage in pleasurable activity
	present	to show
	release	to let go
	serve	to wait upon
	sketch	to draw
	stage	to produce for public view
	supply	to provide
	surrender	to give over
	transfer	to convey from one person, place, or situation to another
	work	to expend energy toward labor
Attitude	adopt	to accept formally
	advocate	to plead in favor of
	champion	to support
	complete	to finish
	conclude	to decide
	cull	to select from a group
	decide	to come to a conclusion
	decree	to determine
	defend	to take a position

Learned Capability	Verb	Definition
Attitude (cont'd.)	determine	to settle or decide
	discover	to make known or visible
	discriminate	to distinguish
	distinguish	to perceive a difference
	divine	to discover or locate
	elect	to choose freely
	embrace	to take in or include as part of
	encompass	to include
	endorse	to express approval
	espouse	to support
	fancy	to like
	favor	to lean toward
	include	to take in as part of a whole
	incorporate	to unite or work into something that already exists
	judge	to form an opinion of
	opt	to choose or select
	perform	to act out or dramatize
	pick	to choose or select
	prefer	to like better; recommend
	resolve	to conclude
	select	to choose by preference
	settle	to resolve or decide
	take up	to accept or adopt

SAMPLE CASE STUDY

This case study demonstrates how information from assessment and analysis are organized to determine the final outcome of a solution to an organizational issue. You can read the basic information from the business case and then see the results of technology analysis, issue analysis, objectives analysis, and media analysis. The solution is provided at the end with an explanation of how it was arrived at for this issue.

Business Case

Beta Northern is a 5,000-member financial organization with divisions located in thirty-four countries throughout the world. The organization is very loosely structured. Each of the authorities in the thirty-four countries operates its divisions pretty much autonomously as long as it reaches quarterly and yearly goals. Beta has a centralized executive committee at its headquarters in Chicago. Each division has a division vice president, operations managers, and analysts.

The organization uses twenty common financial processes. Some processes are used by analysts many times a day, other processes once a year. Any analyst can receive a phone call from a vendor or customer with any inquiry that requires following one or more of the processes. Not only do analysts not know the steps to follow for unfamiliar processes, but they don't know who to refer inquiries to in order to find answers. The procedures are poorly documented, but can be found on a shelf in the storage room of each division office if you really need them.

The analysts are highly paid and there is very little turnover, even though the company does not have a bonus or incentive plan. Benefits are comparable to those in similar organizations, the offices are always modern, and the equipment is state-of-the-art. The company values the skills of these analysts but is not pleased with the decreasing market share.

The company uses a 360-degree performance evaluation process that is administered by managers once a year. These evaluations are administered as a matter of routine; the results are presented to the analysts during a performance review and then filed in their personnel files. There are no development plans or prescriptions for improving in areas needing improvement.

On being hired, analysts are paired with senior analysts for a period of four weeks for individual training, including coaching on the company's policies and operating procedures. Other training consists of company-sponsored conferences and courses to maintain certain certifications required by the profession.

Customers and vendors are very dissatisfied because they are transferred an average of three times per call. In 25 percent of the inquiries, incorrect information is provided to them.

On the following pages, you'll see the results of various analyses conducted jointly by the training, performance improvement, and organization development groups to reach a solution for this organizational issue.

Technology Assessment Tool

1. List the types of technology available. For example, if employees have access to e-mail, put Yes in the "Availability" column of the tool, next to "e-mail."

2. Determine the capability of the technology. The capability is the strength of the technology, not the capabilities of those who use it. For example, if e-mail is used for communication, but the e-mail system has little functionality, mark "Low" in the "Capability" column.

   ☐ High indicates a sophisticated capability that can be used for the issue involved in this analysis.

   ☐ Medium indicates a capability that can be adapted for use for the issue involved in this analysis.

   ☐ Low indicates a capability that would not be useful for the issues involved in this analysis.

3. Document the percentage of users potentially involved in this issue who have access to the technology.

Table B.1
Technology Assessment Tool

Technology Use	Examples of Technology Use	Availability	Capability	Access (percent)
Communication	Phone conferencing	Yes	**Low** Med High	50
	E-mail	Yes	Low Med **High**	100
	Chat rooms	No	Low Med High	
	Newsgroups	No	Low Med High	
	List servers	No	Low Med High	
Reference materials, online help	Websites	Yes	Low **Med** High	100
	Work process and procedures	Yes	**Low** Med High	100
	Databases	Yes	Low Med **High**	100
	Phone lists	Yes	Low Med **High**	100
	Course catalogs	No	Low Med High	
	Scheduling appointments	Yes	Low **Med** High	100

Table B.1
Technology Assessment Tool, Cont'd.

Technology Use	Examples of Technology Use	Availability	Capability			Access (percent)
Reference materials, online help	Course notes	No	Low	Med	High	
	Instructor's notes	No	Low	Med	High	
	Abstracts	No	Low	Med	High	
	Technical manuals	Yes	**Low**	Med	High	100
	Videos	No	Low	Med	High	
	Graphics and photos	No	Low	Med	High	
Testing and assessment: online testing, tracking, reporting	Electronic self-assessment databases	No	Low	Med	High	
	Electronic tracking databases	No	Low	Med	High	
	Electronic reporting databases	No	Low	Med	High	
	Security (access, authentication, confidentiality	Yes	Low	**Med**	High	100
Distribution: sending throughout the organization	LAN	Yes	Low	**Med**	High	100
	CD-ROM	Yes	Low	**Med**	High	75
	Diskette	Yes	Low	**Med**	High	100
	Video	No	Low	Med	High	
	Audio	No	Low	Med	High	
	Downloading	No	Low	Med	High	
Delivery: receiving throughout the organization	Dedicated audio and video servers	No	Low	Med	High	
	Multimedia computers	Yes	Low	**Med**	High	50
	Video teleconferencing	No	Low	**Med**	High	
Design and development expertise: infrastructure design, development, maintenance, resources (include anticipated upgrades)	Video production	No	Low	Med	High	
	Audio production	No	Low	Med	High	
	Graphics production	Yes	Low	Med	High	5
	Online help and reference system production	Yes	Low	Med	High	5
	CBT authoring	No	Low	Med	High	
	Web authoring	Yes	**Low**	Med	High	1
	Testing database	No	Low	Med	High	
	Statistical program	Yes	Low	Med	**High**	50

Issue Analysis Tool

Instructions: Identify all of the information determined from your analysis thus far and place the information in the right-hand column under the appropriate level and activity. A particular piece of information may have components at more than one level. Attempt to separate the components of information into the level and type of activity they represent.

Table B.2
Issue Analysis Tool

Level	Activity	Definition	Information from Analysis
Organizational	Corporate Culture	Will the corporate culture support the solution you propose? • Respect for the individual • Leadership style of management • Acceptance and use of employee ideas	Organization is very loosely structured across the 34 countries. Managers have had the ability to run their divisions pretty much as they choose.
	Retention	Is keeping valuable and experienced employees a high priority?	These are highly paid financial and accounting employees so the company is very interested in keeping them.
	Incentives	Are users motivated by the organization to use the solution you propose? • Pay structure • Bonuses • Recognition • Performance Reviews	Employees are well paid but company has no bonus or recognition plan. Performance reviews are generic and company-wide; seen mostly as a formality; no pay-for-performance structure attached.

Table B.2
Issue Analysis Tool, Cont'd.

Level	Activity	Definition	Information from Analysis
	Organizational Structure	Hierarchical structure of the organization Decision-making authority	The organizational structure is vertical corporate-wide but each division VP has the authority to make his or her own decisions about operating his or her own division.
	Communication	Are people informed of what, how, and why decisions are made? Do people receive feedback?	(See information under corporate culture.)
Performance	Tools	Do employees have the required equipment to complete their jobs • Computers • Software • Forms	Employees do not know the processes or procedures or who the process owner is. There are antiquated paper based references to look up information but they are too cumbersome, few people know where the references are, so the sources are not used.
	Work Environment	Does the environment where work is done permit people to do their jobs? • On-the-job training after or in place of formal training	Employees work in very modern physical environment. There is no old system. Employees are expected to learn the processes and

Level	Activity	Definition	Information from Analysis
		• Removal of old systems	procedures from experienced employees.
		• Coaching	
		• Management support for solution	
		• Temperature	
		• Ventilation	
	Processes and Procedures	Do employees understand ways to do their jobs?	Poorly documented processes and procedures.
		• Are processes and procedures in place for employees to follow?	
		Do employees know who their internal/external customers and partners are?	
		• What are the interdependencies between people/groups to complete work?	
		Are ways of doing work effective?	
		• Are there too many steps?	
		• Are there unnecessary steps?	
		• Are there unnecessary delays?	
	Expectations	Do people know what performance levels they are held to?	Employees are made aware of customer dissatisfaction and the

Table B.2
Issue Analysis Tool, Cont'd.

Level	Activity	Definition	Information from Analysis
		What constitutes a "job well done"?	need for better and more accurate information but have no solution; neither does management.
	Quality Standards	Is the emphasis on quality and effectiveness rather than quantity and efficiency? • Are employees expected to perform their jobs well? • Do employees know the criteria for performance?	Employees are rated by the number of calls they handle per hour.
Training	Knowledge	Do employees have the information they need to do the job?	No
	Skills	Do employees have the ability to do their jobs?	Yes
	Attitudes	Do employees know the importance of doing their job?	Yes, they care about doing well. Hard-working group.

Objectives Analysis Worksheet

Instructions: Write a terminal objective for each piece of information you found from issue analysis under the same level and activity as they were located on the Issue Analysis Tool.

<table>
<tr><td colspan="3" align="center">Table B.3
Objectives Analysis Worksheet</td></tr>
<tr><th>Level</th><th>Activity</th><th>Objective</th></tr>
<tr><td>Organizational</td><td>Corporate Culture</td><td>1. The company will establish mechanisms for communication between managers within two months.

2. Employee opinion survey will indicate an increase of employee perceptions of upper management working together across organizations within one year.</td></tr>
<tr><td></td><td>Retention</td><td>No issue</td></tr>
<tr><td></td><td>Incentives</td><td>3. The company will implement an incentive plan within one month that will provide profit sharing—50 percent based on individual performance and 50 percent on group performance. Individual performance will be based on attaining a minimum of 4.5 on a 5.0 scale on a 360-degree performance evaluation.</td></tr>
<tr><td></td><td>Organizational Structure</td><td>No issue</td></tr>
<tr><td></td><td>Communication</td><td>See Corporate Culture</td></tr>
<tr><td>Performance</td><td>Tools</td><td>Tools are not the issue. See Processes and Procedures</td></tr>
<tr><td></td><td>Work Environment</td><td>4. Quality experts will monitor ten analyst calls per month and provide feedback on meeting expectations of providing 95 percent correct information.</td></tr>
<tr><td></td><td>Processes and Procedures</td><td>5. Analysts will use processes and procedures to provide accurate information to customers, the quality standard to be 95 percent.</td></tr>
</table>

Table B.3
Objectives Analysis Worksheet, Cont'd.

Level	Activity	Objective
	Expectations	6. Analysts will provide 95 percent correct information to customers.
	Quality Standards	7. Analysts will transfer callers no more than one time to receive information.
Training	Knowledge	8. Analysts will state or locate the correct policy and procedure with 95 percent accuracy.
	Skills	9. Analysts will always use the policies and procedures to provide customer information.
		10. Analysts will always state process owners for each financial process.
	Attitudes	11. Analysts will always positively state the importance of providing accurate information to customers and its relation to increased customer satisfaction.

Media Analysis Rating Scale

Instructions: Complete the rating scale as follows:

1. Consider each factor on the rating scale as to its importance to the situation you are analyzing, using the key provided.

2. When you have completed the Media Analysis Form, tally the number of occurrences of each media ranked as a 4 or 5 and record this number in the High Occurrences column on the Media Analysis Summary Sheet.

3. Tally each media ranked as a 1 or 2 and record this number in the Low Occurrences column.

4. Ignore those ranked as 3.

5. Subtract the number of low occurrences from the number of high occurrences and record that number in the Difference column.

6. Determine the weight of each media by dividing the Difference by the All Occurrences number and record that percentage in the Weight column.

7. The media with the highest weight are probably the most likely media for your solution.

Rating Scale
5 = Very important consideration
4 = Important consideration
3 = Neutral consideration
2 = Unimportant consideration
1 = Not a consideration at all

Table B.4
Media Analysis Form

	Factors	Considerations	Suggested Media
1	1 ② 3 4 5 Content requires interactivity (computer).	Does the content involve computer software, simulation or practice? Computer-based training simulations can facilitate learning.	Computer-based Web-based
2	1 ② 3 4 5 Unintended learning may occur.	Do you need to control for participants learning positive habits, eliminating or avoiding undesirable habits? Are learning attitudes important?	Instructor-led Satellite broadcast Video teleconference
3	① 2 3 4 5 Collaborative learning is desired.	Do group learning experiences, including opportunities to build relationships or share information, need to occur?	Instructor-led Satellite broadcast Video teleconference Web-based
4	① 2 3 4 5 Content requires interactivity (human).	Will participants gain interpersonal and communication skills from immediate feedback from an observer about their performance? To what extent does the learner need to use or demonstrate interpersonal or communication skills such as presentation, teamwork, leadership or facilitation?	Instructor-led Satellite broadcast Video teleconference
5	1 ② 3 4 5 Audience requires motivation.	How motivated are the learners? *Note:* Self-instruction or distance education requires higher intrinsic motivation for successful learning.	Instructor-led Videotapes Web-based Satellite broadcast
6	1 2 3 4 ⑤ Audience requires convenience, training at or near the work site.	Is time away from work not possible because of work schedules, project requirements, variable shifts or time sensitive performance? Are participants dispersed and require decentralized training?	Computer-based Video teleconference Performance support Web-based Audio teleconference

Table B.4
Media Analysis Form, Cont'd.

	Factors	Considerations	Suggested Media
7	(1) 2 3 4 5 Audience has limited access to required technology.	What technology is available? Is there a barrier to technology?	Audio teleconference Instructor-led Computer-based
8	1 2 3 4 (5) Audience has limited access to required expertise.	Is there limited expertise that must be leveraged across the organization?	Computer-based Satellite broadcast Videotapes Web-based Video teleconference
9	(1) 2 3 4 5 Students resistant to new media.	How receptive is the audience to using a new medium? To what extent does attitude toward lecture style help or hinder learning? *Note:* Learners often enjoy instructor-led training because it allows them to be with other learners. Although they enjoy it, they may learn less. They may fear technology, have only experienced mainframe CBT, or do not want to spend more time at a computer screen. Take that fear into account and move toward a technology solution whenever possible.	Instructor-led
10	1 2 3 4 (5) Employees must review the information frequently.	Will reference materials be required? Is there a need for "look-up" capabilities?	Performance support Web-based
11	1 2 3 4 (5) There is an immediate need for application of expertise to the job.	How critical are the knowledge or skills to the performance of job related tasks?	Performance support

Table B.4
Media Analysis Form, Cont'd.

	Factors	Considerations	Suggested Media
12	1 2 3 ④ 5 Wide variation in entry level background knowledge.	How wide is the gap in entry level knowledge? *Note:* CBT provides the ability to branch users to different levels of training.	Computer-based
13	1 2 3 ④ 5 Content has a short shelf life or is changing rapidly.	Is the content stable? Is it still under construction or development? How does the stability of the content affect the frequency of revisions? How difficult or is it to make revisions using this medium? Revisions to audiotapes, videotapes, and CBT, are time-consuming and expensive.	Video teleconference Audio teleconference Web-based Satellite broadcast Instructor-led
14	1 2 3 4 ⑤ Global audience multiple cultures or languages.	Will reading, hearing, or understanding English be difficult for audience members? Are there varying levels and types of information need? *Note:* A variety of non-print media can deliver text, graphics, sound, and motion, allowing for learner control	Computer-based Satellite broadcast Videotapes
15	1 2 ③ 4 5 Materials must be available in a variety of formats.	Do you need to re-purpose materials? *Notes:* Video can be reused in a variety of media. Electronic media can be delivered in a variety of formats	Videotapes Satellite broadcast Video teleconference Computer-based
16	1 2 3 4 ⑤ Fewer than two hundred per year need training/ performance support.	How many learners are in the target audience? What is the size of the audience over expected shelf life of the training?	Performance support Instructor-led Video teleconference Audio teleconference

Table B.4
Media Analysis Form, Cont'd.

	Factors	Considerations	Suggested Media
17	1 2 3 4 ⑤ More than two thousand per year need training/ performance support.	How many users are in the target audience? What is the size of the audience over the expected shelf life of the training?	Satellite broadcast Computer-based Videotapes Audiotapes
18	1 2 3 4 ⑤ Must train large numbers of employees quickly.	How quickly must the intervention be developed? How much time is available to build, buy, or revise products? For shortened time frames, consider buying or revising existing products.	Video teleconference Audio teleconference Audiotapes Instructor-led Satellite broadcast
19	1 2 3 4 ⑤ Requires compression of training time.	Is it important to reduce the time participants spend in training? *Note:* CBT has typical training compression ratios of 50 to 70 percent.	Performance support Computer-based Satellite broadcast Self-paced workbook
20	1 ② 3 4 5 Keep development cost per hour of instruction low.	What is the cost per learner for developing or acquiring this medium?	Video teleconference Audio teleconference Satellite broadcast
21	1 ② 3 4 5 Keep travel expenses low.	Is travel a barrier due to budgets, distance, and business considerations? How can you reduce travel expenses?	Performance support Computer-based Web-based Satellite broadcast Self-paced workbook Video teleconference Audio teleconference Videotapes Audiotapes

Table B.4
Media Analysis Form, Cont'd.

	Factors	Considerations	Suggested Media
22	1 2 3 4 ⑤ Keep implemen- tation, delivery, maintenance cost low	What are means of distribution? How will changes be accomplished? Can they be made quickly and easily? Will changes make previous distri- butions obsolete?	Performance support Video teleconference Audio teleconference Self-paced workbook
23	1 ② 3 4 5 Testing, evalua- tion, or tracking of student per- formance is necessary.	Can the assessment be self-scored? Is certification necessary? *Note:* Assessment of interpersonal and communication skills requires observation. Some observation requires a trained expert.	Self-paced workbook Computer-based Satellite broadcast Instructor-led
24	1 2 ③ 4 5 Tracking course completion necessary.	Can media assess course completion?	Computer-based Satellite broadcast Instructor-led

Media Analysis Summary Sheet

- All Occurrences is the total number of times a media appears in the Suggested Media column.
- High Occurrences is the number of times a given media received a rating of 4 or 5.
- Low Occurrences is the number of times a given media received a 1 or 2.
- The Difference is the number of Low Occurrences subtracted from the number of High Occurrences.
- The Weight is determined by dividing the Difference by All Occurrences for each media.
- The highest weighted media are the ones most likely for the solution.

You must now return to the Objectives Analysis Worksheet and match each performance objective with the most appropriate media. Remember that you might present one objective using more than one type of media.

Table B.5
Media Analysis Summary Sheet

Media Type	All Occurrences	High Occurrences (4 or 5)	Low Occurrences (1 or 2)	Difference (High − Low)	Weight (Diff. ÷ All Occ.)
Audiotapes	3	//(2)	/(1)	+1	34 percent
Audio teleconference	8	//////(6)	//(2)	+4	50 percent
Computer-based	12	//////(6)	////(4)	+2	17 percent
Satellite broadcast	15	///////(7)	/////(5)	+2	13 percent
Instructor-led	11	//(2)	///////(7)	-5	
Performance support	7	//////(6)	/(1)	+5	71 percent
Self-paced workbook	4	//(2)	//(2)	0	0
Video teleconference	12	///////(7)	////(4)	+3	25 percent
Videotapes	6	///(3)	//(2)	+1	17 percent
Web-based	8	////(4)	////(4)	0	0

Media/Objectives Mapping Tool

Instructions: This tool is for matching media types with the objectives. Record the objective beside the type of media that will be used to deliver the content of an objective.

Table B.6
Media/Objectives Mapping Tool

Media Type	Objective
Audiotapes	
Audio teleconference	The company will establish mechanisms for communication between managers within two months.
	Employee opinion survey will indicate an increase of employee perceptions of upper management working together across organizations within one year.
Computer-based	
Satellite broadcast	
Instructor-led	
Performance support	Analysts will state or locate the correct policy and procedure with 95 percent accuracy.
	Analysts will always use the policies and procedures to provide customer information.
	Analysts will always state process owners for each financial process.
Self-paced workbook	
Video teleconference	
Videotapes	
Web-based	

Solution

An electronic performance support system (EPSS) is the chosen medium for delivery with six high occurrences and one low occurrence. With an overall weight of seven occurrences, performance support is a highly rated delivery medium. Since most of the issues and objectives relate to knowing and using the processes and procedures, and since the procedures are already in document form, the processes and procedures will more likely be used if they are automated and put on the company's LAN, which 100 percent of all employees have access to.

No formal training will be required for this solution, as indicated by the media analysis, where instructional media ranked very low. Employee performance and quality assurance will be evaluated by the call monitoring system that is already in place. A Help system will be included in the EPSS, consisting of a process flow diagram of the main menu system that leads to the process and then the steps of each procedure. The Help system will also consist of screens that explain the functionality of the system.

An audio teleconference message arranged with the company's long distance telephone carrier will send a message from the CEO to each employee in the financial organization introducing the new EPSS system under development and when to expect it to go online.

The division head will also announce the initiation of a customer evaluation rating system that will result in a pay-for-performance reward system. These customer satisfaction ratings will be the measurement of the effectiveness and use of the processes and procedures through increased customer satisfaction and reduced number of complaints. These initiatives will address the performance and organizational level issues found during analysis.

Upper management will begin to communicate with employees more openly through e-mail, informing employees of the state of the company, as well as decisions that are being made and considered about the company, and soliciting employee input. Executive committee members and other upper management will begin to become more visible to employees by holding company meetings followed by social events. The effectiveness of this effort will be measured on an employee satisfaction survey that will be administered at the end of one year and every year thereafter.

Upper management will use e-mail and meetings with the CEO to begin working more as a unified team and make decisions that benefit the company rather than just his or her own division. Since video teleconferencing has such a high rating on the media analysis, the company will invest in a video teleconferencing system to hold virtual meetings with managers in remote locations other than headquarters. The cost of this system will be more than offset by the reduced cost of managers traveling to headquarters.

THE FOG INDEX

The Fog Index, developed by Robert Gunning (1968), expresses readability as the number of years of schooling required to read a text with ease. Follow these steps to check readability:

1. Select a representative sample of text.

2. Count the number of words the sample contains.

3. Count the number of sentences it contains.

4. Count the number of difficult words in the sample. Difficult words are those defined as having three or more syllables or ending with -ly or -ing. However, note the following exceptions:

   - Capitalized words should not be counted as difficult.
   - Combinations of short, easy words such as vice-chairman, teacher-coach, and so on, count as one word.
   - Verb forms made into three syllables by adding -ed or -es, such as adjusted, inserted, and assesses, should not be counted as difficult.

5. Determine the average sentence length. Divide the number of words by the number of sentences.

6. Determine the percentage of difficult words in the sample:

   Percentage of difficult words =
   (number of difficult words ÷ number of words) x 100

7. Use this formula to calculate the Fog Index:

   Fog Index = (average sentence length [step 5] +
   percentage of difficult words [step 6]) x 0.4

8. Repeat the process by selecting a couple of other samples. Use random samples from the beginning, middle, and end of the material, or from different authors in the same piece, to check for uniformity.

Note: You may average the samples to determine an average readability level. It is permissible to have an escalating reading level from the beginning of a work to the end, as long as the level does not increase by more than about a year and a half.

APPENDIX C: DEVELOPMENT AND IMPLEMENTATION

SCRIPT STANDARDS

General

A script is a recipe that tells the video production crew what they need to know. Here we offer a template, a sort of fill-in version of such a recipe, defining the standard parts that need to be determined for the particulars of each script. We offer just enough of a sample script to illustrate commonly encountered ingredients and instructions for the video recipe.

Start with a title:

<u>UNDERLINED AND CENTERED</u>

Now proceed with the body of the script.

1. *Slug line.* Begin each video scene with instructions for the director, the set, and the lighting crew. The slug line indicates interior or exterior, location or set, and lighting—day or night—in ALL CAPS. Example:

   FADE IN

   INT. RESTAURANT—EXPO WINDOW—DAY

2. Next, indent and describe the scene, including who is in it, what the scene looks like, and what is going on. Include camera directions that are critical to the sequence in ALL CAPS. Use CAPS the first time a character is seen onscreen so that the number of characters can be counted in a quick scan of the script and so that actors can quickly locate the place where their role begins. Example:

   CHRIS stands at the Expo window and looks back and forth between the ticket and the plate. He is wearing a server uniform. He pauses and the CAMERA MOVES IN for a TIGHT SHOT of the ticket in his hand.

3. Insert dialogue and sound effects. Always refer to characters in the dialogue with the same names used in the narrative. Dialogue is indented even further, single spaced, with the character in ALL CAPS. Example:

   SFX: Sound of a busy restaurant in the background.

   CHRIS
   Whoops. Did you forget the tomatoes?

   KATY
   You've got to be kidding.

Check the dialogue to make sure it is realistic by reading it out loud. Avoid tongue twisters such as "So send us seven servers singing, Sir."

4. If the scene continues onto additional pages, write CONTINUED at the top of the page. Be sure to include a slug line and narrative for each new scene.

Terminology

Here are some common terms used in a video script to provide direction.

- FAVORING or ANGLE ON: Focus on or center a person, place, or thing in a shot.
- NEW ANGLE or ANOTHER ANGLE: Shoot the same scene from another angle.
- WIDER ANGLE: Change the focus of a scene to include more of the surroundings.
- INSERT, CLOSE IN, MOVE IN, or TIGHT SHOT: Used to emphasize an object.
- POV: Shoot from a person's point of view.
- REVERSE ANGLE: Change the perspective (usually the opposite of POV).
- MATCH CUT: Matching something in the shot exactly with something in a follow-on shot.
- MOVING SHOT: Focus on the movement of an object such as a car moving through a restaurant parking lot.
- TWO SHOT or THREE SHOT: Subject of the shot is two or three people.
- SFX: Sound effects.
- TIME DISSOLVE: Show a time progression using a fade-in-and-out technique.
- FADE IN: Begin the video.
- FADE OUT: End the video.

APPENDIX D: EVALUATION

COMPLETED EVALUATION STRATEGY
FOR TRAINING AND CONSULTING SOFTEK

Table D.1
Evaluation Strategy

Introduction

< > recognized the necessity to establish a systematic evaluation strategy to ensure the quality of the solutions it implements. All solutions are implemented for the purpose of improving the company's position in the industry. Improvement involves satisfaction of internal partners and employees as well as external customers. Satisfaction is evaluated against the company's balanced scorecard.

The company has established a hierarchical evaluation process to accomplish the requirement of using a systematic evaluation strategy. That hierarchy involves four levels of evaluation as espoused by leaders in the field of measurement and evaluation listed in the Resources section of this document. Each member of the functional group has read these resources and the principles are followed to consistently implement this strategy.

Level 1 Surveys	The portion of the strategy will be implemented in a phased method. All (100 percent) existing solutions will have a survey developed within six months. All new solutions will have a survey developed as part of the design and development process.
	Questions on the surveys will address specific components of the solution with respect to the content of the solution, the delivery interface, and supplementary components, as well as demographic data. Surveys will be developed using a Likert-type scale of four choices to require forced choices for consistency of results. The scale should be Strongly Agree, Agree, Disagree, and Strongly Disagree. Strongly agree should be defined in the survey as a component that is consistently contained in the solution; agree should be defined as a component that is usually contained in the solution; disagree should be defined as a component that is usually not found in the solution; strongly disagree should be defined as a component that is never found in the solution. Each survey should contain space for comments where users can type individual reactions to the solution. The data fields required for demographic data are ethnic origin, age, sex, number of years with company, number of years in the function, and number of e-learning courses previously taken.

Table D.1
Evaluation Strategy, Cont'd.

	Comparing survey questions against the performance objectives of the solution will validate surveys.
	Data will be collected using online survey forms that are returned to a database file on the company's LAN. The data will be in the form of ASCII text. Data will be transferred to an Excel spreadsheet. An Excel survey analysis spreadsheet will be developed to manipulate the data and produce reports.
	A measurement team will review data on a weekly basis and report results to the development and design team as well as to the managers from the user groups.
	Results will be reported to all stakeholder groups in a measurement report.
Level 2 Tests	Each solution that has a training or learning component, a certification requirement, or has some sort of regulatory component will contain a knowledge-level test to determine that a sufficient level of knowledge has been attained as a result of completing the learning portion of the solution.
	Tests will be validated using one of the methodologies found in Schrock and Coscarelli's book (see Resources section of this document).
	The data will be collected electronically and returned to a database on the company's LAN. Data will be collected in ASCII format and transferred to the company's statistical analysis package. This data will be summative in nature to determine overall learning. There may be a need for a formative tracking system. If formative tracking is required, it will be incorporated into the design of the solution and the program will control progress through the solution.
	Results of data analysis will be used to judge the effectiveness of the learning components of the solution. Data collected during a pilot test will be used to conduct distractor analysis and establish criterion levels for sufficient acquisition of knowledge.
	A measurement team will review data on a weekly basis and report results to the development and design team, as well as to the managers from the user groups.

Table D.1
Evaluation Strategy, Cont'd.

	Results will be reported to all stakeholder groups in a measurement report.
Level 3 Performance	Use of any solution is a critical aspect of its value to the organization. All solutions that require transferring skills to the workplace will contain an instrument that measures improved performance.
	Performance may be measured by direct observation of use of acquired skills or by observing the end result of the use of the solution.
	Principles of transfer of training from Broad and Newstrom's book (see Resources section of this document) will be incorporated into the design of a solution to better ensure the use of a solution.
	Performance measures will be validated using techniques found in Schrock and Coscarelli.
	Data will be collected from observations or end results of performance improvement and analyzed against performance of other groups or against the performance of the user before and after using the solution.
	The company's statistical package will be used to analyze data for significant levels of performance improvement when numerical data can be collected. A panel of experts will be used to analyze anecdotal data.
	A measurement team will review data on a weekly basis and report results to the development and design team as well as to the managers from the user groups.
	Results will be reported to all stakeholder groups in a measurement report.
Level 4 Results	This level of evaluation will be used to determine the return on investment the company receives for implementing solutions. Four projects will be evaluated at Level 4 during the first year of implementation of this strategy. In subsequent years, increasing emphasis will be placed on this level and more projects will be

Table D.1
Evaluation Strategy, Cont'd.

evaluated at this level. Chosen projects should always align with the balanced scorecard of enterprise projects.

Formulas found in Phillips' book (see Resources) will be used to establish ROI. Sources of data should be sought and validated for accuracy. Assistance from the financial organization in charge of tracking data for this solution will be engaged in collecting and analyzing this data.

A measurement team will review data on a weekly basis and report results to the development and design team as well as to the managers from the user groups.

Results will be reported to all stakeholder groups in a measurement report.

Resources

Broad, M., & Newstrom, J. (1992). *Transfer of training.* Reading, MA: Addison-Wesley.

Kirkpatrick, D. (1994). *Evaluating training programs: The four levels.* San Francisco: Berrett-Koehler.

Lee, W., & Owens, D. (2004). *Multimedia-based instructional design* (2nd ed.). San Francisco: Pfeiffer.

Phillips, J. (1997). *Return on investment.* Houston, TX: Gulf.

Phillips, J., & Stone, R. (2002). *How to measure training results.* New York: McGraw-Hill.

Schrock, S., Coscarelli, W., & Eyres, P. (2000). *Criterion-referenced test development.* Gaithersburg, MD: ISPI Publications.

DIRECT-INTERVIEW INSTRUCTIONS

Process

During needs assessment, direct interviews are often used to gather information on job-related needs. These instructions apply to constructing instruments for both assessment and evaluation.

Interviews have several advantages:

1. They are a direct link to people who have unique information about the problem you are investigating.

2. They are structured by the elements of schedule and planning, contain specific rules, and have a specific focus.

3. They allow collection of immediate follow-up information.

Note that, although this section focuses on structured interviews, don't overlook valuable information that might come out in informal conversation with individuals. Anything you hear or read may be useful later. Take notes, organize your information, and remember to review it as you proceed with your assessment and analysis.

Procedure

The interviewer must prepare for the interviews, maintain control during them, and analyze the results.

Preparation includes studying available handbooks and dictionaries to learn the jargon of the people you will be interviewing, developing questionnaires for interviews, and presenting the questionnaires to the customer for final approval.

Once the interview questions are approved by management, the next step is to choose who will be interviewed. Customers often want to give you a list of hand-selected interviewees. Discourage them from doing so because these people might not represent a random sample of the population being investigated, and instead might be those who are generally perceived positively by management. Request a list of all persons who are among the population to be interviewed. Randomly select names based on the total number of names on the list, divided by twice the number of interviewees desired for the sample. If you are given a list with one thousand names and wish to have a 10 percent sample (one hundred interviewees), you need to select two hundred names (every fifth name on the list) for a random sample.

Contact everyone whose name appears on this derived list and attempt to enlist their cooperation for the interview.

If the customer insists on hand selecting those persons to be interviewed, explain the drawbacks to this type of selection process but abide by the customer's wishes. However, you should note the selection process in the analysis report.

A confidentiality agreement must be made with the customer, in writing, to show to interviewees. This assures them of the anonymity of their responses and leaves them inclined to give you "just the facts." We have included an example in the Assessment and Front-End Analysis Tools section of Appendix E.

When calling potential interviewees, you need to explain what the purpose of the interview is and enlist their cooperation. During this contact, tell them

- The purpose of the interview
- Their role in the interview
- The confidential nature of the interview
- How the information collected in the interview will be used and who will receive the data
- The potential impact on the organization
- That the interview will be taped (and ask if they have any objections)

Continue calling those on the derived list until you have scheduled the desired number of interviews (in the example above, call until you have commitments from one hundred people). If anyone scheduled for an interview fails to show up, either follow up with that person or return to the derived list and continue calling names until you have a replacement.

Consider all of these factors when scheduling interviews:

- Schedule a specific time and place for the interviews.
- Leave a break of thirty to forty-five minutes between interviews so that you can go over your notes and fill in information while it is still fresh in your memory (if the interview is not taped).
- Don't schedule interviews before or during lunch, or late in the day.
- Make appointments directly with the interviewee rather than leaving messages.
- Be present when the interviewee arrives.
- Conduct the interviews in a neutral location.

Don't begin questioning immediately. Instead:

1. Put the interviewee at ease by explaining the purpose of the interview again.

2. Show him or her the confidentiality statement from management.

3. Ask if he or she objects to having the session tape recorded.

Explain that taperecording helps get all of the information exactly as the interviewee expresses it and eliminates the need to interpret notes later, which might lead to omitting important points. Very few people object to having the session taperecorded. However, if they do object, you must slow the pace of the interview to get the detailed information through note taking.

After establishing rapport with the interviewee, begin. Here are some suggestions for making the interview successful:

- Arrange the room comfortably. Sit opposite the subject so that eye contact is possible, but avoid putting a desk or table between yourself and the interviewee. A table or desk puts up a subtle barrier that might influence the interview results. Rather, put two chairs on either side of a low, small table that can hold the taperecorder. Be certain that the table has a pad or cover so that if the beverage you offer is set on the table or papers are shuffled, there will be little distortion on the recording.

- Focus your attention on the interviewee; don't let your mind wander. You might want to question the person further on a particular statement.

- Sequence questions from general to specific. Ask for concrete examples about statements made, ask key questions in more than one way, and rephrase questions that the interviewee does not understand.

- Ask for constructive criticism, but keep the criticism focused on the problem, not on specific people. Don't encourage long discourse on private gripes. Use the next question on the questionnaire to ask for a specific example to refocus the interview.

- Ask if the opinions expressed by the interviewee are held generally throughout the organization or whether they are his or hers alone.

- Admit an error if you make one.

- Avoid disagreeing with the interviewee as well as expressing sarcasm, correcting, and contradicting. If you find yourself in a personality conflict or a power struggle, simply terminate the interview.

- Don't bring the interview to a stop abruptly. Conclude the interview by summarizing the points made by the interviewees and thanking him or her for the time and valuable information provided.

- Above all, when personally interviewing someone, be a good listener. Remember, you are present to learn. Don't monopolize the talk. Good interviewers have certain requisite skills; you must be able to

Initiate. Use questions or statements to get the session going and keep it moving.

Regulate. Pace the session through periodically summarizing or, if necessary, pointing out time restrictions.

Inform. Clarify a point or offer information that the interviewee might not know.

Support. Discourage the interviewee from attacking the viewpoints of the organization or other members of the group. Regularly remind each interviewee that the purpose of the session is to get his or her point of view, not a critique of the views of others.

Evaluate. Provide a reality check by reflecting back to the interviewee, in summary form, what has been stated.

Remember, one-to-one interviews are expensive in terms of time and money. A well-structured interview minimizes the use of both, while still gaining the maximum amount of information.

FOCUS-GROUP INSTRUCTIONS

Process

If job descriptions and prerequisite skills are not accurate, focus groups should be convened. A focus group consists of current job holders and their supervisors, convened separately or jointly, to determine the KSA required of the job holder.

Procedure

Many of the skills and suggestions that we list in the direct-interview section apply to working with focus groups.

Focus groups are normally organized by the customer, who supplies both the space and the people to attend the sessions. This is usually done at the customer's discretion, but you might want to request that the customer keep the following considerations in mind when selecting focus-group members:

- Members should be those who are considered exemplary workers by their supervisors and peers.
- If the position is being newly created, supervisors who will work with the job holder should participate in writing the job description to delineate which KSA are needed to successfully fill the position.
- Members should be assigned rather than volunteer. This helps ensure that you get a representative sample of the members of the work group.

Regarding this last point, realize that volunteers sometimes have their own agenda precipitating their desire to participate. Even if a personal agenda generates a lot of debate in the focus group, it's counterproductive to the purpose of the session. If the volunteer is highly verbal, has a strong personality, and is very persuasive, he or she might actually dominate the session, which skews the results of the focus group and misrepresents the description of the job holder.

There are several techniques for conducting focus groups, some requiring consensus and some not. What has worked best for us is using a technique that does not require consensus of the group members. This seems to foster discussion and information exchange better than those techniques that do seek consensus. Do, however, prioritize the items in order of relative importance across the entire group. We use a rank-and-order (RAO) technique. With large numbers of items (duties and the like), the first RAO pass might be conducted to arrange the items in some logical structure.

Follow these steps in conducting an RAO procedure:

1. Use a random list of items to be considered by each focus-group member.
2. Request that each member individually prioritize items in the list in order of importance from 1 to n (however many items are in the list).
3. As a group, chart the prioritized number of each item on the list.
4. Sum the group's responses and divide by the number of responses.
5. Rewrite the list in the prioritized format, with numbers closer to 1 at the top, indicating that they are considered more important. (Stop here if this is the second round.)
6. Look for large gaps in the totals that might be natural breaking points for items having high, medium, and low priority.
7. Discuss the highest-priority items with the focus-group members, and elicit expression of why each item has high priority. Ask those members who did not give a high rank to an item to voice their reasons for the lower priority. Their reasoning might be due to misinterpretation of the statement, or the reasoning might change the opinions of others in the group regarding the relative position of an item. Follow the same procedure for medium-priority and low-priority items. Eliminate any items that the group agrees do not belong.
8. Repeat steps 2 through 5.

The resulting list should be the group's estimate of the requirements for successful performance on the job.

OBSERVATION INSTRUCTIONS

Process

Sometimes it is not convenient or practical to collect job-related information in a situation that is removed from where the work is actually carried out. In these cases, a simple yet effective method of collecting information is observation.

Procedure

You should select a subject-matter expert (SME) to observe and write down everything that the person performing the job does. Observations may be made in person, or the individual can be videotaped for later observation. Your job is to develop a behavioral description that consists of the inputs from the observed behavior, actions, and outputs. When collecting information through observations, these steps are helpful:

1. Identify team members (preferably SMEs) to conduct the observations.
2. Develop observation checklists using the recommended techniques of validity in Chapter Thirty.
3. Train observers using the recommended inter-rater agreement techniques of reliability in Chapter Thirty.
4. Identify exemplary (successful) job performers to be observed.
5. Request permission for observation, and give dates and times.
6. Ensure that your observations are as unobtrusive as possible.
7. Mark the checklist, but take a minimum of additional notes. Excessive note taking (if the observer can be seen by the subject observed) can make the subject nervous or self-conscious, which might affect performance.
8. Share observations with the job performers (if appropriate). The fact that information will or will not be shared and the frequency of the sharing should be clarified with the subject prior to the first observation. It would be inappropriate to share information if the subject were going to be observed on subsequent occasions. Sharing information would tip off the subject about what you are observing, which would influence his or her behavior.

SELF-COMPLETION QUESTIONNAIRE INSTRUCTIONS

Process

Questionnaires are an effective way to gain information from a large sample population. Questions must be constructed properly, because poorly constructed questionnaires allow each respondent wide interpretation and therefore yield little valuable information. Constructing useful questionnaires and establishing content validity for questionnaires is covered in Part Four, which is on evaluation.

Questionnaires are limited in that they only elicit the information requested. This limitation can be exacerbated if a questionnaire is returned anonymously. In this case, there is no way to contact the respondent if the answers deviate greatly from the responses of the rest of the sample. It would be valuable to know what unique experiences caused the anonymous respondent to answer as he or she did. One way around this particular difficulty is to send out confidential (instead of anonymous) questionnaires.

Of course, those questionnaires that are intended to be anonymous should remain anonymous. Because this makes it impossible for you to follow up with your respondents, you should carefully consider your options before selecting anonymity.

Procedure

Once you construct the questions you want to ask, have them approved by management or a customer designee with authority to make decisions on the project. There may be some information that you are not allowed to ask for because of labor union agreements or governmental regulations. Give your customer a written plan that details how you will conduct the interviews, select participants, assure anonymity, and analyze and report the information.

If questionnaires are sent out confidentially, a number code system should be developed that can trace a specific questionnaire to a list of names to help retrieve any potentially valuable information. Make sure, however, that you inform all respondents that the confidentiality of their responses will be strictly observed.

Self-completion questionnaires (surveys) have a couple of peculiar characteristics. First, they may or may not have a high return rate. Send a questionnaire to everyone on the list of names that you have. It is not likely that you will be sending to a large group of anonymous persons (as with general surveys through the mail), but if you are, be certain to keep a record of how many surveys you send out and how many are received.

Second, you need a much larger return rate, at least 80 percent. The reason you need such a large return rate is to ensure randomization. The problem with surveys is that you cannot control who returns them. People who return questionnaires may come from a certain group that is not typical of the general population you are seeking information from or on. They might be more civic minded, might have stronger or lesser feelings on the topic than the general population, or (for any of myriad uncontrollable variables) might be otherwise unrepresentative of the group you are surveying. To ensure reliable results, then, if you are given a list of five hundred names, you need four hundred returned surveys to achieve an 80 percent return rate that optimizes the chances that the responses are typical (equivalent to a random sample) of the general population you are surveying.

Consider these points in preparing your questionnaires:

- Ask as few questions as necessary to optimize chances of a high return rate (long surveys are less likely to be returned than short ones).
- Determine the type of response mode to use. Do you want respondents to used open-ended questions, forced choice (yes or no), or scaled scores?
- If you are using scaled scores, do you want to permit a neutral response (use a scale from, say, 1 to 5 or 1 to 7, where 3 and 4 respectively are scores midway on the scale) or not (a scale from, say, 1 to 4 or 1 to 8)?

SAMPLE COMPLETED TEST SPECIFICATION FORM

The test item is valid:
Yes ☐   No ☐
(check one)

Terminal Objective

Objective 1.3.3
Given a diagram of the electronic instrument, the student will discriminate each functional part by circling each major part with complete accuracy.

Test Item

Circle the part of the diagram that shows the oscillator.

Item Attributes

The stem of the sample item written to measure achievement in this objective should

1. State what the student is to do to demonstrate the knowledge.

2. State what part the student must circle to demonstrate the knowledge.

The responses for the sample item should:
[Provide a diagram with the part that the student must circle readily visible and clearly able to be circled without interference or confusion with other parts.]

Comments:

_____

_____

_____

_____

_____

_____

Signature _____

EVALUATION REPORT INSTRUCTIONS

The following is a section-by-section description of how to prepare an evaluation report. A blank template appears on the CD-ROM.

Section I: Executive Summary

This section is a brief overview of the entire report, explaining the basis for the evaluation and the significant conclusions and recommendations.

The following is an executive summary of the main findings of the evaluation:

- [Finding number one]
- [Finding number two]
- [And so on]

Section II: Background Information

Introduction. This section includes a general description of the evaluation and the reasons for conducting the evaluation. It is divided into these components:

- Background
- Purpose
- Roles and responsibilities
- Data-collection methods

Background. The [development activity, course, job aid, mentoring exercise, and so forth] was developed by [name and organization] for the [job family or customer] organization. At the customer's request, an [evaluation level] evaluation was performed.

Purpose. The purpose of the evaluation is to [state the purpose of the evaluation level, what you are measuring, and why]. For this project, the evaluation focused on the following questions:

- [Question number one]
- [Question number two]
- [And so on]

Roles and responsibilities. The following table lists the roles and responsibilities of the cross-functional team that participates in evaluating and reporting the results of the project.

Name	Role	Responsibility
	Sponsor	
	Customer	
	Project Manager	
	Project Team Member	
	Subject-Matter Expert	
	Evaluation Specialist	
	Other Stakeholders	

Data-collection methods. The evaluation is performed by the project manager and project team members, with the support of the evaluation specialist.

[Describe the role of the evaluation specialist.]

Here is a description of the methods and instruments used to collect the evaluation data.

[Briefly describe the process or tools used to collect, analyze, report, and preserve the evaluation data.]

Section III: Findings

This section summarizes the findings of the evaluation. It is divided into two subsections.

Introduction. _____

_____

Findings. _____

_____

Section IV: Conclusions and Recommendations

This section reports the interpretation of the findings.

Conclusions. _____

_____

Recommendations. _____

_____

Section V: Appendices

This section contains the supporting data from the analysis.

EVALUATION GLOSSARY

Concurrent validity Measure of the ability of test items to discriminate between master and novice students. Establishes the superiority of a course in instructional delivery if the course is to be used for certification of competence.

Content validity Measures that use subject-matter experts to review materials to qualitatively validate that there is congruence among the objectives, content, and test items.

Correlation Establishes the relationship among variables regarding whether one variable is dependent on the others for the dependent variable to be true. The result is a number between -1.0 and +1.0. The closer the correlation to +1.0, the higher the positive correlation and the stronger the relationship between the variables.

Criterion-referenced (CR) Measure of performance against a predetermined standard that allows comparison of individuals against that standard.

Difficulty index A rating score by subject-matter experts that identifies how high a degree of expertise is necessary for a student to correctly answer a particular test item.

Distractor analysis Analysis of the possible answers (distractors) on a test to determine whether there are certain questions that students are consistently answering incorrectly and whether a certain one of the incorrect distractors is being chosen more frequently than any other.

Face validity Qualitative measures requiring SME validation that course content approximates that of any other course on the subject. It is the minimum validity required to establish that a course teaches what it intends to teach or test. It cannot be the only form of validity used if reliability measures are also required.

Formative evaluation All activities occurring from the time a customer begins contract negotiations until the final product is delivered, ensuring the instructional soundness, quality, and suitability of a training program.

Instrument validity Developing and evaluating test instruments to ensure that the informational data collected is unbiased and replicable during subsequent administrations of the instrument.

Item analysis A test that compares two independent variables to determine whether individual test items are valid. Item analysis requires that various statistical tests be applied, depending on the information required.

Mastery curve A distribution curve with a mean near the upper or lower end of the distribution indicating that the majority of those whose characteristic is shown on the curve have or do not have the attribute. Also known as a leptokurtic curve.

Normal curve A distribution curve that graphically shows the results from a group in which each is compared on the same variable; the average (mean) score is near the middle of the distribution with equal intervals (standard deviations) both above and below the mean.

Normal distribution A distribution where the mean is near the middle of the distribution with equal intervals (standard deviations) both above and below the mean.

Norm-referenced (NR) Measures of knowledge or performance against a level that is derived from the average of all scores from a large sample of student performance on the test. This measure allows comparison of students who should possess the same characteristic.

Predictive validity Measures of the ability of a test to predict future success in a skill area as a result of success on a test. Establishes superiority of a course in instructional delivery if the course is used for certification of competence.

Qualitative Subjective measure of instructional soundness. May be open to a variety of interpretations.

Quantitative Measure of instructional soundness that employs data and the results of statistical analyses.

Reliability A quantifiable value that describes the degree to which a training program produces consistent results in what it teaches.

Simulations CBT-generated scenarios that contain a high degree of realism. High-level simulations duplicate complex situations in which the student actually experiences and reacts to the scenario; mid-level and low-level simulations demonstrate a situation but have students input answers to questions after the scenario.

Skewed distribution A distribution on a curve where scores are clustered around the top or bottom end of the curve with unequal intervals (standard deviations) on either side of the mean.

Standard deviation A measure of the extent to which individual scores differ from the mean.

Standardized Repeated administrations of a test to refine it to the point where it is both valid and reliable (students score consistently on the test), resulting in a normal distribution curve from any group of people who possess or should possess a certain characteristic.

Summative evaluation Testing the effectiveness of the training program along predetermined criteria.

Test-item validity Statistical analysis of test items to ensure they measure the skills learned to a sufficiently high degree to discriminate between high-achieving and low-achieving students.

Validation Procedures employed to ensure the instructional effectiveness of a training program.

Validity A quantifiable value that describes the degree to which a training program teaches what it claims to teach.

APPENDIX E:
TOOLS

ASSESSMENT AND FRONT-END ANALYSIS TOOLS

CONFIDENTIALITY AGREEMENT

[on customer letterhead]

I [name of customer], as a representative of [customer's organizational name], agree that the information gained from the participation of company employees in the [insert project name] training project will remain strictly confidential and that individual performance or scores need not be divulged to the company. Individual information will be known solely to [your name or organization], whose representatives will guard that data with strictest security.

Only cumulative results of assessment studies or analyses will be divulged to the company in the form of a final report.

[signature of customer]
[date]

[your signature and organization]
[date]

NEEDS ASSESSMENT REPORT FORM

1. Statement of the problem:

   _____

   _____

   _____

   _____

2. Data collection methods used:

   _____

   _____

   _____

   _____

3. Data analysis:

   A. Job goals:

      _____

      _____

      _____

      _____

   B. Potential solutions:

      _____

      _____

      _____

      _____

4. Recommendations:

   _____

   _____

   _____

   _____

   _____

ISSUE ANALYSIS TOOL

Identify all of the information determined from your analysis thus far and place the information in the right hand column under the appropriate level and activity. A particular piece of information may have components at more than one level. Attempt to separate the components of information into the level and type of activity they represent.

Table E.1
Issue Analysis Tool

Level	Activity	Definition	Information from Analysis
Organizational	Corporate Culture	Will the corporate culture support the solution you propose? • Respect for the individual • Leadership style of management • Acceptance and use of employee ideas	
	Retention	Is keeping valuable and experienced employees a high priority?	
	Incentives	Are users motivated by the organization to use the solution you propose? • Pay structure • Bonuses • Recognition • Performance Reviews	

Table E.1
Issue Analysis Tool, Cont'd.

Level	Activity	Definition	Information from Analysis
	Organizational Structure	Does the organizational hierarchy support the use of the solution you propose? • Hierarchical structure of the organization • Decision-making authority	
	Communication	Are people informed of what, how, and why decisions are made? Do people receive feedback?	
Performance	Tools	Do employees have the required equipment to complete their jobs? • Computers • Software • Forms	
	Work Environment	Does the environment where work is done permit people to do their jobs? • On the job training after or in place of formal training • Removal of old systems • Coaching	

Table E.1
Issue Analysis Tool, Cont'd.

Level	Activity	Definition	Information from Analysis
		• Management support for solution	
		• Temperature	
		• Ventilation	
	Processes and Procedures	Do employees understand ways to get their jobs done?	
		Are there processes and procedures in place for employees to follow?	
		Do employees know whom internal/external customers and partners are?	
		What are the interdependencies between people/groups to complete work?	
		Are ways of doing the work effective?	
		Are there too many steps?	
		Are there unnecessary steps?	
		Are there unnecessary delays?	
	Expectations	Do people know what performance levels they are held to?	
		What constitutes a "job well done"?	

Table E.1
Issue Analysis Tool, Cont'd.

Level	Activity	Definition	Information from Analysis
	Quality Standards	Is the emphasis on quality and effectiveness rather than quantity and efficiency?	
		Are employees expected to perform their jobs well?	
		Do employees know the criteria for performance?	
Training	Knowledge	Do employees have the information they need to do the job?	
	Skills	Do employees have the ability to do their jobs?	
	Attitudes	Do employees know the importance of doing their jobs?	

TECHNOLOGY ASSESSMENT TOOL

1. List the types of technology available. For example, if employees have access to e-mail, put Yes in the "Availability" column of the tool, next to "E-mail."

2. Determine the capability of the technology. The capability is the strength of the technology, not the capabilities of those who use it. For example, if e-mail is used for communication, but the e-mail system has little functionality, mark "Low" in the "Capability" column.

   ☐ High—indicates a sophisticated capability that can be used for the issue involved in this analysis.

   ☐ Medium (Med)—indicates a capability that can be adapted for use for the issue involved in this analysis.

   ☐ Low—indicates a capability that would not be useful for the issues involved in this analysis.

3. Document the percentage of users potentially involved in this use who have access to the technology.

Table E.2
Technology Assessment Tool

Technology Use	Examples of Technology Use	Availability	Capability	Access (percent)
Communication	Phone conferencing		Low Med High	
	E-mail		Low Med High	
	Chat rooms		Low Med High	
	Newsgroups		Low Med High	
	List servers		Low Med High	
Reference materials, online help	Websites		Low Med High	
	Work process and procedures		Low Med High	
	Databases		Low Med High	
	Phone lists		Low Med High	
	Course catalogs		Low Med High	
	Scheduling appointments		Low Med High	

Table E.2
Technology Assessment Tool, Cont'd.

Technology Use	Examples of Technology Use	Availability	Capability	Access (percent)
Reference materials, online help	Course notes		Low Med High	
	Instructor's notes		Low Med High	
	Abstracts		Low Med High	
	Technical manuals		Low Med High	
	Videos		Low Med High	
	Graphics and photos		Low Med High	
Testing and assessment: online testing, tracking, reporting	Electronic self-assessment databases		Low Med High	
	Electronic tracking databases		Low Med High	
	Electronic reporting databases		Low Med High	
	Security (access, authentication, confidentiality		Low Med High	
Distribution: sending throughout the organization	LAN		Low Med High	
	CD-ROM		Low Med High	75
	Diskette		Low Med High	100
	Video		Low Med High	
	Audio		Low Med High	
	Downloading		Low Med High	
Delivery: receiving throughout the organization	Dedicated audio and video servers		Low Med High	
	Multimedia computers		Low Med High	
	Video teleconferencing		Low Med High	
Design and development expertise: infrastructure design, development, maintenance, resources (include anticipated upgrades)	Video production		Low Med High	
	Audio production		Low Med High	
	Graphics production		Low Med High	
	Online help and reference system production		Low Med High	
	CBT authoring		Low Med High	
	Web authoring		Low Med High	
	Testing database		Low Med High	
	Statistical program		Low Med High	

JOB OR TASK BREAKDOWN TOOL

Instructions

1. List each job you identified during job or task analysis in the order each must be performed.

2. List each duty associated with the identified job.

3. List each task associated with each duty in the order each must be performed.

4. Eliminate any jobs and associated duties and tasks you deselect during critical incident analysis.

5. Write the number of the objective associated with the job duty or task after you complete objective analysis.

Here are definitions important to the use of this tool:

Job: A collection of duties and tasks constituting the total job responsibilities.

Duties: Major subdivisions of the job responsibilities performed by an individual. Duties are usually stated as a general area of responsibility, with action words ending in -ing.

Task: A specific function or meaningful unit of work that must be performed to accomplish the overall duty. This task achieves a single objective or output.

KSA: Knowledge, skills, and attitudes.

	Objective Number*
Job	Course objective
Duty 1.0	Terminal objective
Task 1.1	Lesson objective
Task 1.2	Lesson objective
Duty 2.0	Terminal objective
Task 2.1	Lesson objective
Task 2.2	Lesson objective

*To be completed after objectives are written.

Multimedia-Based Instructional Design, Second Edition. Copyright © 2004 by John Wiley & Sons, Inc. Reproduced by permission of Pfeiffer, an Imprint of Wiley. www.pfeiffer.com

⚫ TASK INVENTORY TOOL

Here are useful criteria for selecting tasks for training:

Frequency. How often is the task performed?

Number performing. What percentage of the target population is performing or will perform this task?

Difficulty. How difficult is it to learn this task on the job?

Criticality. How important is this task to job performance?

- Noncritical (N): this code identifies tasks not critical to the job.
- Important (I): this code identifies tasks that are important in some situations but not critical.
- Critical (C): this code identifies tasks that must be performed correctly because of their impact on the job.

Time. How long does it normally take to perform this task?

Impact. What is the probability that this task will be performed poorly or incorrectly if the performer is not formally trained?

Delay. How long after training will it be before the trainee encounters this task?

Immediacy or assistance. Must this task be performed on the spot without any assistance?

MEDIA ANALYSIS RATING SCALE

Instructions

Complete the rating scale as follows:

1. Consider each factor on the rating scale as to its importance to the situation you are analyzing using the key provided.

2. When you have completed the Media Analysis Form, tally the number of occurrences of each media ranked as a 4 or 5 and record this number in the High Occurrences column on the Media Analysis Summary Sheet.

3. Tally each media ranked as a 1 or 2 and record this number in the Low Occurrences column.

Ignore those ranked as 3.

4. Subtract the number of Low Occurrences from the High Occurrences and record that number in the Difference column.

5. Determine the weight of each media by dividing the Difference by the All Occurrences number and record that percentage in the Weight column.

6. The media with the highest weight are probably the most likely media for your solution.

Rating Scale

5 = Very important consideration

4 = Important consideration

3 = Neutral consideration

2 = Unimportant consideration

1 = Not a consideration at all

Multimedia-Based Instructional Design, Second Edition. Copyright © 2004 by John Wiley & Sons, Inc. Reproduced by permission of Pfeiffer, an Imprint of Wiley. www.pfeiffer.com

Table E.3
Media Analysis Form

	Factors	Considerations	Suggested Media
1	1 2 3 4 5 Content requires interactivity (computer).	Does the content involve computer software, simulation or practice? Computer-based training simulations can facilitate learning.	Computer-based Web-based
2	1 2 3 4 5 Unintended learning may occur.	Do you need to control for participants learning positive habits, eliminating or avoiding undesirable habits? Are learning attitudes important?	Instructor-led Satellite broadcast Video teleconference
3	1 2 3 4 5 Collaborative learning is desired.	Do group learning experiences, including opportunities to build relationships or share information, need to occur?	Instructor-led Satellite broadcast Video teleconference Web-based
4	1 2 3 4 5 Content requires interactivity (human).	Will participants gain interpersonal and communication skills from immediate feedback from an observer about their performance? To what extent does the learner need to use or demonstrate interpersonal or communication skills such as presentation, teamwork, leadership or facilitation?	Instructor-led Satellite broadcast Video teleconference
5	1 2 3 4 5 Audience requires motivation.	How motivated are the learners? *Note:* Self-instruction or distance education requires higher intrinsic motivation for successful learning.	Instructor-led Videotapes Web-based Satellite broadcast
6	1 2 3 4 5 Audience requires convenience, training at or near the work site.	Is time away from work not possible because of work schedules, project requirements, variable shifts or time sensitive performance? Are participants dispersed and require decentralized training?	Computer-based Video teleconference Performance support Web-based Audio teleconference

Table E.3
Media Analysis Form, Cont'd.

	Factors	Considerations	Suggested Media
7	1 2 3 4 5 Audience has limited access to required technology.	What technology is available? Is there a barrier to technology?	Audio teleconference Instructor-led Computer-based
8	1 2 3 4 5 Audience has limited access to required expertise.	Is there limited expertise that must be leveraged across the organization?	Computer-based Satellite broadcast Videotapes Web-based Video teleconference
9	1 2 3 4 5 Students resistant to new media.	How receptive is the audience to using a new medium? To what extent does attitude toward lecture style help or hinder learning? *Note:* Learners often enjoy instructor-led training because it allows them to be with other learners. Although they enjoy it, they may learn less. They may fear technology, have only experienced mainframe CBT, or do not want to spend more time at a computer screen. Take that fear into account and move toward a technology solution whenever possible.	Instructor-led
10	1 2 3 4 5 Employees must review the information frequently.	Will reference materials be required? Is there a need for "look-up" capabilities?	Performance support Web-based
11	1 2 3 4 5 There is an immediate need for application of expertise to the job.	How critical are the knowledge or skills to the performance of job related tasks?	Performance support

Table E.3
Media Analysis Form, Cont'd.

	Factors	Considerations	Suggested Media
12	1 2 3 4 5 Wide variation in entry level background knowledge.	How wide is the gap in entry level knowledge? *Note:* CBT provides the ability to branch users to different levels of training.	Computer-based
13	1 2 3 4 5 Content has a short shelf life or is changing rapidly.	Is the content stable? Is it still under construction or development? How does the stability of the content affect the frequency of revisions? How difficult or is it to make revisions using this medium? Revisions to audiotapes, videotapes, and CBT, are time-consuming and expensive.	Video teleconference Audio teleconference Web-based Satellite broadcast Instructor-led
14	1 2 3 4 5 Global audience multiple cultures or languages.	Will reading, hearing, or understanding English be difficult for audience members? Are there varying levels and types of information need? *Note:* A variety of non-print media can deliver text, graphics, sound, and motion, allowing for learner control	Computer-based Satellite broadcast Videotapes
15	1 2 3 4 5 Materials must be available in a variety of formats.	Do you need to re-purpose materials? *Notes:* Video can be reused in a variety of media. Electronic media can be delivered in a variety of formats	Videotapes Satellite broadcast Video teleconference Computer-based
16	1 2 3 4 5 Fewer than two hundred per year need training/ performance support.	How many learners are in the target audience? What is the size of the audience over expected shelf life of the training?	Performance support Instructor-led Video teleconference Audio teleconference

Table E.3
Media Analysis Form, Cont'd.

	Factors	Considerations	Suggested Media
17	1 2 3 4 5 More than two thousand per year need training/ performance support.	How many users are in the target audience? What is the size of the audience over the expected shelf life of the training?	Satellite broadcast Computer-based Videotapes Audiotapes
18	1 2 3 4 5 Must train large numbers of em-ployees quickly.	How quickly must the intervention be developed? How much time is available to build, buy, or revise products? For shortened time frames, con-sider buying or revising existing products.	Video teleconference Audio teleconference Audiotapes Instructor-led Satellite broadcast
19	1 2 3 4 5 Requires com-pression of training time.	Is it important to reduce the time participants spend in training? *Note:* CBT has typical training compression ratios of 50 to 70 percent.	Performance support Computer-based Satellite broadcast Self-paced workbook
20	1 2 3 4 5 Keep develop-ment cost per hour of instruc-tion low.	What is the cost per learner for developing or acquiring this medium?	Video teleconference Audio teleconference Satellite broadcast
21	1 2 3 4 5 Keep travel expenses low.	Is travel a barrier due to budgets, distance, and business considerations? How can you reduce travel expenses?	Performance support Computer-based Web-based Satellite broadcast Self-paced workbook Video teleconference Audio teleconference Videotapes Audiotapes

	Factors	Considerations	Suggested Media
22	1 2 3 4 5 Keep implementation, delivery, maintenance cost low	What are means of distribution? How will changes be accomplished? Can they be made quickly and easily? Will changes make previous distributions obsolete?	Performance support Video teleconference Audio teleconference Self-paced workbook
23	1 2 3 4 5 Testing, evaluation, or tracking of student performance is necessary.	Can the assessment be self-scored? Is certification necessary? *Note:* Assessment of interpersonal and communication skills requires observation. Some observation requires a trained expert	Self-paced workbook Computer-based Satellite broadcast Instructor-led
24	1 2 3 4 5 Tracking course completion necessary.	Can media assess course completion?	Computer-based Satellite broadcast Instructor-led

Table E.4
Media Analysis Summary Sheet

Media Type	All Occurrences	High Occurrences (4 or 5)	Low Occurrences (1 or 2)	Difference (High−Low)	Weight (Diff. ÷ All Occ.)
Audiotapes	3				
Audio teleconference	8				
Computer-based	12				
Satellite broadcast	15				
Instructor-led	11				
Performance support	7				
Self-paced workbook	4				
Video teleconference	12				
Videotapes	6				
Web-based	8				

OBJECTIVES WORKSHEET

Write a terminal objective for each piece of information you found from Issue Analysis under the same level and activity as they were located on the Issue Analysis tool.

Table E.5
Objectives Worksheet

Level	Activity	Objective
Organizational	Corporate Culture	
	Retention	
	Incentives	
	Organizational Structure	
	Communication	
Performance	Tools	
	Work Environment	
	Processes and Procedures	
	Expectations	
	Quality Standards	
Training	Knowledge	
	Skills	
	Attitudes	

MEDIA/OBJECTIVES MAPPING TOOL

This tool is for matching media types with the objectives. Record the objective beside the type of media that will be used to deliver the content of an objective.

Table E.6
Media/Objectives Mapping Tool

Media Type	Objective
Audiotapes	
Audio teleconference	
Computer-based	
Satellite broadcast	
Instructor-led	
Performance support	
Self-paced workbook	
Video teleconference	
Videotapes	
Web-based	

EXTANT DATA ANALYSIS TOOL

1. Source of information:

   _____

   _____

   _____

   _____

   _____

   _____

2. Type of information:

   Article _____

   Book _____

   Course material _____

   User manual _____

   Other _____

3. Summary of information found:

   _____

   _____

   _____

   _____

   _____

   _____

   _____

   _____

4. Probability of use:

Very low	Low	Moderate	High	Very high
1	2	3	4	5

EXTANT DATA MATERIALS REVIEW

This form presents questions to aid in evaluating training materials. The purpose of the review is to determine if the program content, materials, and learning activities produce the intended business outcome.

List course materials for review:

1. _____

2. _____

3. _____

After your review, check your response to each of the following questions. Add any comments that you feel might be helpful in making a buy-or-build decision. For example, note items of confusion, parts of the course you feel are helpful, questions, or comments about missing or ambiguous content.

Program Content

	Yes	No
• Were the primary course objectives accomplished?	☐	☐
• Did you feel the content was clearly presented?	☐	☐
• Was the content relevant to job tasks?	☐	☐
• Was the course content at an appropriate level of difficulty?	☐	☐

Comments:

_____
_____
_____
_____

Learning Activities

	Yes	No
• Did the course presentation or exercises meet the primary course objectives?	☐	☐
• Were the media and visuals effective in aiding understanding of the content?	☐	☐

Comments:

_____

_____

_____

_____

Program Materials

	Yes	No
• Were the course materials of high quality?	☐	☐
• Did you feel the materials would be easy to use?	☐	☐
• Will the hardware, software, and scheduling required by the course fit your organization's requirements?	☐	☐
• Is the cost appropriate to the project budget?	☐	☐
• Does the program take too much time?	☐	☐

Comments:

_____

_____

_____

_____

Overall Reaction

	Yes	No
• Overall, are you satisfied that the course meets your requirements?	☐	☐

Comments:

_____

_____

_____

_____

Reviewer: _____ Date: _____

BUILD OR BUY DECISION TABLE

Instructions: Place an X in the Yes or No column in answer to each of the questions in the table. Total the X's in both the Yes and No columns. If the total in the Yes column is greater than the total in the No column, you should consider BUY. If there are more X's in the No column than in the Yes column, consider a BUILD.

Table E.7
Build or Buy Decision Table

Consideration	Yes	No
Is the content in the public domain?		
Can the content be purchased?		
Does your budget permit purchase of the content?		
Is there a professional organization that deals with this subject that provides information on the topic?		
Do you or someone in your company have a contact within the professional organization above?		
Is there information available on the world wide web (www) on the topic?		
Are there experts who consult in this field?		
Does your budget permit hiring a consultant?		
Does your company lack employees with the skills sets to develop the solution?		
Does your company lack the technical infrastructure to deliver the solution?		
Does your company lack employees with the skills sets to deliver the solution?		
TOTAL		

COURSEWARE EVALUATION FORM

Course Title and Number:

Vendor:

Overall Rating

	Great!	Good	OK	So So	Poor
Ease of use					
Breadth of content					
Educational factor					
Fun factor					

Strongly Agree	Consistently found
Agree	Usually found
Disagree	Inconsistently found
Strongly Disagree	Not found

Specifics

Registration/Interface Design	Strongly agree	Agree	Disagree	Strongly disagree	Comments
1. Directions are clear and easy to follow.					
2. No modifications to PC system settings was required.					
3. The interface design is intuitive and provides easy navigation.					
a. Main menu clearly identifies the course layout.					
b. Clear instructions are associated with menu and navigation.					

Multimedia-Based Instructional Design, Second Edition. Copyright © 2004 by John Wiley & Sons, Inc. Reproduced by permission of Pfeiffer, an Imprint of Wiley. www.pfeiffer.com

Registration/Interface Design	Strongly agree	Agree	Disagree	Strongly disagree	Comments
c. Functions of buttons are easily identified.					.
d There is a one-click access to help, exit, and main menu.					
e. Location of where you are in the course is easily identified (module/lesson titles).					
f. Bookmarking feature allows user to exit and resume where they left off.					
g. Pop-up windows are positioned on screen so they do not cover up relevant information.					

Course Design/Content	Strongly agree	Agree	Disagree	Strongly disagree	Comments
1. Objectives clearly stated what I was supposed to learn.					
2. Content of the lesson reinforced the objectives.					
3. The lesson content followed a logical sequence.					
4. Glossary and other reference tools were available.					
5. Important terms or concepts were emphasized or highlighted.					
6. Examples or practice was adequate and related to the material presented.					

Multimedia-Based Instructional Design, Second Edition. Copyright © 2004 by John Wiley & Sons, Inc. Reproduced by permission of Pfeiffer, an Imprint of Wiley. www.pfeiffer.com

Course Design/Content	Strongly agree	Agree	Disagree	Strongly disagree	Comments
7. Adequate number of questions during lesson to check understanding.					
8. Questions were related to important skills.					
9. The courseware includes basic interactions (T/F, multiple choice, multiple choice/ multiple answers, single answer, etc.).					
10. Specific and relevant feedback provided on questions; re-explain or re-teach if response was incorrect.					
11. Opportunity to review questions missed on a quiz.					
12. Material was summarized before introducing a new lesson.					
13. A pre-assessment allows users to test out of certain topics.					
14. Course elements (lessons, quizzes, exams) were of an appropriate length.					
15. Interactivity was used to engage the learner.					
16. Interactivity was appropriate to the content being delivered.					
17. Contained real simulations to practice concepts and skills.					
18. You could use the course as a reference to get specific information on a topic.					

Quality and Use of Media	Strongly agree	Agree	Disagree	Strongly disagree	Comments
1. Graphics reinforce content.					
2. Graphics were easy to read.					
3. Audio was used to reinforce topics.					
4. Audio quality was consistent with online learning.					
5. Animation was appropriately used to reinforce topics.					

Connectivity and Download Speed	Strongly agree	Agree	Disagree	Strongly disagree	Comments
1. Connectivity was consistent.					
2. Speed of access was good.					

Overall Comments:

ROLES AND RESPONSIBILITIES MATRIX

Project: Phase:

Name						
Role						
Tasks	Involvement*					

*Involvement R=Responsible C=Consulted I=Informed

ANALYSIS REPORT TOOL

In this tool, a description of the section content or the source follows each heading, in parentheses.

1. Introduction (brief description of the purpose of this report)

   _____

   _____

   _____

   _____

2. Description of the job analyzed (audience analysis)

   _____

   _____

   _____

   _____

3. Description of the job performer's needs (instructional analysis)

   _____

   _____

   _____

   _____

4. Description of tasks (task analysis)

   _____

   _____

   _____

   _____

5. Attachments:

   - Rejected tasks (critical incident analysis)
   - Objectives list (objectives analysis)
   - Description of delivery media (media analysis)
   - Available materials (extant data analysis)
   - Technical capabilities (technology analysis)
   - Environmental and situational conditions (situational analysis)
   - Cost versus benefit of the solution (cost-benefit analysis)

DESIGN TOOLS

EDITORIAL REVIEW INSTRUCTIONS

An editorial review ensures that incorrect grammar, spelling errors, and poor writing do not detract from the effectiveness of the multimedia. The thoroughness of an editorial review enhances the quality and consistency of the product.

Review Procedures

The CDS is the guide to conducting review of these elements:

- Correct spelling
- Correct punctuation
- Correct grammar

    Person and number

    Tense

    Noun-verb agreement
- Voice

Recording Errors

Record each error you observe.

EDITORIAL REVIEW FORM

Project: _____

Reviewer's signature _____

Be sure that you identify any unique specifications in the space provided. On completing your review, check each item to certify that your review included the item.

☐ **1.** Correct spelling: list any words that have unique form.

_____

_____

_____

_____

_____

☐ **2.** Correct punctuation: list any special punctuation specifications.

_____

_____

_____

_____

_____

☐ **3.** Correct grammar: list any specifications regarding

Person _____

Number _____

Tense _____

Noun-verb agreement _____

☐ **4.** Voice: list any unique specifications.

_____

_____

_____

_____

_____

INSTRUCTIONAL REVIEW INSTRUCTIONS

An instructional review ensures consistency of instructional strategy and design within and among lessons. The thoroughness of an instructional review enhances student learning through improved overall instructional integrity.

Review Procedures

The CDS is the guide to reviewing these elements:

1. *Readability.* Written at the appropriate grade level for the audience, as determined from audience analysis.

2. *Register.* Register is the level of formality or informality of the writing style used in the CBT lessons (that is, formal being highly stylized and impersonal, consultative being instructive and semiformal, and informal being casual). Very formal register is third person singular or plural, using passive voice to a great extent. Casual register uses very familiar language, first person singular or plural.

3. *Vocabulary.* Use terms and vocabulary appropriate for the audience, as determined from audience analysis.

4. *Transitions.* The lesson ties previous topics to current topics.

5. *Conceptual framework.* The lesson contains these events of learning:

   • Introduces the lesson in a way that relates the current lesson to previous and subsequent lessons

   • States the objectives

   • Presents the content by introducing an overview of each topic, breaks the topic into component parts, and ties all components together in a summary

   • Checks often for understanding and extends feedback to learners

   • Provides guided practice where applicable

   • Allows independent practice

6. *Congruence.* There is a natural flow of information and relation between these elements:

   • Objectives

   • Topics associated with the objectives

Multimedia-Based Instructional Design, Second Edition. Copyright © 2004 by John Wiley & Sons, Inc. Reproduced by permission of Pfeiffer, an Imprint of Wiley. www.pfeiffer.com

- Topics summarized
- Topics reviewed
- Topics tested

7. *Question format and feedback.* Questions are in the correct format and refer to the correct objective:
   - Quiz questions refer to a lesson objective
   - Test questions refer to a terminal objective

8. *Mapping strategies.* All information is correctly mapped.
   - All strategies are correctly mapped:
   - Processes
   - Procedures
   - Concepts
   - Principles
   - Facts
   - Systems

Recording Errors

Record each error you observed.

INSTRUCTIONAL REVIEW FORM

Project: _____

Reviewer's signature _____

Be sure that you identify any unique specifications. Check off each item to certify that your review included it.

☐ **1.** Readability (expected level _____)

_____

_____

_____

_____

_____

_____

_____

☐ **2.** Register

_____

_____

_____

_____

_____

_____

_____

_____

☐ **3.** Vocabulary

_____

_____

_____

_____

_____

_____

_____

□ **4.** Transitions

_____
_____
_____
_____
_____

□ **5.** Conceptual framework

_____
_____
_____
_____
_____

□ **6.** Congruence

_____
_____
_____
_____
_____

□ **7.** Question format and feedback

_____
_____
_____
_____
_____

□ **8.** All instruction correctly mapped

_____
_____
_____
_____
_____

STANDARDS REVIEW INSTRUCTIONS

A standards review ensures formatting consistency. The thoroughness of a standards review enhances overall quality of the product by fostering a consistent learning environment.

Review Procedures

The CDS is the guide to conducting review of the following elements:

- Standard pages or screen elements (all standard areas of the pages or screen are in the correct position, using correct fonts)
- Standard pages or screen specifications (all standardized pages are used in the correct place and are identical in appearance)
- Standard page colors (all color standards are adhered to)
- Text (standards for text size are adhered to)
- Standard reference terminology (all informational areas of the document are completed)

Recording Errors

Record each error you observe.

STANDARDS REVIEW FORM

Project: _____

Reviewer's signature _____

Be sure that you identify any unique specifications. Check off each item to certify that your review included:

☐ **1.** Standard page elements (all standard areas of the page are in the correct position and use the correct fonts)

_____

_____

_____

_____

_____

_____

_____

_____

_____

_____

_____

☐ **2.** Standard page specifications (all standardized pages are used in the correct place and are identical in appearance)

_____

_____

_____

_____

_____

_____

_____

_____

_____

_____

_____

☐ **3.** Standard page colors (all color standards are adhered to)

_____
_____
_____
_____
_____
_____
_____
_____
_____
_____

☐ **4.** Text (standards for text size are adhered to)

_____
_____
_____
_____
_____
_____
_____
_____
_____
_____

☐ **5.** Standard reference terminology (all informational areas of the document correct place and are identical in nature)

_____
_____
_____
_____
_____
_____
_____
_____
_____
_____

● TECHNICAL REVIEW INSTRUCTIONS

A technical review ensures that correct information is presented in course materials. The thoroughness of a technical review enhances student learning through improved accuracy and relevance in the courseware.

Review Procedures

The CDS is the guide to reviewing these elements:

- All topics required to thoroughly teach the lesson are covered.
- All topics are covered in the order they should be presented.
- All topics are covered to the proper depth considering the audience.
- All technical terms are explained accurately and completely as listed in the documentation for the course.
- All technical terms are spelled correctly.

Recording Errors

Record each error you observe.

⊙ TECHNICAL REVIEW FORM

Project: _____

Reviewer's signature _____

Be sure that you identify any unique specifications. On completing your review, check each item below to certify that your review included all items.

☐ **1.** All topics required to thoroughly teach the lesson are covered.

_____
_____
_____
_____
_____
_____
_____
_____
_____
_____
_____
_____

☐ **2.** All topics are covered in the order they are listed.

_____
_____
_____
_____
_____
_____
_____
_____
_____
_____
_____
_____

☐ **3.** All topics are covered to the proper depth considering the audience.

_____

_____

_____

_____

_____

_____

_____

_____

_____

☐ **4.** All technical terms are accurate and complete as listed in the documentation for the course.

_____

_____

_____

_____

_____

_____

_____

_____

☐ **5.** All technical terms are spelled and explained correctly.

_____

_____

_____

_____

_____

_____

_____

_____

_____

MANAGEMENT REVIEW INSTRUCTIONS

A management review ensures adherence to goals and to any contractual requirements of the project. Adherence to management requirements affirms sponsorship and ensures that the project meets the needs that management staff perceive.

Review Procedure

Use the contract prepared for the project as a guide to conducting the review of these elements of the materials:

- The materials conform to the requirements outlined in the contract.
- The materials meet management goals and objectives.
- The materials conform to the requirements of the system specification.

Recording Errors

Record each error you observe.

MANAGEMENT REVIEW FORM

Project: _____

Reviewer's signature _____

At the completion of your review, check each item to certify that your review included each item.

☐ **1.** The materials conform to the requirements outlined in the contract.

_____
_____
_____
_____
_____
_____
_____

☐ **2.** The materials meet management goals and objectives.

_____
_____
_____
_____
_____
_____
_____

☐ **3.** The materials conform to the requirements of the system specification.

_____
_____
_____
_____
_____
_____
_____

DEVELOPMENT AND IMPLEMENTATION TOOLS

● SHOT LIST

Here is a key to understanding and using the Shot List.

Shot Number	sequentially numbered shots for the lesson
Storyboard Number	the storyboard sequence where the shot will be used
Brief Description	two or three words that will convey the essence of the shot
File Name	to be filled in with the file convention name from the Course Design Specifications or Programmer's Guide
Used/Reshot	This will be filled in after the shot is logged in post-production to determine if the shot was used; if reshot, the number of the new shot should be indicated here
Disposition	Choices are (1) buy (this is the shot chosen for use in the course); (2) OK (this shot can be used if there are no better one available); (3) no good (this shot has errors and cannot be used)
Logged	The camera has a running meter that can tell where a shot began (IN) and where it ended (OUT)

Note: Sections 1 through 4 are filled out during the shoot by the director's assistant. Sections 5 through 7 are completed during review and logging in post production.

SHOT LIST

Lesson Number _____
Unit Number _____
Lesson Title _____

Director _____
Logged by _____
Date Logged _____

1. Shot Number	2. Storyboard Number	3. Brief Description	4. Filename	5. Used or Reshoot (Reshoot No.)	6. Disposition	7. Logged In	7. Logged Out

Multimedia-Based Instructional Design, Second Edition. Copyright © 2004 by John Wiley & Sons, Inc. Reproduced by permission of Pfeiffer, an Imprint of Wiley. www.pfeiffer.com

AUDIO LOG

Here is a key to understanding and using the Audio Log.

Number	sequentially numbered audio segments for the lesson
Storyboard Number	the storyboard sequence where the audio will be used
Brief Description	two or three words that will convey the essence of the audio
File Name	to be filled in with the file convention name from the Course Design Specifications
Used/Rerecorded	This will be filled in after the audio file is logged in post-production to determine if the audio was used; if rerecorded, the number of the audio file should be indicated here
Disposition	Choices are (1) buy (this is the bite chosen for use in the course); (2) OK (this bite can be used if there are no better ones available); and (3) no good (this bite has errors and cannot be used)
Logged	The audio recorder in the sound studio has a running meter that can tell where a segment began (IN) and where it ended (OUT)

Note: Sections 1 through 4 are filled in during recording by the sound expert. Sections 5 through 7 are completed during review and logging in post-production.

AUDIO LOG

Lesson Number _____

Unit Number _____

Lesson Title _____

Sound Director _____

Logged by _____

Date Logged _____

1. Segment Number	2. Storyboard Number	3. Brief Description	4. Filename	5. Used / Rerecorded (Re-record No.)	6. Disposition	7. Logged	
						In	Out

AUDIO REVIEW AND ERROR LIST

Here is a key to understanding and using the Audio Review and Error List.

Segment Number — running list of the number of segments where errors occur

Storyboard Number — the storyboard identification page where the error was found so that the narrator can quickly identify where the segment is that needs to be rerecorded

Description of Error — a brief description of the error identified

File Name — the audio file name

Old Segment — the beginning (IN) and end (OUT) of the old audio segment

New Segment — the beginning (IN) and end (OUT) of the new audio segment

Date Logged — date the new audio segment was logged onto the master audio file list

---

AUDIO REVIEW AND ERROR LIST

Record any errors in the audio on this sheet and return it to the audio production team for re-recording.

Requester _____

Lesson Number _____

Unit Number _____

Lesson Title _____

Date _____

Sound Director _____

Logged by _____

Segment Number	Storyboard Number	Description of Error	File Name	Old Segment		New Segment		Date Logged
				In	Out	In	Out	

Important note: Be sure to record the audio file changes on the audio log.

Multimedia-Based Instructional Design, Second Edition. Copyright © 2004 by John Wiley & Sons, Inc. Reproduced by permission of Pfeiffer, an Imprint of Wiley. www.pfeiffer.com

⊙ GRAPHICS LOG

Here is a key to understanding and using the Graphics Log.

Graphic Number	sequentially numbered graphic segments for the lesson
Storyboard Number	the storyboard sequence where the graphic will be used
File Name	to be filled in with the file convention name from the Course Design Specifications. Each frame in an animation sequence must be logged separately but identified as part of a sequence. (Animation sequences will be specified by the Course Design Specifications but would normally be identified with an alpha/numeric extension on the file name.)
Brief Description	two or three words that will describe the graphic

GRAPHICS LOG

Lesson Number _____
Unit Number _____
Lesson Title _____

Graphic Artist _____
Logged by _____
Date Logged _____

Graphic Number	Storyboard Number	File Name	Brief Description of Graphic

⊙ RESHOOT REQUEST

Requester: _____   Date of Request: _____

Unit Number: _____   Old Shot Counter IN: _____

Lesson Number: _____   Old Shot Counter OUT: _____

Lesson Title: _____

1. Reason for Request

   _____
   _____
   _____
   _____
   _____
   _____
   _____
   _____
   _____

2. Explanation of New Shot Needed

   _____
   _____
   _____
   _____
   _____
   _____
   _____
   _____
   _____

Completed

Date: _____   By Whom: _____

New shot IN: _____   New shot OUT:_____

Logged Date: _____

● RERECORD REQUEST

Requester: _____   Date of Request: _____

Unit Number: _____   Old Segment Counter IN: _____

Lesson Number: _____   Old Segment Counter OUT: _____

Lesson Title: _____

1. Reason for Request

_____

_____

_____

_____

_____

_____

_____

_____

_____

_____

2. New Audio (written here as needed)

_____

_____

_____

_____

_____

_____

_____

_____

_____

_____

Completed

Date: _____   By Whom: _____

New Shot IN: _____   New Shot OUT:_____

Logged Date: _____

GRAPHICS REWORK REQUEST

Requester: _____   Date of Request: _____

Unit Number: _____   File Number: _____

Lesson Number: _____   File Name: _____

Lesson Title: _____

1. Reason for Request

_____

_____

_____

_____

_____

_____

_____

_____

_____

_____

_____

2. Explanation of New Graphic

_____

_____

_____

_____

_____

_____

_____

_____

_____

_____

_____

Completed

Date: _____   By Whom: _____

Graphic File Number: _____   File Name: _____

Logged Date: _____

FUNCTIONAL REVIEW INSTRUCTIONS

A functional review of online lessons and courses assures that the material is free of bugs and is of professional quality. The Course Design Specifications is the guide to establishing the standards for courseware design and development. The functional review determines if all of the functional aspects of the software execute correctly.

Review Procedures

Obtain a current copy of the storyboards from configuration control. Follow the storyboards closely to be sure that the functions to be checked operate in the manner that they were designed. Record any errors on the Functional Review Checklist.

Functions

Function buttons must appear on each screen and work the way they are intended. Press each function button on each screen. Functions to check include:

- Pause/resume
- Back
- Replay
- Continue
- Hypertext
- All main menu items (see specific menu items on checklist)
- Help
- Quit
- Others (list specifics)

Programming

1. Movement between screens should be free of glitches, blips, and fatal errors that make the program crash.

2. Test the branching on each screen, where there are options for where the programming goes, depending on inputs. You will need to test each branching option by backing up to the original screen and choosing each possible option. If backing up is not possible from some screens, mark those areas; it will be necessary to go through the lesson again. Typical branching items that must be checked are

---

- Embedded questions
- Quiz questions of a multiple-choice format (alternate between entering the correct answer first and then the incorrect answer first)
- Expanded information based on incorrect student input (these may be the most difficult to back out of since the lesson will typically move back to the main lesson after the information is delivered)

3. Test the lesson using the longest path first (go through the lesson answering every question incorrectly and taking all remediation available), then review the lesson again taking the shortest path (go though the lesson answering everything correctly).

4. Keep a tally of the number of questions answered correctly and incorrectly on questions that will be tracked and scored. Check this against the score given by the computer at the end of the lesson.

5. Be sure that the branching between lessons also functions smoothly, as intended.

Recording Errors

1. Record errors on the Functional Review Checklist.

2. Use the color assigned to record errors.

3. Be very specific in your description of the error.

FUNCTIONAL REVIEW CHECKLIST

Lesson Number: _____   Date of Review: _____

Lesson Name: _____

Reviewer Signature: _____

Functions

☐ Pause/resume

☐ Back

☐ Replay

☐ Continue

☐ Hypertext

☐ All main menu items (lists specific menu items here)

_____

_____

_____

_____

_____

☐ Help

☐ Quit

☐ Others (list specifics here)

_____

_____

_____

_____

_____

Comments:

Programming

- ☐ Movement between screens is free of jumps, blips, and other problems
- ☐ Branching works correctly
    - ☐ Embedded questions
    - ☐ Quiz questions
    - ☐ Expanded information
- ☐ Branching between lessons
- ☐ Quizzes and other recorded items are scored correctly

Comments:

ONLINE REVIEW FORM

This form is used by subject-matter experts, educational soundness reviewers, and pilot audience members for a post-production quality review of a course. These persons generally will fill out hard copies of these forms as they go through the lessons.

Lesson Number:

Lesson Name: Storyboard Number:

Reviewer's Name: Date Completed:

Editorial	Validated ☐
Comments/notes:	

Reviewer's Name: _____ Date Completed: _____

Standards	Validated ☐
Comments/notes:	

Reviewer's Name: _____ Date Completed: _____

Functional	Validated ☐
Comments/notes:	

Changes Validated by: _____ Date Completed: _____

REVIEW SCHEDULING FORM

The author fills out one of these forms for each lesson as it becomes available. Each reviewer places his or her name in the first column, then schedules the day and time for reviewing the lesson by initialing the appropriate box on the schedule. The reviewer's initials or signature go in the last column to indicate completion of the review.

REVIEW SCHEDULING FORM

Lesson Number and Title _____

Reviewer's Name	Time	M	T	W	R	F	Review Completed
	8:00						
	9:00						
	10:00						
	11:00						
	12:00						
	1:00						
	2:00						
	3:00						
	4:00						
	5:00						

Multimedia-Based Instructional Design, Second Edition. Copyright © 2004 by John Wiley & Sons, Inc. Reproduced by permission of Pfeiffer, an Imprint of Wiley. www.pfeiffer.com

● STORYBOARD TEMPLATE EXPLANATION

Lesson Title — Title of the lesson as it appears on the screen in the header

Sequence Number — A running, sequential page number, such as "1 of 14"

Section — "Introduction," "Objectives," "Lesson," "Summary," "Quiz," "Test," and so forth

Visual — Describes what the student will see on the screen. This can be described in words or with an illustration. Text and questions should be in the identical or corresponding font and size that students will see on the screen. The box at the bottom of the template is for any hand-drawn graphics for the screen.

Audio — Any narration that the student will hear. This can be listed here or referenced to audio scripts. (Write the scripts that accompany the screen on separate pages using the Audio Script Standards found in Appendix C and attach these pages immediately behind the storyboard screen.)

Programming — Any special instructions to the author (including correct answers to question screens). Most standard programming instructions will be in the Programmer's Guide and do not need to be mentioned in this section.

Branching — Explains where the program goes after a student input, expressed using the storyboard number

Previous — Where the program goes if the student goes backward one screen

Next — Where the program goes if the student uses <Continue> to move forward

Variable — A series of if/then statements for variable branching, for example, if the student answers a question correctly, the program moves one screen; if incorrectly, the branching moves to a different screen in the program

Type — The type of screen (for example, graphic text is normally considered graphic depending on how it is created on the screen or video)

Note: The following are completed by the author.

Video In   Identifies the video file number where video begins on the videodisc or CD-ROM

Video Out   Identifies the video file number where the video ends

Files Required Files from other sources (for example, graphic, audio, CD-ROM). *Graphic* includes diagrams, drawing, and other items that reside on the computer software disk but must be called up. *Audio* means logged audio file numbers that must be called up from audio source.

⊙ STORYBOARD TEMPLATE

Lesson title: _____   Sequence number: _____

Section: _____

Visual:

_____

_____

_____

_____

_____

Audio:

_____

_____

_____

_____

_____

Programming:

_____

_____

_____

_____

_____

Branching: previous _____ next _____ variable _____

Type: _____

Video in: _____ Video out: _____

Files required: graphic _____ audio _____

┌───┐
│ Graphic   │
│   │
│   │
│   │
│   │
└───┘

EXPLANATION OF WEB-BASED STORYBOARD

Screen Number   The sequence of the web page in the course.

Screen Description   The visual look of the screen. The placement of components of the screen such as text, video, buttons.

Video   Explanation of the video for the screen.

Audio   Explanation of what the audio for the screen describes. Use the script format found in Appendix C to create an audio script.

Text   The print that appears on the screen.

Branching   The screen number, URL, or other location the screen moves to if any of the buttons on the screen are pressed.

● WEB-BASED STORYBOARD TEMPLATE

Screen Number			
Screen Description			
Video			
Audio			
Text			
Branching			

LESSON PLAN TEMPLATE FOR WEB-BASED/DISTANCE BROADCAST

Time (in minutes): _____

Objectives (learning outcomes):

_____

_____

Materials required (hardware, software, print materials, handouts):

_____

_____

Preparation (instructor activities before the lesson):

_____

_____

Items to Include	Supporting Information
What to ask (Questions)	_____ _____
What to explain (Instructor script)	_____ _____
What to demonstrate	_____ _____
Overhead number	_____ _____
Video segments	_____ _____
Exhibit name and number	_____ _____
Page number of references and text materials	_____ _____
References to handouts	_____ _____
Instructor's self-written notes	_____ _____

EVALUATION TOOLS

⊙ EVALUATION STRATEGY TEMPLATE

Evaluation Strategy for <Name of Company>

Introduction <Purpose for Implementing the Strategy>	
Level 1. Surveys	<How to implement> <What to measure> <How to measure it> <How data will be validated> <How data will be collected, analyzed, and used> <System that will be used to analyze the data>
Level 2. Tests	<How to implement> <What to measure> <How to measure it> <How data will be validated> <How data will be collected, analyzed, and used> <System that will be used to analyze the data>
Level 3. Performance	<How to implement> <What to measure> <How to measure it> <How data will be validated> <How data will be collected, analyzed, and used> <System that will be used to analyze the data>
Level 4. Results	<How to implement> <What to measure> <How to measure it> <How data will be validated> <How data will be collected, analyzed, and used> <System that will be used to analyze the data>
Resources	<Sources used by all members of the group to fully understand and use the evaluation strategy>

Multimedia-Based Instructional Design, Second Edition. Copyright © 2004 by John Wiley & Sons, Inc.
Reproduced by permission of Pfeiffer, an Imprint of Wiley. www.pfeiffer.com

EVALUATION PLAN TEMPLATE

<Company>
<Date>
<Submitted by>

Project Name	
Executive Summary	<The problem> <The solution>
Problem Statement	<The rationale for addressing this issue> <Gap between present state and desired state>
Solution	<Results of analysis for bridging the gap>
Objectives	<Measurable performance outcomes>
Evaluation Plan	
Level 1. Reaction	<Survey Construction> <Data Collection> <Data Analysis> <Expected Results> <Reporting Results>
Level 2. Knowledge	<Test Construction> <Data Collection> <Data Analysis> <Expected Results> <Reporting Results>
Level 3. Performance	<Observation Study Construction> <Data Collection> <Data Analysis> <Expected Results> <Reporting Results>
Level 4. Impact	< Study Construction> <Data Collection> <Data Analysis> <Expected Results> <Reporting Results>

MATCHING QUESTION CHECKLIST

☐ Have more possible answers than terms.

☐ Provide instructions that are clear and concise in specifying how to match the stimulus to the response.

☐ Co-locate stimuli and responses on one page.

☐ Identify stimuli by Arabic numbers (1, 2, and so on).

☐ Have only one correct response for each stimuli.

☐ Identify responses with uppercase letters commencing with A.

☐ Make the ratio of responses to stimuli 3:2.

☐ Place the stimuli column left of center with the responses column right of center.

☐ Keep the lists of terms homogeneous.

☐ Title the lists of terms and answers. (No, don't use the titles "Terms" and "Answers." Devise a short title that conveys the concept.)

☐ Form answers using longer phrases than the terms.

☐ Explain the basis for matching stimuli with responses and whether options can be used more than once.

Multimedia-Based Instructional Design, Second Edition. Copyright © 2004 by John Wiley & Sons, Inc.
Reproduced by permission of Pfeiffer, an Imprint of Wiley. www.pfeiffer.com

⊙ MULTIPLE CHOICE QUESTION CHECKLIST

☐ The question stem should contain a verb.

☐ The stem must clearly formulate a problem.

☐ The stem should contain no extraneous information.

☐ Make interrogatory stems complete sentences punctuated with a question mark.

☐ Should be clearly one correct answer.

☐ Specify in the instructions if the student is to select the one correct answer or the most correct answer.

☐ Dont use the following words: *always, never, simply, all of the above, none of the above*; don't use a combination of correct answers ("both A and C")

☐ Have between three and five choices per question, one correct answer and two to three distractors; this discourages guessing. However, if the question does not lend itself to this many distractors, do not add obviously incorrect answers just to equalize all questions.

☐ Increase the similarity between the possible answers to increase the difficulty of the questions.

☐ Precede choices with an uppercase letter (A, B, C, D, E).

☐ Incorporate video and/or graphic (for example: selecting three of four parts on a video still by clicking on it with the mouse).

Multimedia-Based Instructional Design, Second Edition. Copyright © 2004 by John Wiley & Sons, Inc.
Reproduced by permission of Pfeiffer, an Imprint of Wiley. www.pfeiffer.com

TRUE/FALSE QUESTION CHECKLIST

☐ Make items definitely true or definitely false without requiring additional qualifiers.

☐ Use short stems that eliminate unnecessary material.

☐ Keep statements approximately the same length whether they are true or false.

☐ If opinion is used, attribute it to some source.

☐ Do not make questions either all true or all false.

☐ Avoid using double negative statements.

☐ Randomize the questions after they are all written so that no pattern can develop either intentionally or unintentionally.

☐ The method of responding should be explained at the beginning of the test.

COMPLETION (SHORT ANSWER) QUESTION CHECKLIST

☐ Make wording clear and comprehensive enough to allow the student who is knowledgeable to answer correctly.

☐ Make the missing segment of the incomplete statement important, such as a key element of equipment.

☐ Don't omit so many words as to make the statement unclear.

☐ Specify the degree of accuracy of the answer and the units for computational problems.

☐ Put the completion portion for incomplete statements at the end.

☐ Use direct questions to test for comprehension of technical terms or knowledge of definitions.

☐ Omit only consecutive words.

SIMULATION/ROLE PLAY/PERFORMANCE TEST CHECKLIST

- ☐ Examples depict exemplary performance of the skills.
- ☐ Examples of the situation are positive.
- ☐ Negative examples are only of common errors.
- ☐ Activity is demonstrated before student performance.
- ☐ Practice is permitted before evaluation.
- ☐ Performance criteria are shared with the student before beginning the activity.
- ☐ Evaluate only the end result unless there is a specified or preferred way to achieve the end result or if there is a possibility of personal injury or damage to expensive equipment.

ESSAY QUESTION CHECKLIST

- ☐ Clearly fix the level that you want to write the question to and use appropriate verbs (compare, contrast, give reasons for, give original examples for) in the question.

- ☐ Explain the overall task in the information that precedes the test.

- ☐ Be certain that the task involved in completing the question is clearly defined.

- ☐ Ask for supporting evidence for the student's answer.

- ☐ To ensure test validity, have all students complete the same questions rather than allowing them to choose from a number of questions.

- ☐ When you write essay questions for any type of delivery (paper-and-pencil, CBT, and so on) you must develop the scoring criteria ahead of time. What key words are you looking for in students' answers?

- ☐ Establish a reasonable length for completing a question in number of pages and/or in amount of time students should spend composing the question. (Restricting time and length of responses actually requires students to better compose and express their thoughts.)

- ☐ Use essay questions for those objectives that cannot be measured adequately through objective questions.

PARALLEL TEST ITEM BANK CONSTRUCTION FORM

This form is used for developing equivalent tests that can be administered before and after a lesson or section of a course.

The test developer should complete the following before giving the tests to the judges:

1. Place the number of each terminal objective in the first column.

2. Enter the weight of the objective in column 2.

3. Enter the test item numbers for the test items that match the terminal objective in columns 3, 4, 5, and 6.

4. Provide this form, the terminal objectives, and the test items to the test judge.

Test judges should:

1. Write "Yes" in the Same Level of Difficulty column if all test items for a terminal objective are at the same level of difficulty. Write "No" if any items are not at the same level and circle the test item number in column(s) 3, 4, 5, or 6 that is not at the same level as the others.

2. If all test items are at the same level of difficulty, sign the bottom of the form and return it to the test developer.

3. If all test items are not at the same level of difficulty, return the form to the test developer unsigned.

4. The test developer will modify the questions and return them to you for re-judging.

Project: _____   Date: _____

Evaluator: _____

Terminal Objective Number	Weight	Test Item Number	Test Item Number	Test Item Number	Test Item Number	Same Level of Difficulty?

I concur that the test items matched above are parallel in form.

Signature: _____

EVALUATION REPORT TEMPLATE

Section I: Executive Summary

Section II: Background Information

Introduction

Background

Purpose

Roles and Responsibilities

Name	Role	Responsibility

Data-Collection Methods

Section III: Findings

Introduction

Findings

Section IV: Conclusions and Recommendations

Conclusions

Recommendations

Section V: Appendices

TEST ITEM VALIDITY TOOL

Directions to Reviewers

Your assignment is to determine whether the test items on this form match the objective they are designed to measure. Please follow these steps:

1. Read the objective and be certain that you clearly understand what it intends the person who will answer the question is to know or do.

2. Read the test item, both what it asks and the criteria for the correct answer (if multiple answers are provided or possible, each will be highlighted).

3. Place a check mark in the box beside the test item if you agree that it measures the objective.

4. Leave the box blank beside any test items you feel do not measure the objective.

5. Place a check mark in the box at the bottom of the form to certify that all checked items match the objectives.

6. If the test will not use all of the questions when it is administered, it is important that all of the test items be equally difficult. If you feel that all of the test items are equally difficult, put a check mark in the box beside that statement.

7. Sign and date the form and return it according to instructions.

Test Item Validity Worksheet
Objective: [Completed by the test developer]
☐ Test Item: [Completed by the test developer] Criteria for correct answer:
☐ Test item: [Completed by the test developer] Criteria for correct answer:
☐ Test Item: [Completed by the test developer] Criteria for correct answer:
☐ I agree that the above checked test items accurately measure the objective. ☐ I agree that all of the test items are of equal difficulty. If any item is not checked, explain why you feel it does not measure the objective.
Signature of Reviewer: _____ Date:_____

RETURN TO:

REFERENCES

Abernathy, D. "Authoring Software: It's the Write Stuff." *Training & Development,* 1999, *53*(4), 54–55.

Alley, G., and Deschler, D. *Teaching the Learning Disabled Adolescent: Strategies and Methods.* Denver: Love, 1979.

American Society for Training and Development. *State of the Industry Report.* Alexandria, VA, ASTD Publications, 2002.

Andersen Consulting. *The Future of Airline Training.* Chicago: Arthur Andersen, 1994.

Barron, T. "IDL Options Broaden for Training Providers." *Technical Training,* 1999, *10*(3), 18–21.

Borg, W., and Gall, M. *Educational Research: An Introduction* (4th ed.). White Plains, NY: Longman, 1996.

Briggs, L. (ed.). *Instructional Design.* Englewood Cliffs, NJ: Educational Technology Publications, 1977.

Campbell, D. T., and Stanley, J. C. *Experimental and Quasi-Experimental Designs for Research.* Boston: Houghton Mifflin, 1963.

Coscarelli, W., and Schrock, S. "The Two Most Useful Approaches to Estimating Criterion-Referenced Test Reliability in a Single Test Administration." *Performance Improvement Quarterly,* 2003, *15*(4), pp. 74–85.

Dewey, J. *Democracy in Education.* New York, Macmillan, 1916.

Dick, W., and Carey, L. *The Systematic Design of Instruction* (3rd ed.). Glenview, IL: Scott, Foresman; Little, Brown, 1990.

Equal Employment Opportunity Commission, U.S. Civil Service Commission. U.S. Department of Labor and U.S. Department of Justice. *Uniform Guidelines on Employee Selection Procedures.* Washington, DC: Federal Register, 1978.

Forman, D. "Eleven Common-Sense Learning Principles." *Training & Development,* 2003, *57*(9) 39-46.

Gagné, R. *Conditions of Learning and Theory of Instruction.* Austin, TX: Holt, Rinehart and Winston, 1985.

Gagné, R., Briggs, L., and Wager, W. *Principles of Instructional Design* (3rd ed.). Austin, TX: Holt, Rinehart and Winston, 1988.

Gilbert, T. *Human Competence: Engineering Worthy Performance.* Washington, DC: International Society for Performance Improvement, 1996.

Gunning, R. *The Technique of Clear Writing.* New York: McGraw-Hill, 1968.

Hale, J. *The Performance Consultant's Fieldbook: Tools and Techniques for Improving Organizations and People.* San Francisco: Pfeiffer, 1998.

Hammer, M., and Champy, J. *Reengineering the Corporation: A Manifesto for Business Revolution.* New York: Harper Business, 1994.

Hammond, S. *The Thin Book of Appreciative Inquiry.* Dallas: Kodiak Consulting, 1996.

Harrow, A. (ed.). *A Taxonomy of the Psychomotor Domain.* New York: David McKay, 1972.

Horton, W., and Horton, K. *E-learning Tools and Technologies.* Indianapolis, IN: Wiley Publishing, 2003.

Kirkpatrick, D. L. *Evaluating Training Programs: The Four Levels.* San Francisco: Berrett-Koehler, 1994.

Knowles, M. *The Adult Learner: A Neglected Species.* Houston, TX: Gulf, 1990.

Krathwohl, E. (ed.). *A Taxonomy of Educational Objectives: Handbook II, Affective Domain.* New York: David McKay, 1964.

Lee, W. "Bridging the Gap with IVD." *Training & Development,* 1990, *44*(3), 63–65.

Lee, W., and Krayer, K. *Organizing Change: An Inclusive, Systemic Approach to Maintain Productivity and Achieve Results.* San Francisco: Pfeiffer, 2003.

Lee, W., Mamone, R. A., and Roadman, K. *The Computer-Based Training Handbook: Assessment, Design, Development, Evaluation.* Englewood Cliffs, NJ: Educational Technology Publishing, 1995.

Lee, W., and Owens, D. "Linking Business Needs to Training Objectives and Delivery Media." *Performance Improvement,* 1999, *38*(8), 30–36.

Lee, W. W., Owens, D., and Benson, A. *Design Considerations for Web-Based Learning Systems: Advances in Human Resource Development.* Thousand Oaks, CA: Sage, 2002.

Lee, W., and Roadman, K. "Linking Needs Assessment to Performance Based Evaluation." *Performance & Instruction,* 1991, *30*(6), 4–6.

Lee, W., Roadman, K., and Mamone, R. *Training Evaluation Model.* 1990. Library of Congress copyright number TXu 455–182.

Mager, R. *Preparing Instructional Objectives.* Palo Alto, CA: Fearson, 1962.

Martuza, V. Applying Norm-Referenced and Criterion-Referenced Measurement in Education. Boston: Allyn & Bacon, 1977.

Noonan, J. "How to Escape Corporate America's Basement." *Training,* 1993, *30*(12), 39–42.

Phillips, J. *Return on Investment.* Houston, TX: Gulf, 1997.

Phillips, J., and Phillips, P. "Using Action Plans to Measure ROI." *Performance Improvement,* 2003, *42*(1), pp. 22–31.

Shackleford, B. A SCORM Odyssey. *Training & Development,* 2002, *56*(8), pp. 30–35.

Shrock, S., Coscarelli, W., and Eyres, P. *Criterion-Referenced Test Development: Technical and Legal Guidelines for Corporate Training.* Reading, MA: Addison-Wesley, 1996.

Skinner, B. *The Technology of Teaching.* New York: Appleton, 1968.

Teitelbaum, D., and Orlansky, J. *Costs and Benefits of the Integrated Maintenance Information System (IMIS).* Institute for Defense Analysis, IDA Paper P-1373, Alexandria, VA, 1996.

Toth, T. *Technology for Trainers: A Primer for the Age of E-learning.* Alexandria, VA: ASTD Publications, 2003.

INDEX

Issue analysis: activities used during, 39–40; diagram of, 41*fig*; function of, 39; process of, 39; tips from our experience with, 40–41

Issue analysis activities: collection of data, 39; placing data into appropriate category, 40

Issue Analysis Model, 41*fig*

Item analysis, 255

K

Kinesthetic learning, 118

Kirkpatrick, D., 224, 227

Knowledge-based assessments, 263–264

Knowles, M., 31

Krathwohl, E., 44

KSA (knowledge, skills, and attitudes): relationships among tasks and, 32*fig*; task analysis of, 31

L

Learning: adult learning theory on, 31–32*t*; distance, 214; eight-step metacognitive strategy for, 46–47; four media approaches to, 117–118. *See also* Domains of learning; E-learning; Learning strategies

Learning environments: creating computer-based, 181–189; developing interactive distance broadcast, 214–220; developing Internet, Intranets, Web-based, 190–213

Learning principles: 1: use review in learning, 129–130; 2: include introductions/specified objectives, 130; 3: use of effective verbal content, 130–131; 4: use of examples/demonstrations, 131; 5: build in student success, 131; 6: tailor course to audience, 131–132; 7: keep pace brisk, with variations, 132; 8: include smooth transitions, 133; 9: use clear assignments/directions, 133; 10: maintain proper standards, 134; 11: monitor, circulate, and check work, 134; 12: ask one question at a time, 134–135; 13: work in feedback, 135; 14: follow feedback with appropriate techniques, 135; 15: material should motivate, 135–136; 16: connect material to real world, 136–137; examples of application of, 137–141; four categories of all, 137

Learning strategies: brainstorming, 143; components of, 232–233*fig*; deductive and inductive, 141; defining, 232; games, 143; guided learning, open exploration, 142–143; lecture and demonstration, 142; lecture and discussion, 142; lecture or linear presentation, 142; lecture, recitation, interaction, 142; performance support, 144; role playing, 144; simulation, 144. *See also* Learning

Lecture or linear presentation, 142

Lecture, recitation, interaction strategy, 142

Lecture/demonstration strategy, 142

Lee, W., 6, 32, 100, 167, 246

Lighting designers, 177

LMS (learning management systems): ID and capabilities of, 99*fig*–100; as ID consideration, 96; interaction between LCMS and, 100*fig*; as oversold concept, 103

M

Macromedia, 211

Mager, R., 42

Mamone, R., 246

Martuza, V., 227

Materials developer, 110

Media analysis: activities used in, 57–68; cost factors associated with, 65*t*–67*t*; four levels of blended solution learning environment, 71*fig*; function of, 55; information learned from, 5; process of, 56–57; tips from our experience, 68–72; types of delivery, 55*t*–56*t*; validity/reliability of tools used in, 68

Media analysis activities: compare results and decide on media, 64; document the results, 68; match media advantages/limitations, 58, 59*t*–64*t*; match media to appropriate objectives, 68; place the resulting media in hierarchy, 58;

rate each of the factors, 57; summarize findings, 57–58

Media elements creation/assembly, 186–187

Media specifications: activities used in process of defining, 118–128; design decisions on, 116–117; four approached to learning related to, 117–118; function of, 116; Screen Design Pattern, 120*fig*; theory related to, 117; tips from our experience using, 128

Media specifications activities: decide on animation and special effects, 127; define interaction/feedback standards, 123–126; define the interface/functionality, 119–123; define the look/feel of the theme, 118–119; define the video/audio treatments, 126; indicate text design/standards, 127; prepare the graphic design standards, 127

Metacognitive domain: described, 46; eight-step metacognitive strategy for learning to teach, 46–47; objectives for technical skills in, 51

Microsoft Project, 107

Microsoft Scheduler Plus, 107

Motivation: instructional material which promotes, 135–136; learning principles and, 137

Motor/psychomotor domains: described, 46; levels in the, 47*t*

Multimedia development: of computer-based learning environments, 181–189; e-learning's impact on, 167–169; icons inserted during, 164, 166*fig*; illustrative diagram of, 161; of interactive distance broadcast environments, 214–220; of Internet, Intranets, Web-based learning environments, 190–213; production cycle of, 171, 172*t*, 173–180; strategies to increase efficiencies of, 165, 167; templates used during, 164–165*fig*; tips from our experience with, 169–170

Multimedia development production cycle: post-production and quality reviews, 178–180; pre-production, 171, 173–175; production phase of, 175–178

Multimedia evaluation: collecting and analyzing data for, 265–268; formative and summative, 224; illustrative diagram of, 223; impact of e-learning on, 225–226; instrument development for, 252–264; levels of, 224–225*t*, 227; measures of validity used in, 245–251; overview of, 224–225; plan for, 235–244; purpose of, 227–231; strategy of, 232–234; tips from our experience with, 226

Multimedia evaluation plan: activities used to develop, 236–241; described, 232, 235; process of, 235, 242*fig*–243*fig*; tips from our experience on developing, 244

Multimedia evaluation plan activities: complete executive summary, 241; complete pertinent components of plan, 236–241; complete problem statement section, 236; complete solution section, 236

Multimedia evaluation purpose: determining purpose of solution activity for, 229–231; Evaluation Matrix on variables in, 228*t*; tips from our experience on, 231

Multimedia evaluation strategy: activities used in, 233–234; overview of, 232–233*fig*; process of, 233

Multimedia instruction: developing computer-based, 181–189; e-learning's impact on, 167–169; synchronous or asynchronous delivery of, 168

Multimedia instruction learning principles: building student success into, 131; using clear assignments/directions in, 133; connecting material to real world, 136–137; using effective verbal content, 130–131; examples and demonstrations used in, 131; feedback used in, 135; importance of motivation in, 137; including introductions/specified objectives, 130; including smooth transitions, 133; keeping pace brisk with variations, 132; maintaining proper standards, 134; monitoring/work checked by instructors, 134; motivating material used in, 135–136; use of questions in, 134–135; review of material applied to, 129–130; tailoring course to audience, 132

Multimedia instructional design. *See* ID (instructional design)

Multimedia needs assessment: illustrative diagram of, 3; impact of e-learning on, 4–5

N

Needs assessment: data-collection techniques used in, 8*t*–10*t*; defining, 6; five types of, 6*t*–7*t*; six activities in process of, 7–8, 10–12; tips from our experience on, 12–14

Needs assessment activities: define the job, 11; determine positive areas, 12; determine the present condition, 10–11; identify discrepancies, 11; listed, 7–8; rank the goals in order of importance, 11; set priorities for action, 12

Northwestern University, 169

NR (norm-referenced) measurements, 253, 260

O

Objective analysis: activities used during, 48–53; domains of learning and, 44*t*–47*t*; function of, 42; System Flowchart used during, 43*fig*; theory related to, 42–43; tips from our experience with, 53–54

Objective analysis activities: decide on domains, 49; decide on level, 49; separating lesson/performance objectives, 52–53; separating terminal/performance objectives, 52; write goal statement, 49; write performance objectives, 49–52

Objectives: five parts of an, 49*t*; importance of specified, 130; learned capability/capability verbs for developing performance, 50*t*; matching media to appropriate, 68; ordering, 48*t*; separating lesson from performance, 52–53; separating terminal from performance, 52; writing performance, 49–52; writing within domains of learning, 47

Objectivism design approach: compared to constructivists, 125–126; described, 100; examples of, 121–126; structured feedback used in, 126; structured questioning techniques used in, 124–125

Olfactory learning, 118

Online reviews, 187–188

Open exploration/guided learning strategy, 142–143

Ophthalmology (CBT program), 125*fig*

Owens, D., 100, 167

P

Parallel test validity, 256–257

PeopleSoft, 138

Performance analyst, 112

Performance support, 144

Phillips, J., 227, 257

Phillips, P., 257

Photographers, 178

Photography standards, 126

Point-biserial correlation, 250

Postproduction tasks, 178–180

Preparing Instructional Objectives (Mager), 42

Preproduction tasks, 171, 173–175

Principles of Instructional Design (Gagné, Briggs, and Wager), 42

Producer, 176–177

Production cycle. *See* Multimedia development production cycle

Project manager (leader), 113

Project schedule: described, 104–105; three activities used as part of, 105–107; tips from our experience with, 107–108

Project schedule activities: document general project information, 105; list project deliverables, 105–106; schedule project activities, 106–107

Project team activities: assign roles and responsibilities, 115; list project tasks, 115; list team roles, 109–115

Stanley, J. C., 227

State of the Industry Report (ASTD), 226

Statistical measures, 261*t*

Steam Turbulence Seal System (CBT program), 123*fig*

Storylands: flowchart of constructivist course, 185*fig*; interactive designs for content of, 183*fig*; steps in creating, 182, 184, 186

Stratus (CBT program), 121–123, 122*fig*

Students: building-in success for, 131; promoting motivation of, 135–136, 137; synchronous training of, 207; tailoring course to, 131–132

Summative evaluation, 224

Symposium (Centra program): asynchronous learning solutions, 202; class management features of, 200–201; integration and customization of, 201; real-time interactivity of, 198–199; rich content and multimedia support of, 199–200; security features of, 201–202; structured, live interaction of, 195–198. *See also* Centra Software, Inc.

Symposium Participant Interface, 196*fig*

Symposium Session Leader Main Screen, 197*fig*

Synchronous training, 207

Synchronous web delivery: described, 168; Symposium's (Centra) use of, 194–202

System engineer (or programmer), 114, 178

Systems designer, 114

T

Tactile learning, 118

Task analysis: activities used during, 32–34; adult learning theory and, 31–32*t*; function of, 31

Task analysis activities: define the position title, 33; document the results, 34; identify all job-related duties, 33; identify all tasks, 33–34; order the tasks, 34, 35*t*

Task Analysis Diagram, 33*fig*

A Taxonomy of Educational Objectives (Krathwohl), 44

Technical Training (journal), 218

Technology analysis: activities used during, 22–26; function of, 22; information learned from, 5–6; tips from our experience with, 26–27

Technology analysis activities: analyze available communication technology, 23; analyze technology available for reference/performance support, 24; analyze technology available for testing/assessment, 24–25; analyze technology for delivery, 25; analyze technology for distribution, 25; analyze technology expertise, 25–26; document the results, 26

Templates: created for multimedia instruction, 181; for integrating HTML components, 211–212; Intellinex, 165*fig*; used during multimedia development, 164–165*fig*

Tests of significance, 255

Theories: adult learning, 31–32*t*; related to content structure, 129–137; related to measures of validity, 245–246; related to media specifications, 117; related to objective analysis, 42–43; related to task analysis, 31–32*t*

Toolbook, 170

V

Validity measurements: activities used in development of, 246; comparison of survey question types, 249*t*; described, 245; process of developing, 246; theory related to, 245–246; tips from our experience with, 249; types/establishment of, 247*t*–248*t*. *See also* Instrument development

Vendor analysis, 5

Verbal content, 130–131

Video director, 174

Video editor (or technician), 114

Video producer, 114–115

Video reshoots, 176

Video scripts, 174

Video standards, 126

Video teleconferencing, 218

Videographers, 175
Visual learning, 117

W

Wager, W., 42
WBT (web-based training), 139
WWW (World Wide Web) delivery: Centra's synchronous, 194–202; comparing CBT to, 193–194, 211; designing for, 193–194; differentiating between Internet, intranets and, 191; PSS (performance support system) for, 203–206; rapid adoption of, 191–193; testing security of, 202–203. *See also* Internet delivery

WWW (World Wide Web) development: activities for, 206–209; methodology used for, 172*t*; process of, 206; tips from our experience on, 209–213

WWW (World Wide Web) development activities: assemble components, 208; conduct reviews, 208; conduct the session, 209; determine type of product/platform, 206–208; rehearse the presentation, 208

William W. (Bill) Lee is director of research and education for the American Heart Association in Dallas, Texas.

Bill specializes in measurement and evaluation, multimedia instructional design, designing evaluation strategies and evaluation plans, e-learning, competency models, and organizational change.

Bill has worked for several Fortune 100 and 500 corporations, including American Airlines, EDS, Siemen's ElectroCom, and Ferranti Defense Educational Systems. He has also been a full time professor at Penn State University, Virginia State University, and Clarion University of Pennsylvania. He is currently on the faculty of the University of Oklahoma and the University of Texas at Dallas.

Bill is the lead author of *The Computer-Based Training Handbook* (1995), *Multimedia-Based Instructional Design: Computer-Based Training, Web-Based Training, Distance Broadcast Training* (2000), and *Organizing Change: An Inclusive, Systemic Approach to Maintain Productivity and Achieve Results* (2003). He has authored numerous articles in professional journals and has been a featured speaker at regional, national, and international conferences. He holds several copyrights.

Bill is active in ASTD and ISPI at the local and national levels. He served on the Dallas ASTD board of directors for four years and serves on several volunteer committees for International ASTD. He was the chair of the 2003 ASTD TechKnowledge Conference and is a reviewer for ASTD's Excellence in Practice Award.

Bill received his bachelor's degree from Clarion University of Pennsylvania and his master's and Ph.D. from Penn State University.

Diana L. Owens is the owner of Training Consultants Softek (TCS). Diana has more than twenty years' experience in human resources development, personnel management, performance technology, and adult education. She manages the overall operation of TCS, including marketing/sales, budget, customer relations, program design, and program production/coordination. She also acts as senior human resources professional supporting projects in the areas of instructional design, development and implementation of performance support programs, and strategies that target improvements in productivity, performance, and profitability.

Diana has consulted on the analysis, design, development, and implementation of performance support, communication, and training websites. Diana has also consulted on the design and development of interventions that address the communication, training, and change management issues inherent in enterprise software implementations. Acting in the role of TCS senior instructional designer, Diana managed the analysis, design, and production of a two-year, associate's degree program at Concord Career College. She consulted with EDS on the design and production of a comprehensive instructor-based IT training program. She also managed the analysis, design, and development of the thirteen-week Restaurant Management Essentials training course at Carlson Restaurant Worldwide. She is currently on assignment at Verizon, consulting on programs that target improvements in productivity, performance, and profitability.

Before becoming an independent consultant, Diana worked for CAE Link, Multimedia Learning, EDS, and Idea Integration.

Diana is the co-author of *Multimedia-Based Instructional Design: Computer-Based Training, Web-Based Training, Distance Broadcast Training* (2000). She has authored numerous articles in professional journals and is a featured speaker at regional, national, and international conferences. Diana is an active member in the Dallas ASTD and Dallas/Fort Worth ISPI and is currently instructing an ASTD-sponsored Performance Improvement Certification program at the Center for Management Education at the University of Texas, Dallas.

Diana holds a bachelor of education degree from The University of Nevada, Reno, and a master of science degree in human resources training and development from Chapman College, Orange County, California.

HOW TO USE THE CD-ROM

SYSTEM REQUIREMENTS

Windows PC

- 486 or Pentium processor-based personal computer
- Microsoft Windows 95 or Windows NT 3.51 or later
- Minimum RAM: 8MB for Windows 95 and NT
- Available space on hard disk: 8 MB Windows 95 and NT
- 2X speed CD-ROM drive or faster

Macintosh

- Macintosh with a 68020 or higher processor or Power Macintosh
- Apple OS version 7.0 or later
- Minimum RAM: 12MB for Macintosh
- Available space on hard disk: 6MB Macintosh
- 2X speed CD-ROM drive or faster

NOTE: This CD-ROM requires Netscape 3.0 or MS Internet Explorer 3.0 or higher. You can download these products using the links on the CD-ROM Help Page.

GETTING STARTED

Insert the CD-ROM into your drive. The CD-ROM will usually launch automatically. If it does not, click on the CD-ROM drive on your computer to launch. After you click to agree to the terms of the Copyright Page, the Home Page will appear.

MOVING AROUND

Use the buttons at the left of each screen to move among the menu pages. To view a document listed on one of the menu pages, simply click on the name of the document. To quit a document at any time, click the box at the upper right-hand corner of the screen.

To quit the CD-ROM, you can click the Exit button or hit Alt-F4.

TO DOWNLOAD DOCUMENTS

Open the document you wish to download. Under the File pulldown menu, choose Save As. Save the document onto your hard drive with a different name. It is important to use a different name, otherwise the document may remain a read-only file.

You can also click on your CD drive in Windows Explorer and select a document to copy it to your hard drive and rename it.

IN CASE OF TROUBLE

If you experience difficulty using this CD-ROM, please follow these steps:

1. Make sure your hardware and systems configurations conform to the systems requirements noted under "Systems Requirements" above.

2. Review the installation procedure for your type of hardware and operating system. It is possible to reinstall the software if necessary.

3. Have a question, comment, or suggestion? Contact us! We value your feedback, and we want to hear from you.

For questions about this or other Pfeiffer products, you may contact us by:

E-mail: customer@wiley.com

Mail: Customer Care Wiley/Pfeiffer
10475 Crosspoint Blvd.
Indianapolis, IN 46256

Phone: (U.S.) 800-274-4434
(Outside the U.S. 317-572-3985)

Fax: (U.S.) 800-569-0443
(Outside the U.S. 317-572-4002)

To order additional copies of this product or to browse other Pfeiffer products visit us online at www.pfeiffer.com.

To speak with someone in Product Technical Support, call 800-762-2974 or 317-572-3994 Monday through Friday 8:30 a.m. to 5 p.m. (EST). You can also contact Product Technical Support and get support information through our website at http://www.wiley.com/techsupport

Before calling or writing, please have the following information available:

- Type of operating system
- Any error messages displayed
- Complete description of the problem

It is best if you are sitting at your computer when making the call.

Pfeiffer Publications Guide

This guide is designed to familiarize you with the various types of Pfeiffer publications. The formats section describes the various types of products that we publish; the methodologies section describes the many different ways that content might be provided within a product. We also provide a list of the topic areas in which we publish.

FORMATS

In addition to its extensive book-publishing program, Pfeiffer offers content in an array of formats, from fieldbooks for the practitioner to complete, ready-to-use training packages that support group learning.

FIELDBOOK Designed to provide information and guidance to practitioners in the midst of action. Most fieldbooks are companions to another, sometimes earlier, work, from which its ideas are derived; the fieldbook makes practical what was theoretical in the original text. Fieldbooks can certainly be read from cover to cover. More likely, though, you'll find yourself bouncing around following a particular theme, or dipping in as the mood, and the situation, dictate.

HANDBOOK A contributed volume of work on a single topic, comprising an eclectic mix of ideas, case studies, and best practices sourced by practitioners and experts in the field.

An editor or team of editors usually is appointed to seek out contributors and to evaluate content for relevance to the topic. Think of a handbook not as a ready-to-eat meal, but as a cookbook of ingredients that enables you to create the most fitting experience for the occasion.

RESOURCE Materials designed to support group learning. They come in many forms: a complete, ready-to-use exercise (such as a game); a comprehensive resource on one topic (such as conflict management) containing a variety of methods and approaches; or a collection of like-minded activities (such as icebreakers) on multiple subjects and situations.

TRAINING PACKAGE An entire, ready-to-use learning program that focuses on a particular topic or skill. All packages comprise a guide for the facilitator/trainer and a workbook for the participants. Some packages are supported with additional media—such as video—or learning aids, instruments, or other devices to help participants understand concepts or practice and develop skills.

- *Facilitator/trainer's guide* Contains an introduction to the program, advice on how to organize and facilitate the learning event, and step-by-step instructor notes. The guide also contains copies of presentation materials—handouts, presentations, and overhead designs, for example—used in the program.

- *Participant's workbook* Contains exercises and reading materials that support the learning goal and serves as a valuable reference and support guide for participants in the weeks and months that follow the learning event. Typically, each participant will require his or her own workbook.

ELECTRONIC CD-ROMs and web-based products transform static Pfeiffer content into dynamic, interactive experiences. Designed to take advantage of the searchability, automation, and ease-of-use that technology provides, our e-products bring convenience and immediate accessibility to your workspace.

METHODOLOGIES

CASE STUDY A presentation, in narrative form, of an actual event that has occurred inside an organization. Case studies are not prescriptive, nor are they used to prove a point; they are designed to develop critical analysis and decision-making skills. A case study has a specific time frame, specifies a sequence of events, is narrative in structure, and contains a plot structure— an issue (what should be/have been done?). Use case studies when the goal is to enable participants to apply previously learned theories to the circumstances in the case, decide what is pertinent, identify the real issues, decide what should have been done, and develop a plan of action.

ENERGIZER A short activity that develops readiness for the next session or learning event. Energizers are most commonly used after a break or lunch to stimulate or refocus the group. Many involve some form of physical activity, so they are a useful way to counter post-lunch lethargy. Other uses include transitioning from one topic to another, where "mental" distancing is important.

EXPERIENTIAL LEARNING ACTIVITY (ELA) A facilitator-led intervention that moves participants through the learning cycle from experience to application (also known as a Structured Experience). ELAs are carefully thought-out designs in which there is a definite learning purpose and intended outcome. Each step—everything that participants do during the activity— facilitates the accomplishment of the stated goal. Each ELA includes complete instructions for facilitating the intervention and a clear statement of goals, suggested group size and timing, materials required, an explanation of the process, and, where appropriate, possible variations to the activity. (For more detail on Experiential Learning Activities, see the Introduction to the *Reference Guide to Handbooks and Annuals*, 1999 edition, Pfeiffer, San Francisco.)

GAME A group activity that has the purpose of fostering team spirit and togetherness in addition to the achievement of a pre-stated goal. Usually contrived—undertaking a desert expedition, for example—this type of learning method offers an engaging means for participants to demonstrate and practice business and interpersonal skills. Games are effective for team building and personal development mainly because the goal is subordinate to the process—the means through which participants reach decisions, collaborate, communicate, and generate trust and understanding. Games often engage teams in "friendly" competition.

ICEBREAKER A (usually) short activity designed to help participants overcome initial anxiety in a training session and/or to acquaint the participants with one another. An icebreaker can be a fun activity or can be tied to specific topics or training goals. While a useful tool in itself, the icebreaker comes into its own in situations where tension or resistance exists within a group.

INSTRUMENT A device used to assess, appraise, evaluate, describe, classify, and summarize various aspects of human behavior. The term used to describe an instrument depends primarily on its format and purpose. These terms include survey, questionnaire, inventory, diagnostic, survey, and poll. Some uses of instruments include providing instrumental feedback to group members, studying here-and-now processes or functioning within a group, manipulating group composition, and evaluating outcomes of training and other interventions.

Instruments are popular in the training and HR field because, in general, more growth can occur if an individual is provided with a method for focusing specifically on his or her own behavior. Instruments also are used to obtain information that will serve as a basis for change and to assist in workforce planning efforts.

Paper-and-pencil tests still dominate the instrument landscape with a typical package comprising a facilitator's guide, which offers advice on administering the instrument and interpreting the collected data, and an initial set of instruments. Additional instruments are available separately. Pfeiffer, though, is investing heavily in e-instruments. Electronic instrumentation provides effortless distribution and, for larger groups particularly, offers advantages over paper-and-pencil tests in the time it takes to analyze data and provide feedback.

LECTURETTE A short talk that provides an explanation of a principle, model, or process that is pertinent to the participants' current learning needs. A lecturette is intended to establish a common language bond between the trainer and the participants by providing a mutual frame of reference. Use a lecturette as an introduction to a group activity or event, as an interjection during an event, or as a handout.

MODEL A graphic depiction of a system or process and the relationship among its elements. Models provide a frame of reference and something more tangible, and more easily remembered, than a verbal explanation. They also give participants something to "go on," enabling them to track their own progress as they experience the dynamics, processes, and relationships being depicted in the model.

ROLE PLAY A technique in which people assume a role in a situation/scenario: a customer service rep in an angry-customer exchange, for example. The way in which the role is approached is then discussed and feedback is offered. The role play is often repeated using a different approach and/or incorporating changes made based on feedback received. In other words, role playing is a spontaneous interaction involving realistic behavior under artificial (and safe) conditions.

SIMULATION A methodology for understanding the interrelationships among components of a system or process. Simulations differ from games in that they test or use a model that depicts or mirrors some aspect of reality in form, if not necessarily in content. Learning occurs by studying the effects of change on one or more factors of the model. Simulations are commonly used to test hypotheses about what happens in a system—often referred to as "what if?" analysis—or to examine best-case/worst-case scenarios.

THEORY A presentation of an idea from a conjectural perspective. Theories are useful because they encourage us to examine behavior and phenomena through a different lens.

TOPICS

The twin goals of providing effective and practical solutions for workforce training and organization development and meeting the educational needs of training and human resource professionals shape Pfeiffer's publishing program. Core topics include the following:

Leadership & Management

Communication & Presentation

Coaching & Mentoring

Training & Development

E-Learning

Teams & Collaboration

OD & Strategic Planning

Human Resources

Consulting

What will you find on pfeiffer.com?

- The best in workplace performance solutions for training and HR professionals

- Downloadable training tools, exercises, and content

- Web-exclusive offers

- Training tips, articles, and news

- Seamless on-line ordering

- Author guidelines, information on becoming a Pfeiffer Affiliate, and much more

Discover more at www.pfeiffer.com

Customer Care

Have a question, comment, or suggestion? Contact us! We value your feedback and we want to hear from you.

For questions about this or other Pfeiffer products, you may contact us by:

E-mail: **customer@wiley.com**

Mail: **Customer Care Wiley/Pfeiffer**
        10475 Crosspoint Blvd.
        Indianapolis, IN 46256

Phone: **(US) 800-274-4434** (Outside the US: 317-572-3985)

Fax: **(US) 800-569-0443** (Outside the US: 317-572-4002)

To order additional copies of this title or to browse other Pfeiffer products, visit us online at **www.pfeiffer.com**.

For **Technical Support** questions call **(800) 274-4434.**

For authors guidelines, log on to www.pfeiffer.com and click on "Resources for Authors."

If you are . . .

A **college bookstore, a professor, an instructor, or work in higher education** and you'd like to place an order or request an exam copy, please contact jbreview@wiley.com.

A **general retail bookseller** and you'd like to establish an account or speak to a local sales representative, contact Melissa Grecco at 201-748-6267 or mgrecco@wiley.com.

An **exclusively on-line bookseller**, contact Amy Blanchard at 530-756-9456 or ablanchard @wiley.com or Jennifer Johnson at 206-568-3883 or jjohnson@wiley.com, both of our Online Sales department.

A **librarian or library representative**, contact John Chambers in our Library Sales department at 201-748-6291 or jchamber@wiley.com.

A **reseller, training company/consultant, or corporate trainer**, contact Charles Regan in our Special Sales department at 201-748-6553 or cregan@wiley.com.

A **specialty retail distributor** (includes specialty gift stores, museum shops, and corporate bulk sales), contact Kim Hendrickson in our Special Sales department at 201-748-6037 or khendric@wiley.com.

Purchasing for the **Federal government**, contact Ron Cunningham in our Special Sales department at 317-572-3053 or rcunning@wiley.com.

Purchasing for a **State or Local government**, contact Charles Regan in our Special Sales department at 201-748-6553 or cregan@wiley.com.